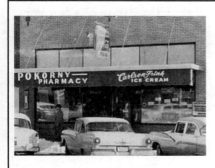

BRYAN L. JONES

Mark Twain
Made Me Do It
& Other Plains
Adventures

University of Nebraska Press

Lincoln and London

ACKNOWLEDGMENTS

Lonnie and Pam Schilz of McCook loaned the vintage
automobiles for the author photos. Al Cuellar of
McCook took the photos. Dr. Gary Zaruba, Department of Art and Art History, University of Nebraska at
Kearney, generously shared both his considerable
knowledge of Aaron Pyle and his slide collection of
Aaron Pyle paintings. Dr. Ward Newcomb graciously
answered all questions, no matter how stupid,
on Indian Charlie, Aaron Pyle, and famous Chappell deni-
zens of the 1950s. Dale and Jeanine Kastens of Lodgepole ignored considerable inconvenience to produce
photos of their Indian Charlie portrait. Dale also shared
freely his knowledge of Indian Charlie's life and times.
The Nebraska Department of Health made special
collections available on the polio epidemic of 1952.

The illustrations at the front of the book are from
"Chappell: Brochure of a Beautiful City of Western
Nebraska," courtesy of the *Chappell Register* and
the Chappell Chamber of Commerce. *Indian Charlie*
on page 40, courtesy of Dale and Jeanine Kastens.

Library of Congress Cataloging-in-Publication Data
Jones, Bryan, 1945–. Mark Train made me do it and
other plains adventures / Bryan L. Jones. p. cm.
ISBN 0-8032-7592-7 1. High Plains (U.S.)–Social life
and customs. 2. Jones, Bryan, 1945–.–Childhood and
youth. 1. Title. F595.2.J66 1997 978–dc20 96-8534 CIP

For Judith Ann,
Miriam Ruth, and
Linda Mary

CONTENTS

Mark Twain Made Me Do It

and Other Plains Adventures

Pot Roast Every Sunday

The bishop is coming to dinner. I am awed by the presence of such an august personage in our living room. My older sisters, Judith Ann and Miriam, eavesdrop on the conversation by running spurious errands in and out of the room. Not yet old enough for kindergarten and self-conscious around strangers, I sit just out of sight on the front stairs, where my father's quiet voice is barely audible. The bishop's stentorian speeches roll over me, dropping bits of largely indecipherable gossip. A Methodist preacher has been caught smoking a pipe. Another has had a nervous breakdown. I wonder if the Camel cigarettes I tried last week will get me in trouble with the bishop. I wonder if the preacher with the breakdown has lost his transmission. If so it must be a serious matter. Our own car suffered such a breakdown last year on a dusty road outside of town. After the car rolled to a clanking stop and my father said, "Doggone it!" rather emphatically, he explained to my mother the treacherous habits of 1941 Chrysler transmissions. I still hadn't the foggiest notion of what a transmission was, but I knew when they went bad the folks that owned them got grumpy and stayed that way.

Church services have concluded over an hour ago, my father's suitably impressed parishioners long departed for family dinners and more casual clothing. My own neck is constricted by a frayed brown tie sporting cowboys on horseback; my legs itch inside heavy wool trousers. There is a small shriek from the kitchen as a heavy metal lid bounces off the stove a couple of times before going into a rhythmic spinning as it settles inexorably to the floor. The conversation in the living room pauses, then resumes. My mother has been known to break a few dishes, especially when she is under pressure. The kitchen door swings open and my sisters, stifling red-faced laughter, burst through, the unmistakable sound of breaking glass following in their wake. They rush past my roost on the stairs. A bedroom door slams on their wild giggling.

The bishop seems not to have noticed. He drones on, moving from one weighty matter to another, money for apportionments, money for missions. He talks about helping the Japanese people now that the war is over. He is much concerned over atomic bombs. We know in a general way that the bishop is important to our future. We sense the adoration of my father's northeast Nebraska congregation, largely composed of small businessmen, corn and hog farmers, and their wives. Somehow the knowledge has filtered down that our father is respected by his bosses in the Nebraska Methodist Conference and that some sort of promotion might be in the offing. My mother hopes to impress the bishop with a pot roast dinner, something that graces our table most non-holiday Sundays of the year. Today she has added several side-vegetables gleaned from our garden and a fancy multicolored Jello concoction rich with pineapple and a thick garnish of white salad dressing.

Dinner, when it finally arrives, goes smoothly enough. My mother, slightly flustered and pretty in her only good dress, is all smiles and flashing brown eyes. The bishop, at my mother's request, delivers a convoluted blessing, offering up obsequious thanks for everything from President Truman to the pot roast on the table. I decide he must not be nearly as hungry as I am. When we are finally allowed to eat he continues to expound on worldly topics, his prayerful reference to President Truman apparently stimulating a vast reservoir of heartfelt opinion. I concentrate on chewing with my mouth closed, on the correct positioning of my knife after I apply gobs of apple butter to my mother's refrigerator rolls. Our normal table banter checked by the bishop's presence, my sisters and I listen in respectful silence. We nod agreeably when we see someone else nodding. The bishop, like any other incorrigible gasbag, mistakes our politeness for interest, leaving his own food to cool as he expounds on one ponderous inanity after another. I grow concerned about his gravy, which has congealed on top of his stewed potato. There is nothing more poisonous to the human body, in my somewhat imprecise understanding, than cold gravy. Hundreds of toxic germs lie in wait, ready to dive into any gravy incapable of scalding the tongue.

The bishop appears unaware of the growing threat now sitting solidly on top of his cold potato. It would be plain bad manners to tell him to shut up and eat. I decide to interrupt, hoping he will be jarred into some much-needed knife and fork usage.

"I gotta potty."

The bishop favors me with a benevolent smile. He thinks I am cute. As I slip out of my chair he sticks a fork into his little heap of potatoes and gravy. I hope it is not too late and, if it is, that the bishop will not drop dead until he is well away from our parsonage. I do not want my father to get into trouble and maybe lose his transmission.

In the sanctuary of the upstairs bathroom I look around for a source of diversion. Against the wall, next to the much-used toilet plunger, sits a fresh can of cleanser. I sprinkle the turquoise crystals into the bowl, where they fizz pleasantly. I add a few generous squirts of white toothpaste and a dollop of Miriam's bubble bath. Perhaps I think a dose of just the right mix of chemicals will cure our toilet of its chronic habit of overflowing at inopportune times. Maybe I am so bored by the bishop's speeches I will seek relief in any novelty.

Once the pot is perking merrily, I become curious whether toilet paper will float on its surface. Soon a sizable navy of toilet paper wads is bobbing around the bowl. I shoot streams of toothpaste down on them until they sink gracefully beneath the blue foam.

"Dessert!"

My father's command floats up from the front hall. I study my handiwork with regret. Toilets have never been as fascinating. I pull the lever on the tank and head downstairs. Before I reach the second-floor landing, the dining room erupts. I arrive to see everyone kicking back chairs, pulling dishes from the table. My mother's best crocheted white tablecloth, reserved for only the most exalted company, is drenched a lovely shade of blue. From the yellowed crack in the dining room ceiling flows a steady stream of pungent, extravagantly colored water, puddling on the remaining dishes, plinking musically into our water glasses. The bishop stands out of range in a corner, the pot roast platter gripped tight as any offering plate. Miriam and Judith Ann point accusing fingers in my direction between fits of merriment. Surely punishment will come from somewhere. My mother is too wrapped up in the salvage operation to pose much danger. I glance at my father, whose unflappable good nature might be under some strain. Against all odds, he seems to be amused. He winks at me before relieving the bishop of his platter.

"That toilet," he says, "has been acting up lately."

*

We are fated to eat hundreds of pot roast dinners in the coming years. Moving from one small-town parsonage to another, always a square two-story structure with porous walls and erratic plumbing, we will traverse the state of Nebraska. Our universe in the late 1940s and through much of the 1950s will be defined largely by the city limits of our small-town pastorates and by the periodic visits we make to our relatives in other parts of the state. My father's congregations, flush with postwar prosperity and innocent optimism, exhibit, for the most part, a tolerant congeniality. In many ways, it is an idyllic milieu in which to grow up. Our precarious state of genteel poverty represents our greatest menace. Somewhere over the horizon lurk the evil Joes, Stalin and McCarthy, doing bad things to innocent people, but they remain mere abstractions. My parents, whose harsh life during the Depression only made them more fearless, inoculate us from birth with confidence in our own curiosity. We will test our capabilities with a kind of supreme assurance unimaginable in less benign surroundings. I will persist in flushing balky upstairs toilets secure in the knowledge that no matter how awful the consequences, someone in my family will find them humorous.

Bloomers Eldon

Alight with the fullness of June, the farmstead meanders down the north bank of Indian Creek. Fifty yards west of a large yellow bungalow sit a square-sided barn, a machine shed, and a large granary, all on sound foundations, all freshly painted deep barn-red with clean white trim. The farm prosperity of the recent war against the Germans and Japanese has purchased plenty of paint. Down the hill from the barn is the loafing shed, with its hay-thatched roof angling out of the side hill. Twice a day, wary of the prying eyes of unexpected company, Grandma Edith tucks her loose cotton housedress into a pair of worn jeans and scurries down the hill to wheedle a few quarts of thin milk from her cantankerous brockle-faced shorthorn. Beyond the barn, down a gently curving driveway, are a smattering of corn cribs and small granaries, then neat hog pens filled with grunting red Duroc sows. Just north of the driveway are the all-important weigh scales. No B. J. Tupper farm ever lacks the means of checking against the suspicious weight tickets grain-elevator operators and livestock buyers are apt "to put over on a fella." South of the clear-running creek, fenced hog pastures dotted with ruddy A-shaped farrowing sheds spread over twenty acres of cottonwoods and willows. The Tupper orchard, a hog-tight fenced island in a sea of buttermilk-fed Durocs, bends under a bumper crop of early sauce apples.

Four years old and temporarily orphaned by my parents' trip to the Methodist annual conference, I am seeing my grandparents' farm with the first eyes of memory. Judith Ann and Miriam have been sent to the chicken houses to snatch eggs from grumpy, hard-pecking hens. My sisters learn early in life to loathe chickens. I have been banished from the house to "look for something to do." A calico English shepherd dozes under the lilac bush near the bungalow's east porch. Corpulent from a late breakfast of pancakes and hard-fried hamburger, I step off the porch and venture toward him, thinking to make a new friend. He twitches a cockleburr-bejeweled ear. Faintly to the west echoes the pop-pop-pop of a two-cycle A John Deere tractor. The shepherd wakes up barking. He tears out of the bush and on down the lane, leaving a wake of frantic excitement. My grandfather putts into view riding the distinctive green tractor, which trails a flatbed hayrack loaded with freshly emptied buttermilk hogsheads. Great clouds of juicy black flies swarm over the barrels. The dog spins himself in mad circles, then dashes to lead the tractor to the machine shed. I trot out to the tractor, buttermilk ambrosia swimming in my nose.

Grandpa, red-faced under a clean engineer's cap, shuts off the tractor. The now-silent dog sniffs at the dusty tractor tires, unhurriedly marks all four, then, with an air of high accomplishment, makes his way back to the cool dirt under the lilac bush.

"That dog sure knows his tractors, Bryan Lee. Al'ays barks for a John Deere. Never barks a'tall for an International. You git plenty of breakfast?" His high-pitched bellow carries far over my head. Any squirrel sitting in a cottonwood twenty rods away could make out every syllable. My grandfather is smiling, but his mouth is snagged with cruel yellow teeth, his face fierce with flashing eyes and bushy red eyebrows. I am too petrified to speak.

"Puttin' up hay down on Hunsickers today. Milton's already mowin' down there. He was supposed to check that dam on the way down. Cows mebbe out of water. He probably forgot.

"Eldon! That kid's wilder than a March hare. Thinks he works for the gummit fifteen-sixteenths of the time. Did Eldon git those teams up?" I stand mute, not knowing an Eldon from a fire hydrant. "Eldon!" A slight teen-aged Indian boy waves at us from the open barn. Behind him towers the mammoth black rump of one of my grandfather's Percherons. "I'll bet you a day's pay at even money he's forgotten the fly nets," Grandpa grumbles, marching off for the barn and the day's serious business.

My sisters are on the back stoop washing eggs. They assign me the dirtiest ones to clean. I resist, choosing instead to fiddle with the nearby cider press. They are talking about Eldon, who turns out to be the wayward son of a woman Grandma befriended in the Hastings hospital while both were recovering from gallbladder surgery. A summer on the farm is supposed to save Eldon from a life of crime. Judith Ann has already discovered Eldon is easy to rile. She dubs him Bloomers Eldon, for obscure creative reasons of her own, and plans to burn his ears at every opportunity.

My grandfather's voice boils out of the distant barn, rolling over our stoop in waves. "Git them blacks some feed, Eldon. They ain't a high-lifed team, but they ain't partial to starvin' to death. That collar on Gypsy ain't right. You'll rub a hole in her. Git that one with the yella hames over there on the south wall." Hames? None of us knew what those might be. Some hames were evidently colored differently than others.

"Lucky's stall is full of manure. I won't allow a horse to stand in manure like that. He i'n't much of a horse, but I don't imagine he'll git better with his hooves rotted off. There's a saddle sore on him where you left the cinch too tight. Come night you better take the saddle clear off him and git some salve on that bad place."

"Bloomers Eldon has to scoop poop," Judith says, making us all snicker.

"You git those fat cattle fed down south, take the horse over west with a sack of salt to them yearlings. See if there i'n't some pinkeye. And that bull on Hunsickers has been crawlin' the north fence. That neighbor fella put some heifers in there next to me. I run accrost that fella the other day. I don't imagine he knows too much. I told that fella he should al'ays tell a man when he's about to git some heifers slid in next to him. You find that bull out, run him in, and fix the fence. Take the pliers and staples layin' on the east bench in that north shed."

By now I am sure that whoever is in the barn with Grandpa has been blasted unconscious, perhaps stone dead, by the decibel level. Maybe Grandpa is now talking to Eldon's corpse. We approach the barn like Apache scouts, sliding along the barn, sneaking furtive peeks into the hazy interior. Grandpa and the still-functioning Eldon are harnessing two teams, a nervous set of sorrels with flaxen manes and a docile pair of thick-necked blacks. Eldon, oblivious to the instructional avalanche, darts in and out of the stalls, fastening harness buckles in no apparent order. He spots us, in spite of our crafty approach. A well-aged egg splatters the ground at Judith's feet. We retreat, gagging, to our stoop. Eldon smirks at us from the barn door.

"Bloomers Eldon scoops poop," we chorus. Eldon makes a face and disappears. Grandpa's order list rolls on and on:

"That gilt up north with the late litter needs some a that bran feed in the east bin. You tote that up there see if she needs a drink. That pail on the north side of the west crib'll still hold water. Put it back down there when you git done so we can find it. Still ain't found the last one you toted water in. That tin on the west crib i'n't fixed. I told you about that yesterday. You git back from rakin' this evening take that ladder layin' in there under that north mulberry and git them long-shank nails from under the bench in west of that old shel-ler. There's a hammer in there with 'em. Wind don't al'ays give no-tice when it's going to raise up in this country. I don't want my crib roof spread over Webster County and half of Franklin."

"Bloo-mers El-don for-got to do his jo-ob," Judith sings.

"Bloomers scoops poop, Bloomers scoops poop," I hant, proud of using *poop*, the newest and wickedest word in my entire vocabulary.

"My boy Milton don't see to keepin' stuff up like he ought to," Grandpa continues. "He al'ays thinks he can do more'n he can. I imagine that boy could pick corn with just about anybody. I told that fella lives over east how Milton would fill a wagon before his two boys had their breakfast. Don't think he liked that any too good. 'Course his boys don't amount to much; al'ays goin' to town when there's things need doin'. And that fella ain't much of a hand at mendin' his harness, nor workin' in a young team once in a while. You let your stock git old and purty soon everything goes to pot all at once, and you got nothin' a bank would lend a nickle on."

I am puzzled by the references to corn picking. I wonder if it is like picking apples. Do the farmers use ladders and five-gallon buckets?

"You git done with them little chores and check that rammy white-face bull, you ride on to where that west hayfield runs on the bottom south of the highway. Edith's going to send a little lunch down, and that hay will be ready to rake about the time you git done eatin'. You watch them high-lifed sorrels on that rake. You or them neither one ain't had that much rakin', an' if you jaw at 'em too much or hit 'em with a whip like I seen you do the other day, they're just liable to get frisky and bust up good machinery."

Judith says we have permission to ride Lucky tomorrow if Eldon isn't using him. Grandma has warned her not to get bucked off. I decide that "bucked off" is the same as being killed. If I ride this horse I'm going to stay on, no matter what happens.

Grandpa drives us down to the hayfield in his new Ford auto-mobile, Grandma's overflowing picnic hamper riding between my sisters on the back seat. B. J. cranks up the first of the many economics lectures I am to hear over the years:

"Most of this land is awful high, Bryan Lee. I al'ays said I'd rather rent a good farm than own a poor one. This grass won't pay interest and taxes. I imagine a man could get around three per cent on gum-mit bonds, and they're worth one hundred cents on the dollar on your inheritance taxes. Time you buy some posts and wire and pay the county's taxes, there i'n't hardly two per cent left. I wouldn't know enough to run a popcorn wagon, but I know if you can git three per cent on a U.S. gummit bond you'd be ahead to do it and go rent the grass."

Pretending to understand any particle of this, I nod and put on what I think might pass for a serious financial expression.

"You take these good white-faced cattle, Bryan Lee. Any money that's ever been made in this country on cattle has come from white-faces. Milton, he thinks a lot a them Angus. But anybody knows cattle will tell you an eighty per cent calf crop with Angus is as good as ninety per cent with your good white-faces. Then your Angus cow is kinda like a toy. You cull 'em off they might not weigh six-seven hundred pounds. We weighed them two Wally Bean white-face bulls when they went to pasture, and neither one missed much of seventeen hundred and fifty pounds. I ain't seen an Angus bull much over thirteen hundred."

I look out over the dash at a dusty landscape of three-wire fences and eroded banks and try to conjure proper cattleman thoughts. I wonder if Milton, my Mom's brother, knows his cattle are so puny.

After lunch Uncle Milton lets us take turns riding on his new Ferguson tractor as he makes his mowing rounds. He is bemused by all my questions: Why is this tractor painted gray and Grandpa's is green? Which one can go faster? What does that lever do? Why do you have your foot on that pedal? Milton answers everything in his soothing drawl. He lets me steer once in a while, his unobtrusive thumb never quite leaving the wheel. He says I have the makings of a "toppy kind of tractor hand." Milton immediately goes to the front of my favorite-uncle list, edging out Uncle Malvin Jones, who has won my capricious affections with the gift of two BB guns. The alfalfa, short and dry, is alive with big yellow grasshoppers. Milton says they came up from Kansas, having eaten everything there is to eat in that poor state.

Eldon shows up late, long after Grandpa has tired of waiting, and is out with the sorrels raking the stubby crop into paltry windrows. We can hear him talking to his horses from the far side of the field. My sisters tease Eldon unmercifully about his bloomers. His pimply face turns red. He says, "You just think you're a couple of real smartypants, don't ya?" Judith Ann solemnly promises never to tease him again.

Eldon produces a pocketful of firecrackers, and we blow up yellow grasshoppers for half an hour. He has some fine thread with him, like he's planned the whole deal. Our job is to catch the biggest hoppers we can find while he ties one-inch firecrackers to their backs and sets them on the hood of Grandpa's new car. The grasshoppers wait patiently while Eldon lights the fuses. Once in a while a hopper gives a great doomed leap just before the explosion. Legs and wings fly everywhere. It is wonderful. When we tire of vaporizing grasshoppers, Eldon blows up a toad and a whole set of blind, bald baby mice he digs out of the bed of a nearby hayrack. B. J. Tupper's car hood is a mess, but Eldon doesn't seem to notice. He is scouring the hayrack for a garter snake to explode when Grandpa drives up. Eldon is up on the rake seat and has the team turned onto a swath before Grandpa has time to chew more than fifteen-sixteenths of the little guy's behind into bits.

Judith Ann and Miriam bon-voyage Eldon with a raucous chorus of "Bloomers Eldon, Bloomers Eldon, Bloo-o-o-o-o-mers Bloo-o-o-o-o-o-o-o-o-mers El-don" before collapsing in a pile of giggles. Grandpa says he has to go see about getting the stacker put on "that tractor of Milton's," meaning one of those no-account International tractors he so despises. We go home by a long, circuitous route, checking all manner of windmills, stock dams, cattle, fences, everybody's crops. It is soon evident that Eldon hasn't finished all his day's assignments, at least not to Grandpa's satisfaction. Judith Ann is sure Bloomers Eldon is going to "get told" when he gets home that night and says we should spy on the proceedings. We do, and he does.

I have the job of fetching Grandpa for supper. The late-afternoon sun slants into my eyes, making me stumble. He is where he is supposed to be, down on the creek turning his new sorrel team out to pasture. They are itchy from the day in harness. He faces them, yells at top volume, cracks a long buggy whip over their heads. Like twin trained pups the horses go to their knees and roll, first to one side, then another, then up on their backs, hooves pawing the air. At first, with all the bawling, I am worried the horses have seriously displeased Grandpa, and he is going to punish them with the whip. But before long it is clear the horses are enjoying their roll in the sandy dust, a reward for a day's hard work. I don't try to get Grandpa's attention, not wanting to interrupt the frolicking of those magnificent beasts, even if I could. He cracks the whip, issues more orders. The sorrels rise, give themselves a good shaking, like spaniels coming out of the water. He leads them through the gate, turns them loose, then stands for a moment watching them gambol and snort their pleasure. He comes up the hill toward the barn, his toe-heavy walk kicking up dirt and clods ahead of him. He starts talking a hundred yards away. I get the strong impression he has known I am there all along.

"Well, they're not much of a team yet, Bryan Lee. But they're young. One's four, and the other's just above five. It's about all I can do to get 'em to pay attention."

*

The three of us are yelling "Whoa!" with no noticeable effect. We are returning down the long lane from the mailbox. Lucky's stiff-legged gait bounces us around on the worn stock saddle. I am stuck behind my sisters, holding on to the cantle with all my might. Judith saws on the reins. Lucky's jarring trot turns into a canter, then a full-strided run. Someone yells from the house yard as we pass. Judith says we should jump before Lucky runs us into the barn. She thinks Lucky has this all planned. Judith and Miriam disappear over the side. I am supposed to follow, but the ground is too far away. I slide down Lucky's heaving side, find the stirrup with my left foot. We are almost to the barn. Lucky does not slow. Voices behind order me to jump. I step off into space just as Lucky veers to miss the barn. The ground is moving faster than I am. I roll hard against the corner of the barn, knocking myself slightly goofy. When I stop crying, I tell the solicitous assemblage that Miriam and Judith are "fraidy cats" who jumped off for no good reason. There I was, the last and bravest member of my family, tall in the saddle, in total control, willing to ride that headstrong horse as far and as fast as he wanted to run. But then he'd put on a terrific bucking exhibition, hadn't he? Not even an experienced buckaroo like myself could be expected to hang on through all of that. Everyone lets me get away with this balderdash—everyone except my dear sisters. I blithely ignore taunts of "Liar, liar, pants on fire," secure in the knowledge that my version of that historic ride will always prevail. He who jumps last, after all, reserves some prerogatives.

*

Eldon, while ensconced in the family's pink outhouse, is attacked by a hornet. Judith asks him if he had his bloomers on at the time. Eldon vows to teach those hornets a thing or two. He locates the source of his troubles, a large round hornet's nest hanging in a sapling three feet east of the outhouse door. Eldon tromps down the path, cudgel in hand, thirty seconds' worth of long-range strategic planning swimming in his skull. We are watching from the safety of the screened porch. Judith is pessimistic about Eldon's mission.

Eldon smacks the nest a Ruthian swat, dislodging it cleanly, sending it rolling twenty feet down the bank toward Indian Creek. "I got 'em," Eldon yells. The hornets, who ordinarily spend all of their waking and sleeping moments in a seething homicidal rage, become overtly grumpy. They seem to have a pretty good idea of who is responsible for their troubles. Suddenly Eldon is streaking up the creek, a fog of highly motivated insects hammering him at every step. His yowling fades away in the west. Judith Ann and Miriam are laughing. I know this by their crimson faces, their mouths propped open by long strings of saliva, though no sound is coming out. Grandma worries about rounding up some ice.

The hard lumps on Eldon's head and back are the size of Easter eggs. One eye is puffed shut. His swollen lips protrude sideways, like some drunken platypus. His shirt is missing in action. All of Eldon is slick with rank black mud. A track of dark wet clods leads to the back door from his seat by the kitchen sink. "I didn't shake 'em," he tells Grandma, "until I jumped in that swamp west of the orchard. I kept duckin' under water till they finally give up." Miriam and Judith Ann, perhaps entertaining small pangs of sympathy, stand meekly by the enameled cookstove, promising Eldon to never, never again refer to him as Bloomers Eldon. They take their mounting hysterics out on the east sleeping porch. All the while Grandma is ministering to Eldon's injuries, we hear the occasional snorts and blurts of suppressed laughter.

*

It is Armistice Day. We are bundled into the Red Cloud Methodist Church for Uncle Leo's reinterment services. Leo, small and smart, always the favorite, died during World War II crossing a minefield in Sicily. Sophie and Anita, Leo's widow and daughter, sit in the front pew between my grandparents. Grandpa has his arm around Sophie. Sometimes when the minister is talking, Sophie cries and Grandpa pats her shoulder. Grandma is tending to little Anita, dark-eyed and perky, dressed in a bright red jumper. Perhaps Grandma is thinking of the windswept Wyoming homestead where Leo was born. It was, after all, her favorite place in the whole world.

The previous night, during the house-shaking blizzard that drove us deep under the feather tick, Grandma came upstairs with three hot sadirons wrapped in newspapers. She carried a kerosene lantern, which warmed the walls with yellow light. Perched on the side of our bed, she fussed with our covers, worried we didn't have enough. While we toasted our feet and the wind threatened to blow the bedroom down around our ears, she told us Wyoming stories—stories of homesteading, emigrant cars, crazy people, violent birth, and suicide, her measured voice as tinny as brand-new galvanized roofing.

Bryan, as she called Grandpa, was the hero of most of these ballads. People called on him to fetch a doctor, consult on a sick horse, do chores for a neighbor in trouble. So when a crazed man with a gun drove a family from their home into subzero snow, the neighborhood asked Bryan Tupper to do what he could. He planted himself within easy shooting distance, finally talking his way into the house. Then he maneuvered the nutty guy around until another man could conk him on the head with a stick of cordwood. They tied up the unconscious man, and Grandpa crawled back on his horse to ride twenty miles in lowering dark for the sheriff.

"It was late when he got home," Grandma said, "and I was worried about what might have happened, don't you know. When he rode in, it was bitter cold. I can see it yet, his horse, his clothes, everything was white. You never saw anything like it." She paused, and I thought we were through with stories for one night. But she was only shifting gears.

"That winter of 1918 when Leo was born there was no doctor in Upton. So on Friday Bryan went over on Kara Creek and got Mrs. Frederickson. He went out in the pasture and got her horse, and they rode back. But she was Seventh-Day Adventist, don't you know. She wouldn't work on Saturday at all. Mr. Jurgenson knew that, and he was going into town. He always had trouble with his horses or something. While he was in there, he found out there was a new doctor, and he brought him out. Leo was born about two o'clock on Sunday morning. He was in pretty bad shape, too. He was little. He weighed four pounds and a half. He'd just sleep, sleep, sleep. You'd have an awful time getting him awake enough to feed. Sometimes it got so terrible cold in that house I had to build a tent over the stove. I'd put a little water to boil and set his bed under the tent right in front. It kept the chill off and let the little guy breathe. He was always scrappy, you know. He and Clinton would fight something awful. Leo was just a mite of a boy, but Clinton would have to half kill him before he'd quit. Next day he'd be ready for more."

Grandma's voice trailed off. She gave us each a hug and took her work-weary bones to bed, leaving us in a state of mild surprise. We had been warned not to talk about Leo or war or guns or killing around Grandma. "Grandma is still having a hard time about Leo," we were told. She put away all his things, banished any household mementos with the faintest connection to war, even taken her World War I–vintage sheet music from the piano bench and packed it away. What had gotten into her?

Grandpa talks about Leo all the time. From his favorite over-stuffed chair, he fills the living room with rage. My father listens. We listen through the open heat register in the bedroom floor. He is disgusted with Leo for not having arranged some sort of deferment. Surely a married county agent of Cherry County, the largest county in the state, was entitled to some consideration. Sophie had been ex-pecting Anita, but Leo hadn't pushed for a deferment. Grandpa is also angry at himself, convinced that he didn't do all he could, that he should have known what was happening with the draft board so he could have done more talking to Leo, maybe changed his mind. Grandpa takes no comfort from raising a dead patriot, not when the farm that was supposed to be Leo's sits empty on Thompson Creek, the western border of B. J. Tupper's growing empire. Mostly he is angry at governments that manage their affairs so poorly that good young men die for no good reason. To Grandpa, no reason is good enough to "kill boys," and he ridicules anyone silly enough to think such a justification exists. Warlike in business, combative in his household, B. J. Tupper, in the tiny corner of his world that includes national military matters, has become a total pacifist.

*

Looking back on Leo's funeral service with the perspective of the hours I was to spend with Grandpa, I wonder at his self-control. He squirms in that exposed front pew as one speaker after another extols his son's sacrifice, praises a merciful God's ultimate judgment, asks us to take our comfort from the inscrutable maneuverings of divine will. If Grandpa had any notion of approaching the podium and throttling the idiots, it was abandoned to the greater duties of tending to Sophie and the family's public face. He will deliver his version of things at a later date.

Outside the church fat snowflakes swirl in a freshening wind. In the pew beside me, Dad worries that a new blizzard will strand us in Red Cloud. Snow has postponed Leo's rites to a Saturday, and Sunday services in Neligh, our current home, are 250 miles of tenuous roads to the north. Our car is something of a family joke, bald tires and not much of a heater.

*

The snow has lifted. We are in the Red Cloud cemetery watching the American Legion burial detail go through the drill. I stick my fingers in my ears after the first volley. A uniformed man presents my cousin Anita with the folded flag. "Thank you," she says. Some people in the crowd chuckle at her precocity. Sophie is crying. She has the fairest skin and the blackest hair of anyone I have ever seen. I think she is beautiful. Grandpa and Grandma have installed, next to Leo's modest military headstone, a large marble stone inscribed with their own names and birthdates. How do they know already they are going to die? I find an empty brass cartridge in among the frozen clods by Leo's grave. It has ".30-06" inscribed on the bottom.

*

Our car creeps toward Neligh along an ice-blackened highway, past ditches scattered with snow-drifted vehicles. Sometimes a rooftop shows, sometimes only a bumper. I am worried all these derelicts are the tombs of frozen dead people. The atmosphere inside our car is unusually tense, no endless Susabelle Band-Aid stories from Judith Ann, none of the everyday sisterly bickering. Overcoated state patrolmen wave us through one-way stretches with dim flashlights. When Dad questions them about the road ahead, they shake their heads. We keep going. The heater gives up all pretense of producing warmth and begins to spout foul fumes. I throw up over everything—several times. With the windows cracked open our car is even colder. When we pull into Neligh in the wee hours of Sunday morning, great banks of new snow along the highway block the view of our house. There is no place to park. We abandon our cold, vomit-spattered car in the Safeway parking lot, the only cleared space within walking distance. Sunday services are canceled. Three weeks pass before Dad is able to move our car. The winter of 1948–49 has arrived.

*

Another Methodist annual conference. The crops around Indian Creek are stunted by drought. Bloomers Eldon is older, more serious. He rides Lucky to a growing list of responsibilities, always at a full gallop. The losing war with blazing skies and cracked earth has Grandpa is a state of near-apoplexy. All through breakfast he rants about Eldon's laziness, complains that no one sees the things that "need doin'." Eldon's appetite does not seem much affected. He takes a third helping of sausage gravy. Grandpa makes fun of Milton's International tractor, says it burns too much fuel, that it is too expensive to overhaul. Milton quietly disagrees. Grandpa turns purple. He stands up yelling. There is a flurry of arms and legs. Milton flies out the screened porch door. Through all of this, I am holding a brimming bowl of sausage gravy, waiting to hand it to Grandpa. My arms weaken. I dump half the scalding bowl in my lap. I screech and blubber, sure I am killed. Grandpa is suddenly all smiles. He helps Grandma wipe off the searing gravy. In no time I have clean clothes and a plateful of Grandma's puffy biscuits. Grandpa ladles fresh gravy. He tells me I must be "purty strong" to have held that heavy bowl so long. I can help Miriam and Judith Ann tote lunch to the silage crew in a few hours. The gravy is delicious. So are the biscuits.

We cross Indian Creek over the fragile stone dam we erected only that morning. The current has torn a three-foot hole in our handiwork. We take turns broad-jumping, handing across the food hamper and the sloshing Thermos. The orchard is full of surprises. We stop to nibble and discard several varieties of hard green pears and apples. Under a barren peach tree we find a well-bleached horse skull. Judith Ann thinks the poor horse was probably killed and eaten by wolves. She thinks perhaps she saw twenty or thirty wolves skulking about this morning while we were building our dam. She says wolves have a particularly strong appetite for small children. We become eager to get on with our trip to the field.

We pass through a large grove of heavy cottonwoods. I feel the eyes of a hundred ravenous wolves on me. My BB gun is back under the bed in Neligh, where Mom made me leave it. I pick up a fallen branch and begin to swing it menacingly above my head. Maybe the wolves will notice I am ready to go down fighting. Judith Ann begins to speculate about our own funerals. How sad our parents will be sitting in front of three little caskets, with three little well-gnawed bodies inside. Miriam starts bawling. This is an ear-splitting, very open-mouthed procedure. Judith says if only we had some Susabelle Band-Aids, we could slap them on the wolf bites and survive nicely. She plucks some currant leaves and pronounces them a good substitute.

"Remember that time, not so very long ago," Judith asks, "when Susabelle was walking through a grove of trees just like this one?" Miriam dries up a little. "She walked and walked, because it was a

lovely summer day, just like this one. After a little while Susabelle
heard a noise. She turned around, just like this, and looked and
looked but couldn't see anything. So she walked and walked until
she heard it again. She turned and there stood a big ugly wolf with
big yellow teeth!" Miriam starts sniveling again. I wave my stick.
"What do you suppose that big wolf did?"

"Eat Susabelle?"

"Well, he certainly tried. He snapped off her head with one big
bite and swallowed it whole."

"Did she bleed?"

"The blood came up out of her neck like a fountain. It poured and
poured, just like our upstairs toilet when it overflows, until the
ground was covered two feet deep. And just at the last minute, just
before Susabelle was about to faint from lack of blood, she reached
in her pocket for one of her new-fangled currant-leaf Band-Aids.
She stretched her arm way down in that old wolf's tummy and stuck
a Band-Aid on the top of her head and yanked it right out. She
slapped it back on her neck with a couple more new-fangled currant-leaf Band-Aids and was as good as new."

"What did the wolf do?"

"He was a very hungry old wolf and he wasn't about to give up a
meal as tasty as Susabelle. He opened his mouth wide, wider than
he'd ever opened his mouth in his entire life, because he intended to
swallow all of little Susabelle down to the bottom of his ugly old
stomach."

"What did Susabelle do?"

"What do you think Susabelle did? She whipped out one of her
super-duper extra-strength and anti-wolf Band-Aids and, quick as a
wink, wrapped that Band-Aid around his mouth. The wolf growled
and tore at the Band-Aid with his paws, but he couldn't get it off. It
was one of Susabelle's very best Band-Aids. You're probably thinking that wolf never did get that Band-Aid off his mouth, but Susabelle felt sorry for him. He was such an old wolf. Maybe he'd been a
nice wolf when he was younger. So Susabelle made him promise to

never eat any more children as long as he lived, and he did and she took off the Band-Aid."

"Did he keep his promise?"

"Of course he did. Wolves always keep their promises. But as she walked along in the woods, a woods a lot like this one, she heard a funny noise. It sounded like buttercups being trampled. She turned, and there right behind her stood a polar bear and he was terribly hungry . . ."

*

Grandpa stands on a small hill barking orders in several directions. Milton and some neighbors are cutting silage in a field of bleached stalks no more than three feet tall. A Caterpillar tractor, belching oily smoke, digs a narrow trench in a cut bank at our front. Grandpa's face is drawn, his neck corded with yelling. Sometimes he hollers at the distant silage cutters, sometimes at the oblivious Caterpillar operator. All is harsh sun and wind and noisy machinery and dust and yelling. Once he looks up into the cloudless sky and begins to curse. He curses everything and everyone. He curses the lazy neighbors and their poor equipment. He curses the Caterpillar guy, who can't understand what he's supposed to do or when he's supposed to do it. He curses Milton for not starting this project earlier in the day. But mostly he curses the weather for daring to burn up a B. J. Tupper crop. He uses words we have never heard to excoriate the weather. They are terrible words, words so full of spleen that we suspect the weather has made a fatal mistake in irritating our grandfather. We are afraid, too afraid to come closer. We leave Grandma's lunch a safe distance away and retreat to the creek and serious dam repair. Judith Ann does not talk any more of wolves or polar bears.

Eldon rides up in late afternoon. He wants to show us something in the haymow. He talks mostly to Judith Ann. I instantly suspect he has an unhealthy interest in my sister. The air in the mow is heavy with decomposing alfalfa. Eldon points out several abandoned nests of rotten hen eggs. He throws several against the barn wall, leaving blotches of stinking green slime. We turn down his suggestion of a rotten egg fight. A large cluster of eggs near the top of the mounded hay begins to move. A long garter snake slithers away down the other side. My sisters backpedal toward the ladder. Eldon heaves an egg in the general direction of the snake, saying garter snakes don't scare him none, that he's cut the heads off so many poisonous water moccasins he's plumb lost track of the total. He produces a large yellow onion and a pocketknife. He explains that an application of raw onion will make my sisters' eyelashes grow long and black. Soon the three of us are lying stupidly on the hay while Eldon cuts the onion into slices. We are not to open our eyes until the "medicine" has a chance to work its magic. Our eyes, covered with neat slabs of stinging onion, begin to water; our noses run. Soon we are headed for the house, half-blind, eager to find Grandma to tell on Eldon.

Stepping into the kitchen is like entering a furnace. Grandma is sweating over a green-bean canning project, her face composed in the worried expression she wears during serious work. "Land o' Goshen!" she exclaims once we list our complaints. "That Eldon does beat all!" We are directed to the wash-up sink in the kitchen. She rummages through the medicine cabinet for a jar of "special" salve, guaranteed to soothe onion-burned eyes in a jiffy. Before I know I am cured, she sends me out to gather any late eggs. Judith Ann and Miriam peel potatoes on the screened porch, muttering dark plots of revenge on Bloomers Eldon. They have noticed that their eyelashes are not yet growing.

The first hen I reach under pecks me smartly on the hand. I find a big stick and poke the heck out of the old bag until she gives up, floundering awkwardly out of the nest squawking her outrage. I learn to poke first. Grandma beams at my motley collection of eggs, several of them cracked by errant pokings. I scrub "my eggs" operating-room clean. Grandma says I am becoming a good worker.

Our twin aunts, Irene and Ilene, recently graduated from high school, come home from their work at the county ASCS office. They are pretty and stylish, talking a mile a minute, finishing each other's sentences. We are scooted out on the sleeping porch for a nap while they occupy the kitchen, taking turns in the washtub. Judith Ann says the Twins have boyfriends and are going to the movies. We are going to the movies too; Grandpa promised this morning, right after I nearly castrated myself with sausage gravy. Judith Ann says we should sit behind the Twins and their dates during the movie and see if they kiss. We practice exaggerated kissing sounds until we are hysterical. Grandma sticks her head in the door and tells us to shush, says we are "just a bunch of silly goofs." If we don't take this nap business seriously, maybe she should give us a good dose of castor oil to "settle you down." I don't know what castor oil might be, but I'm pretty sure I don't want any, even before Miriam, who has experience in being settled down, says, "It tastes icky and makes you BM every five minutes." We pretend to sleep. Pretty soon we do sleep.

*

Grandpa lets us sit on the front seat. He is wearing a white shirt and suitpants and a satin-banded snap-brimmed hat. He feeds us red-and-white striped peppermints from a big paper sack in the glove compartment. I think Grandpa must own all the candy there is. At seventy miles an hour the rutted dirt road behind us becomes a boiling mass of dust. As we top each little hill the car loses contact with the road; our stomachs jump for our throats. We tell Grandpa to go faster. He does. It is the best roller-coaster ride we've ever had. Grandma sits quietly in the back seat looking straight ahead, her hands twisting a handkerchief in her lap. Grandpa says this Ford has a good v-8 engine and an overdrive transmission. I decide my father should get an overdrive transmission so we can go over hills at seventy miles an hour and make our stomachs jump.

The sidewalks of Red Cloud are crowded with freshly bathed farmers and their loud kids. Everyone is in town to trade—eggs and cream for groceries. We let Grandma off at the big Farmer's Union grocery store and help carry in the eggs and cream. She stays to shop and talk with her friends. Grandpa takes us across the street to the Chief Theater. Every seat is taken except for three in the back. We cannot locate the Twins and their boyfriends among all these people. Grandpa brings us popcorn and boxes of licorice candy, then stands in the aisle beside us. During the cartoons he has a conversation with everybody coming in or going out. He is as loud as usual, but after the movie starts I pay no attention.

The credits roll to the sound of Indian war drums. Something bad is about to happen. A covered wagon comes into view. The guy driving the wagon is happy as a clam, talking to his cheerful sunbonneted wife on the seat beside him. They must not hear the war drums, which are getting louder and louder. The drums stop. An arrow thuds into the guy's chest. He grabs at the arrow and pitches over backward. Sunbonnet screams. I have seen enough violence. Judith Ann, who usually has to take me home early from scary movies, is disgusted. "It'll get better in a little bit," she says. "Just don't watch." I don't watch, but I sure can hear. Sunbonnet is screaming her fool head off. I peek. A grinning Indian in full war paint is approaching with a big old knife. Sunbonnet's hair is about to be lifted. I run. Grandpa catches up with me in the lobby. I tell him what is going on. He seems to be amused about something. He takes me by the hand out to the sidewalk. He says we will look up Milton.

We find Milton in the smoky darkness of the two-lane bowling alley. A shirtless boy not much older than Judith Ann works the manual pinsetters. Two guys are bowling, and a hundred people are watching. Every time one of them knocks all the pins down, a big cheer goes up. I notice the pin boy is smoking cigarettes. Grandpa says he is going back to the movie "to see what those girls are up to."

Milton and I wander through the crowd, stopping every once in a while to visit with the clumps of overalled farmers standing under the streetlights. He introduces me to each group as if I'm an important visitor. I shake dozens of work-hardened hands, just like a grown man. Everyone seems glad to see Milton. He is, without question, the handsomest guy in town—strong chin, deeply tanned face around a white-toothed smile, moving easily from group to group, passing a gentle word or a casual wave to everyone.

We find an empty tall-backed booth in the Palace Cafe. Ceiling fans turn silently below the high metal ceiling. Milton orders me a "Homestyle" at the largest, most elaborate soda fountain I have ever seen. The ubiquitous Homestyle is fifteen scoops of malt ice cream covered with malt powder, chopped nuts, butterscotch sauce, and whipped cream. At twenty-five cents it is the most expensive concoction in the place. It is delicious, a kid's hedonistic dream-come-true, more sugary sticky gunk than I can eat in a month. I do my best, but have to give up without inflicting much damage. Milton, eating so slowly I am afraid the whole mess will melt, finishes for me.

Barbara Bunch slides in the booth next to Milton. She is young and big-eyed beautiful. She and Milton seem to be in thunderbolt love. I am infatuated as well. I can't take my eyes off her cupid mouth, her every gesture. Milton fetches her an RC Cola, much superior to both Coke and Pepsi, she says. I peer suspiciously at the unfamiliar camels and pyramids on the label. Milton and Barbara hold hands while she finishes the bottle. I think I am getting more exposure to romance than my sisters with their scary Indian movie and no Twins in sight. Barbara says she has to get home. Her friends are waiting by the door. Milton reluctantly lets her go. He says her parents are "not too hot on this deal." I decide Barbara's parents must be real ding-dongs to disapprove of Milton, who is not only the best-looking, most likable guy in the entire country but a man who treats his buddies to Homestyles and lets them drive Ferguson tractors practically by themselves.

*

The Jones kids sleep on the screened porch that night. Indian Creek is alive with lightning bugs flitting in and around the goldenrod and nettles, much better than any fireworks display. Long after Susabelle has applied her last Band-Aid to the last life-threatening wound, when I have drifted off to the faint murmerings of my sisters' Bloomers Eldon plots, Judith Ann shakes me awake. The Twins have arrived. We tiptoe through the screened porch door out onto the front lawn. A four-door sedan is parked just beyond the yard fence. We can see four heads. They are far apart. Doors open, Twins and boyfriends walk to the back door. Judith Ann and Miriam sneak down to spy on the back stoop. I am too afraid to go with them. They run back snickering, triumphant. They have seen the

Twins get kissed. The car pulls away, we scamper back into bed. We hear muffled voices from the side yard. We hunker down, silent as wool. The Twins stroll by, arm in arm, through shifting clouds of lightning bugs. We cannot make out what they are saying. Judith Ann and Miriam burn with curiosity. Maybe the Twins are talking about important business, like kissing. My sisters get out of bed and follow with barefooted stealth. I worry that they will be caught, and we will all have to drink castor oil and make BMs every five minutes.

They are gone a very long time. I have stopped being nervous and have begun to get sleepy again. They come to bed breathless. They have heard everything, they say. The Twins are having some sort of romantic crisis. Ilene is dubious about her future with her boy-friend, who does not get along well with Richard, Irene's beau. "No man," Ilene is supposed to have said, "is more important than my sister." Judith Ann is sure Ilene's boyfriend is about to get his walking papers.

"Why did she kiss him if she doesn't like him anymore?" I ask. For once my sisters are stumped.

*

We are to be handed over to Uncle Clinton and Aunt Doris for the balance of our stay. We are looking forward to spending time with our fun-loving cousins, Ann and Dick. They live north of Riverton on Thompson Creek, a clear-running sand creek half again as large as Indian Creek. This is the much-storied Tupper family farm, where B. J. returned from his sojourn in Wyoming. My mother and father courted here, were married next to the lilac bush in the front yard. Leo sang at their wedding. The second-largest barn in the Thompson Creek valley sits east of the house. Grandpa, holding the Ford at a steady seventy-five miles an hour, is telling about building the barn:

"I was just short of sixteen, Bryan Lee. Dad hired a set of carpenters out of Omaha. They was all right, but didn't want to work any too fast. Dad put me in there to see to it they paid attention. We got 'er up in two weeks an' had them guys back on the train. They said next time they'd charge by the job instead of the hour. They wasn't sore, just makin' conversation."

Miriam wants to know if Grandpa really faced down an armed man out in Wyoming. "Oh it weren't any big deal. I just told him it was too cold to be standing around outside. It was terrible cold. That other fella's the one hit him with the stovewood. I was just kinda there is all. It was 'bout as cold the time that crazy Renfro woman ran off. They lived way out on the flats and the neighbors looked all over for a couple days. 'Bout froze my feet. Like to rode Edith's little horse plumb out. We finally found her up in the timber there. She was dead, of course. Couldn't nothin' live in weather like that. She'd been walkin' around this pine tree, walked down through the snow, wore a little ring in the dirt. Musta been purty confused."

We stop in Riverton to visit B. J.'s parents. Western-style storefronts and warped wooden sidewalks border the broad dusty main street. At midmorning of a hot June day, nothing but the tail of an occasional town dog is moving. The house rests at the base of a large hill on the west edge of town. This is where my parents watched the crest of the 1935 Republican River flood roll down the valley with the roar of a hundred freight trains, a roar so loud Grandma heard it six miles north on the Thompson Creek farm.

Willis J. Tupper shows us a big wooden barrel of buttermilk. Every so often a fierce beaked head appears at the top of the yellow slurry and fixes us with a baleful gaze. Buttermilk is supposed to leach the river taste out of snapping turtles. Great-Grandpa pays town kids ten cents for big snappers. Looking at those cruel jaws I think maybe it would take a dollar to get me much interested. Great-Grandpa has a big-bellied, easy disposition. If we come to Sunday dinner we can eat some fried turtle. I begin to hope we are a couple of hundred miles away by Sunday. He shows us his milk goat. I think the goat is too small and scruffy to give much milk, but Great-Grandpa says it gives way more than they can use. A substantial garden stretches north of the house. We admire rows of giant tomatoes. He whispers that his secret is the judicious application of turtle-scented buttermilk fertilizer.

All the while we are touring the grounds, the house buzzes with a high-pitched voice. Grandpa is listening to his mother. I begin to understand that he has come by his verbosity honestly. The modest square house smells of musty old age. We file into a marginally clean kitchen. Rows of canned mulberries sit on a counter. Great-Grandma says her relatives in the Sandhills are short of "eatin' fruit." She has birdlike arms and a small potbelly that pushes her mulberry-stained apron out into space. Her eyes blink brightly behind rimless spectacles. Her mouth snaps open and shut, like one of Great-Grandpa's buttermilk swimmers. She offers us soda crackers and cold goat milk. We take the crackers. Once we are settled, she resumes her querulous lecturing of my grandfather. He listens without interrupting. I begin to wonder if he has taken sick. After she pounds on him a while, she blisters Great-Grandpa about something else. We know she is smart because her talk is full of arithmetic. She spills out so many computations we become mesmerized.

"Will's been payin' seventy cents for good forty-pound oats. I'd rather be buyin' than sellin' at that kind of price, wouldn't you? I don't believe you could go too far wrong putting oats over on those two west patches next spring. You get an average kind of yield, mebbe eighty bushels, that'd get you fifty-six dollars an acre less'n interest on your ground of, say two-and-a-quarter, a dollar for seed and mebbe another three dollars and a dime for wear and tear on your overalls and a little charge on machinery. That'd leave forty-nine dollars and sixty-five cents times, oh, what is there? Eleven-and-a-third in that one and mebbe five-and-a-half in the other? Take that times forty-nine sixty-five and just round it off for easy figgerin'. That'd be eight hundred and thirty-five dollars and a hair over seventy-five cents. Sounds like a pretty likely way to make eight hundred and thirty-five dollars and a little over seventy-five cents to me."

Grandpa answers with even more arithmetic:

"Well, in the first place all them forty-pound oats is shipped in here from somewheres up in the Dakotas where the ground don't hardly get around to thawing no matter how hot it gets. Most likely after we got some a those hot Kansas winds we'd get closer to thirty-two pounds than we would forty. In the second place, that ground over west is sandy. Never did hold any moisture. We'd be lucky to get twenty-five bushels of light oats in an average year. We might get 'em in the ground for around what you say, but mebbe you should add a nickel onto that overall-and-machinery charge. Last time I bought rings for my A John Deere they wanted fifteen dollars and twelve cents. These parts are getting awful steep. So you add a nickel there. That brings your expenses up to six dollars and forty cents. You take twenty-five times fifty cents, which is what these elevator men are offering for light oats, less your land-and-expense charge, and you come up with six dollars and a dime times sixteen point eight three acres. In round figures that'd give you a hair over one hundred and two dollars and sixty-six cents. I think I'd just as soon plant Sudan grass over there and turn them yearlings onto it in August when the grass gets thin. Some a them bigger steers will gain three pounds a day on a good stand of Sudan. We can run a bunk over there and grain 'em a little. Might be a man could add a half-pound a day with a little rolled corn."

Great-Grandma fixes Grandpa with an unblinking predator's stare. "What would those pounds be worth on a yearling?"

"If we ship 'em to Kansas City, on today's market they'd bring around twenty-six and one-quarter cents. Cost you three per cent shrink and two cents in commission and freight. If twenty steers'd pick up a little over a hundred pounds in thirty days at twenty-six and one-quarter cents less commission and freight and death loss and a dab of interest charge, you'd end up with a shade less than five hundred dollars for your trouble."

Great-Grandma peers out the window at the garden. "I don't know why I got to thinking about oats. Will always thinks that goat ought to have anything she wants, even if it costs nine prices." Grandpa takes a bill from his billfold and slips it in her apron pocket. She protests a little, says it is too much, says they are managing just fine. But she takes the money. Turning cheerful, she urges us to work hard while we are at Clinton's and sends us on our way with crackers and an invitation to Sunday dinner. Platters of squirming turtle meat torture my imagination for months afterward.

*

We head north up the serpentine Thompson Creek road. We pass Riverton High School, from which my mother graduated at a precocious fifteen. We have recently uncovered some of her high school mementos in the Neligh parsonage attic, including a book of school cheers. Our favorite:

Boola, Boola, Boola, Boola
We will kick them in the knee
Boola, Boola, Boola, Boola
We will stomp them in the floor
Boola, Boola, Boola, Boola
Yea Riverton High School!

Any mention of Boola, Boola throws us into stitches. Mom does not share our amusement. The cheer book disappears into a new hiding place, along with several of Dad's unabashedly mushy courting letters. It takes us days to find them again.

Half a block north of the high school is the tiny parsonage Dad lived in for the year he served the Riverton–Spring Valley charge. He drove a twenty-five-dollar Model T into town in the fall of 1934 with the idea of commuting to his studies at Hastings College. The car proved to be a complete dud, however, and he made the best of his unplanned year's sabbatical by launching the successful courtship of B. J. Tupper's eldest daughter.

Grandpa, however, is not talking about farmer's daughters or capital-disadvantaged ministers. He is talking about a horse:

"That pure-bred Hamiltonian mare was awful high-lifed, had a nice easy rack. She could haul a buggy as fast as most saddle horses can run. We'd be comin' back from town on this road, and these other fellas with rigs would want to bet. Edith didn't care for it, but sometimes I did take 'em up. Those fellas didn't know too much. That Hamiltonian mare was never beat. She was as good a horse as I ever owned."

As we careen around the sharp curves, tires chattering on the washboarded surface, the idea of Grandpa tearing up Thompson Creek road in a buggy does not seem particularly farfetched.

Grandpa zooms through Clinton's farmstead without stopping, but he does take a quick inventory as we pass. He says Doris might have a few more hens than last year. We head north along the edge of the cornfield. He wants to see firsthand Clinton's new project, irrigating a few acres by pumping out of Thompson Creek. Grandpa is not sure it is worth the added expense. We find Clinton knee-deep in sand and water, trying to extract a drowned mud turtle from the intake pipe. Clinton is well-muscled, all bronze and sun-bleached, with a wide-brimmed straw hat tipped back. He is mighty peeved at the turtle, but he acts glad to see us. The corn in the watered patch is rank and green compared to the nonirrigated balance of the field. Clinton and Grandpa launch into an animated debate loaded with turtles, gallons of tractor fuel, bushels of corn, and lots of arithmetic. I can't tell who, if anyone, prevails. Clinton goes back to his stubborn turtle.

*

Ann and Dick have to show us everything at once—Rocket, Clinton's black Morgan stud horse; the rope swing in the haymow; the baby pullets in the barn cellar; the new Guernsey bucket-calf; their new accordions. Ann's enthusiasms are of the breathless variety. She is mad about Rocket. He is the fastest, most stylish horse in the neighborhood, and she can ride him anywhere. Dick and Ann are taking accordion lessons. We will hear their first duet. Maybe we would like to go swimming in Thompson Creek. There is a deep hole where we might see actual water moccasins. We should take some tin cans and a shovel so we can build dams and canals and sand houses. Dick says we will have a blast.

We sit waist-deep in cool water. Dick and I dig big handfuls of gravel from the creekbed and let the ambitious current carry it all away. Our hole does not grow as rapidly as we would like. On the east bank Ann and Judith debate the shape of their sand castle. Miriam scoops sand into her bucket until it is brimming, then carefully levels it off with a stick. She dumps her sand in front of the architects, content to let them decide how to use it. Our hole fills as fast as we can empty it. We decide to build a dam to divert the current. Then we can sink a hole six feet deep, maybe put up a diving board. We persuade Miriam to join our project. She assumes the position of principal engineer. We supply all the backbreaking labor. Ann and Judith scarcely pause to admire their finished castle before launching their own water-diversion projects. Soon there are three different dams under construction. A nation of beavers could not have been busier. Our dam is finished first, creating just the sort of backwater necessary for proper hole digging. We have a three-foot hole dug before Judith and Ann have their projects completely rip-rapped with flat rocks. They abandon construction to sit neck-deep in our new pool. Dick and I discover we can use our cupped palms to splat our sisters' eyes with great sprays of creek water. A general water fight breaks out. Dick and I make a coordinated attack. The girls retire in total defeat. Or perhaps they are bored. We assume it is a full surrender.

The fetid scent that has been floating around all morning begins to intrude. Dick and I head upstream. Entangled in a barbed-wire fence that stretches across the creek is a dead fat hog. The water we so recently splashed into eyes and mouths has flowed over and around his stinking carcass. Lodged in the drift sand, flyblown and waterlogged, the hog auditions for the job of chief bogeyman. Lately this spook, who whimsically switches locations between my closet and the dark dangerous area under my bed, has closely resembled the menacing Indian who was about to take Sunbonnet's hair when I made my untimely exit from the Red Cloud movie theater. For the next few nights the scalp-hunting Indian will take a back seat to platters of squirming turtle meat and the grinning eyeless skull of a maggoty pig.

Our discovery is a great success, of course. The girls are suitably impressed. They poke the poor hog with sticks and examine him from every angle. "That," says Miriam, using her stick as an audio-visual aid, "is where he made BMs." Someone raises the issue of cause of death. There is careless speculation about predators. Certain sisters seem a bit infatuated with wolves. Ann thinks there is a good chance the hog died from disease, perhaps the cholera she has heard her dad talk about. Miriam wants to know if humans can catch cholera from pigs. Ann is not sure. Gradually the realization that we are standing knee-deep in germ-rich hog-polluted water drives us out of the creek to pursue new castle- and moat-building projects on the bank. When Doris calls us for lunch, we hurry up to the house, not just because we are hungry.

Doris has laid on a spread. The table is crowded with bowls of fried chicken, new potatoes and cream gravy. The intensely pleasing aromas and tastes crowd visions of rotting hogs almost clear of the screen. Clinton asks each of us all sorts of questions. He is particularly interested in anything Judith Ann has to say about her school work. This is the first time I realize the creator of two or three thousand Susabelle and her magic Band-Aid stories might be considered intelligent by other folks.

We spend the early afternoon in the haymow, swinging off the oat bin roof on the knotted end of a thick hay rope anchored to the rafters forty feet above our heads. We all know the legend of Clinton and the hay rope; it came with our mothers' milk. How one day, while Edith and B. J. were gone, the rope broke under the weight of several kids. How Clinton, carrying one frayed end, climbed up in the rafters, where he braced himself, and in an astonishing show of strength, gave one sibling after another a ride on the end of the thirty-five-foot hay rope, swinging them high, wide, and handsome across the entire length of the haymow with only his strong hands as anchors. B. J., returning home to an empty house, wandered into the haymow to see what all the laughter was about. There is no dispute that Grandpa was horrified by what he saw. There is no dispute that he "warmed Clinton purty good" for such a fool stunt. There is also no dispute that Grandpa tells this story regularly to any unenlightened soul who crosses his path. Grandpa's boys seldom hear his praise unless it is secondhand.

Dick and I get a bedroom to ourselves, away from giggly girls.

Hanging out with a solid citizen like Cousin Dick reveals by contrast the astounding amount of silliness girls are apt to exhibit. While they are being goofy in the north bedroom, getting themselves shushed by Doris every five minutes, we are discussing the intricacies of catching dangerous wild animals with steel traps. A badger has made a costly visit to the barn's basement section, killing dozens of Hy-Line pullets. Dick has acquired a large beaver trap and has set it in the foundation crack he thinks the badger used. "I'll get him tonight," Dick says. "He won't be able to resist coming back for another meal."

We stare out the open screen door at the west end of our bedroom. The air above the creek bottom is alive with warm-night song. A few lightning bugs fly convoluted paths through the trees. We strain to hear the snap of the beaver trap, but the only metal sounds are the occasional clangs of hog-feeder lids from far up the creek. We know all about this second-story screen door. Didn't Milton, who as a boy often walked in his sleep, go through this door and out onto the hard ground below? Wasn't that the time he sprained both ankles so badly he was on crutches for weeks? I vow not to let myself sleepwalk. I concentrate so hard I am almost too far under to hear Dick when he promises me "a real blast" tomorrow.

*

Grandpa and Grandma have moved into Red Cloud. We make two quick late-winter trips down from snowbound Neligh. During the first Dad marries the Twins in a lavish double ceremony. Lloyd, Ilene's new intended, gets along with Richard much better than her old boyfriend. Miriam and Judith get new dresses. I get a new jacket for my ring-bearer duties. There are so many rings Dick has to carry half of them. Dad marries a Twin to the wrong guy and has to back up and start over. This creates considerable merriment in the crowd. Dad laughs as much as anyone. Dick and I help my sisters and Cousin Ann fill the lone honeymoon car with as much rice as we can heave.

Two weeks later we are back for Milton and Barbara's wedding. I sense that Milton has won only a grudging consent to his suit. The marriage rituals are now familiar, but the air is full of tension. Barbara's mother appears to be making most of the decisions. Neither I nor Dick is toting rings in this one, and I am grumpy, feeling much abused by the slight. Our rival, the sniveling wretch of a designated ring-bearer, gets a severe case of the fantods and is carted out in complete ignominy. Serves Mrs. Bunch right, I think, for not picking one of the pros. I forget all this when the wedding march is played and Barbara, even more stunning than I remember, comes down the aisle. I think Milton is one lucky guy.

Milton and Barbara will move onto the Indian Creek place. Grandpa, at sixty, is officially retired, although he plans to lend a hand in a supervisory role. He will run his herd of ninety Hereford cows for another twenty-eight years. Ilene and Lloyd and Irene and Richard are temporarily farming outside of B. J. Tupper's orbit. In the living room of his new house in town, Grandpa worries about them all. Farm prices, buoyed by the Korean Conflict, are bound to crash. Higher interest rates are as near as the next Republican victory. None of his offspring or in-laws are anticipating these catastrophes, and worse, in spite of his best efforts at sounding the alarm, no one is making any plans to deal with them.

On the living room wall to Grandpa's right is an oval frame. Grandpa has hired the local photographer to make it on special order. Leo's picture, taken in his first lieutenant's uniform, has been superimposed on one of Sophie with the baby Anita in her arms. Sophie is lovely, her warm smile looking straight into the camera. Above and a little to one side, hanging in a celestially vague background, is Leo, looking grimly at something way off to his right, in the opposite direction of his family. The total effect is of ghostly dissonance. I wonder if Leo knew he was going to hit a mine, if that's the reason he stares off in the distance toward fateful Sicily. If he knew, I ask myself, why did he go?

Grandpa moves to the price of wheat, then corn, then hogs. He tongue-lashes the Republicans on their high-tariff trade policies. He blasts the Democrats for coddling the labor movement. People who go looking for communists under every bed "don't know too much," he says. I wonder if communists look anything like maggoty hogs. Grandpa says that while he "doesn't hold much with sky pilots," the new Methodist minister "seems to be a nice fella." He speculates on where the stock market might go from here. My father, who at this point in his life does not have a checking account and is sitting on our entire accumulated capital, nods agreeably in the appropriate places.

Outside, the early March wind whistles through bare branches, skitters gravelly snow over the hard-crusted drifts. Our road back to Neligh may blow shut again. Grandma hollers in from the kitchen that all the talk about money makes her tired. Grandpa says, "She's al'ays been like that." He worries about some local young men who have recently been drafted. He informs my bemused father, who asked to be classified a conscientious objector just prior to World War II, that these boys could have used a little-known section of the draft law to declare themselves conscientious objectors. "I told those fellas," Grandpa complains, "but none of 'em would pay any attention."

Heading West

The moving van is backed up to the parsonage's high-roofed front porch. Two swarthy men, violet tattoos glistening under a sweaty sheen, wrestle our ancient piano up the loading plank. I have been watching the movers all morning from my perch on a stack of blankets inside the van. Initially they responded to my barrage of questions with gruff good nature. Now, after six hours of uninterrupted labor, my former buddies seem to resent my presence. Innocent questions like "Why did you wrap the green floor lamp in a blanket and not the gold one? Where are you going to put my tricycle? How long will it take you to drive this truck from Neligh to Chappell? Why did you drop that box of dishes? Do you think anything is broken?" are answered with mutters and grunts. The oldest mover, the one with tattooed snakes encircling his skinny arms, glares at me. He reminds me a little of the sleepy prisoners behind the barred windows over at the Antelope County jail after the Stefel boys and I shoot them with water pistols. Maybe it would be a good time to see what my sisters Judith Ann and Miriam are doing.

They are up in the attic sorting through old playthings. They pack up Judith Ann's chemistry set, although she will be using a fresh variety of serious chemicals at her new high school. I hope to take sole possession of the old set once we get moved. Miriam, blessed with a middle child's skills at manipulating parents, may have other ideas. It is hardly a prize worth fighting over. Although packed in an impressive red tin box, the good stuff has been used up long ago, mostly during one botched experiment. In their attic lab, Judith Ann and Miriam, choosing the chemicals with the most unpleasant odors, mixed up a dangerously smoking purple concoction. Fearing that it was about to explode, they dumped it out on the roof, where it cascaded into the gutter, staining the shingles the color of old peas and eating a fist-sized hole in the gutter. Judith Ann and Miriam live in constant fear that someday a church board member will step out of the sanctuary and let his gaze float up to the parsonage's third story, where the coppery evidence of their perfidy will betray them.

They are leaving behind their dress-up clothes, great heaps of clunky high-heeled shoes, piles of stained hats and musty out-of-style dresses. On the attic walls hang brilliantly colored satin banners proclaiming every new Studebaker model year since 1948. Mrs. Mahood, who lounges around her apartment in a mink wrap and wears her heavy stockings rolled down around her ankles, commandeers advertising pennants from her car-dealer husband. She gives them to us, along with generous tips, when she pays her monthly *Omaha World-Herald* bill. We convert these banners into the gaudy togas and Holy Land cloaks needed to stage bloody conflicts between early Christians and the Roman Empire. I find my role as a highhanded centurion immensely satisfying, especially the dramatic floggings of my piteously weeping sisters who play, with great conviction, their roles as martyred Christian maidens. My mother has declared the old clothes and Studebaker banners casualties in the war against accumulated junk. We box them up, assuming the next set of parsonage children will use them to great advantage.

Judith Ann and Miriam haul a lone carton of special keepsakes down to the second-floor landing for the movers' convenience, then begin packing the sparse collection of mementos from their bedroom—Miriam's doll collection, a box of garish jewelry, some Blue Waltz perfume. Eager to get to western Nebraska, I have finished my boxing up days ago. My sisters are less enthused but have resigned themselves, knowing it is the lot of a Methodist minister's family to be periodically uprooted. They wish they weren't leaving behind their bosom friends, and hope, with little confidence, that school in Chappell will be as challenging as in Neligh.

I wander downstairs, where my mother is on her hands and knees scrubbing the floor of the empty kitchen. She is singing. The adventure of going to a new place always has that effect. It strikes me as odd that she isn't sad to be leaving the newly remodeled kitchen, with its sparkling sink and clean-smelling cabinets. I am remembering when the carpenters tore out the old cabinets and uncovered a maze of mice and rat burrowings in the wall. "No wonder," my mother said, "I could never get rid of them."

The church is less than thirty feet from our side door. My father is in his office packing up the last of his books. He moves with deliberate care, stacking each full box within easy reach for the movers' next trip, scrawling hieroglyphics on the boxes that no one but he can read. He motions in a westerly direction.

"I understand Chappell has a nice swimming pool."

"Will we be able to swim?"

"Probably. I don't think they've had as much trouble with polio out there. I hope not."

"Will I be able to get my own dog?"

"Might be."

My own dog. No more secondhand, part-time pets. No more subverting the neighbor's dog with table scraps. I will get a pup, train him the right way. In no time we will be exploring the world, a pair of grim-visaged adventurers equal to any challenge. My sisters can grump around all they want, but to me this moving deal is sounding better and better. I have no idea, of course, that by moving from the subsistence corn-and-hog farm economy of northeastern Nebraska to the wheat-rich Panhandle our family is about to get a solid boost in income. No one, least of all my father, has let on that the Chappell ministry, with its large, warm-hearted congregation, is considered a plum appointment for a pastor of his age and experience. All I know is the powerful entity my parents call "The Cabinet" has decreed that we move. If my mother is singing in an empty kitchen, it must be all right.

*

My optimism turned out to be paltry downpayment on our seven years in Chappell, Nebraska, a world filled with strange and wonderful characters. How could I, eight years old and four hundred miles away, have predicted the existence of J. Steinway Stoble, arguably the world's most successful hitchhiker; Indian Charlie, implacable foe of Wyatt Earp; Jackrabbit Vincent, hunter *par excellence*; Mrs. Keister, the mad banshee; or my soon-to-be blood enemies, the Churtedepriches? Blind to anything that was about to happen, I was merely a hopeful child, anxious to commence the roll westward, just ahead of a couple of tattooed soreheads in a Mayflower moving van.

Indian Charlie
by Aaron Pyle, from the collection
of Dale and Jeanine Kastens

Indian Charlie

Indian Charlie rode a fat horse. Mostly he rode the alleys in the late afternoons, scouring trash barrels for the grass clippings his roly-poly pinto turned into lard. Charlie made time for any kid to climb up behind for a short trip around the block. And if any town within a day's ride threw a parade, Charlie would be there, big white smile, riding easy in the black-and-silver saddle, short legs stuck out over the pinto's barrel belly. Parades brought out the hoarded turquoise, a heavy conch belt, lots of rings, one massive bracelet. Brought out his best shirt too, a silky western cut with pearl snaps. Must have cost at least four dollars. Afterward he'd stick around the celebration, give kids rides until he wore them out or until it was time to ride home before dark.

Before he became famous a second time, Charlie, semiretired off the famous Lisco Ranch, drifted down from the southern Sandhills in the early forties to our little railroad town. Charlie Barnett was his chosen handle, although the Lisco crowd thought he'd been Juan Flores when he'd wandered in from Arizona. He came north by way of Vernon, Texas, sometime before the Great War, maybe about the time Pancho Villa was tying a can on Black Jack Pershing's tail down in old Mexico. Sometimes the cowboys up there called him Jack Barnett, sometimes Indian Jack, which he liked, or Nigger Jack, which he didn't. They didn't call him Nigger Jack unless they wanted to fight. No one knew for sure if he was Spanish, Apache, or Hottentot. Charlie wouldn't say. Wouldn't say how old he was either, ever. When the locals buried him in 1963, they put a best guess down as a birthdate.

Old as he was, and he couldn't have been a day less than seventy-five when he came to town, Charlie remained a hard worker. When he wasn't hauling and piling grass clippings down by his shack near the railroad tracks, he scraped paint for the local body shop and tended the gaited American saddlebred horse kept by a local businessman on some nearby vacant lots. Charlie knew diddly-squat about gaits, but he knew horses and could soothe that hot-blooded gelding with a few quiet words of his mumbo-jumbo talk that wasn't quite Spanish and sure as hell wasn't English.

The boys I ran with thought Indian Charlie was Mexican. He was "short-coupled" like most of the brown men that rode handcars out to repair the Union Pacific tracks every morning. But he had a peculiar coppery skin and a voice that rose up from somewhere down around his boots. He was Indian all right, any fool that ever heard Jay Silverheels say "Yes, Kemo Sabe" knew that by gut instinct. I was dead certain he had a war bonnet stashed under his bed, a bow and flint-tipped arrows, some solid evidence of Indianness hidden in a clever Indian way. Surely he wasn't simply a retired Mexican herder just off one of the last big spreads in Nebraska. Nope, he was a 100 percent pure D Indian who was pretending, for his own inscrutable savage reasons, to be a retired Mexican sheepherder.

The fact that Charlie smiled as easily as breathing didn't mean we took him for a patsy. Anyone else riding a lard-ass pony up and down my alley would have come to immediate grief. Shooting that fat tub of goo full of BBs would have been the first order of business, and if that didn't work, we'd have thunked him good with some rocks, or stuffed a lighted M-80 under his tail, or dropped a Molotov cocktail in front of his fat face. We would have done what it took to make him buck, pile his rider in the most painful way imaginable. However, even though the alley was our sacred territory, we didn't mess with Indian Charlie, and I never knew anyone who did. He was just too damned good-natured and too damned unflappable. And after all, who knew with Indians? Next parade might see my mangy little scalp hanging from Indian Charlie's silver-plated saddle horn.

*

From a kid's viewpoint, Pokorny's Pharmacy had a couple of things going for it. The rowdiest soda fountain in town, it was the only business that consistently stocked the kind of lurid magazines that featured naked women. We never actually purchased the magazines; that would have been way too mortifying. The clerks were always high school girls. We'd have no more walked up to the cash register with one of those well-thumbed little black-and-white sleaze collections than we'd have asked an actual girl for a date. No, much simpler all around just to steal the magazines. Wasn't a kid worth his salt that didn't have a low-cost batch of Pokorny cheesecake photography stashed where his mother wouldn't stumble over it.

Pokorny soda jerks, also girls but more approachable than the clerk types, turned out the entire soda-fountain repertoire of that era: lime phosphates; ice-cream sodas; chocolate, lemon, cherry, and graveyard Cokes; malts with real malt powder; obscenely huge ice-cream sundaes; and the inimitable tin roof. A tin roof was anything topped with marshmallow creme, which possesses all sorts of interesting chemical properties. Mixed with anything fizzy, marshmallow creates a steady foaming action, inundating the table with gluey stickiness.

Once the fountain personnel cleaned up three or four of those little messes and were showing signs of shutting off our marshmallow creme supply, we switched to our real mission for the day, shooting straw wrappers up at the ceiling. Tear off one end of the paper straw wrapper, dip the other end in marshmallow creme, aim at the lofty tin ceiling, and blow hard. Pokorny's ceiling, at any given time, downsprouted several hundred of these gummy little missiles, waving gently in the slight breeze, waiting patiently for those dog days of summer, just before wheat harvest, when the temperatures climbed above a hundred, when the furnace winds blew up from some unimaginably hot portion of the Texas panhandle, making the wheatfields smell like fresh baked bread. It was then the marshmallow creme stickum would sort of give up, not all at once, but gradually, so that no more than four or five straws an hour would come floating down to attach themselves with equanimous precocity to the hot-water bottles, suntan lotion, patent medicines, and Dr. Scholl's foot-care products that stuffed Old Man Pokorny's shelves. And it was a rare magazine purchased or stolen during the warm months that didn't bear some telltale white gunk on its cover. Pokorny hated all of this, of course. He'd come roaring out of his little drug cage, swearing and threatening us all with lost soda-fountain privileges. On rare occasions he lapsed into a state of abject depression, and we desisted for a day or two. Otherwise we waited only for him to get back in his cage before resuming our love affair with marshmallow creme. We all expected him to stop serving tin roofs or to buy the kind of plastic straws without a wrapper. That he never did either remains one of those youthful mysteries that still gnaws a bit.

We were also puzzled when Pokorny turned his place into a makeshift art gallery. Aaron Pyle, student of Thomas Hart Benton and local semi-hermit, lived and painted just outside of town. Pyle had experienced some personal troubles of the vague unmentionable sort. Rumor had it he painted sporadically, that his best work was done back in the thirties and forties when he'd been as crazy as a raccoon. Those in the know whispered that wife number one, who shared the first name of wife number two, had surprised a straight-arrow Aaron Pyle, newly returned from the service, with a right good dose of syphilis. Aaron had unloaded the wife, the story went, but had to paint his way out of his depression. Silly bugger couldn't feed himself if he didn't have a few hogs around to pay the bills. Lord knows how that new wife put up with him. Hogs weren't much of a status symbol in fifties wheat society. A man raising hogs was seen as motivated by some deep financial desperation. Why else would he put up with the stink?

Recently Pyle had taken to splashing up precious little egg tempera portraits of Herefords and windmills. Benton showed up periodically, taking Pyle off to the Sandhills or the Tetons for extended paint-offs. Despite Benton's reflected stature, Pyle's work found its way into only a few local homes. If some knowledgeable messenger had told us that Aaron Pyle often collected $60,000 from a single Kansas City show, we would have signed the commitment papers on the spot.

Somehow Pyle talked Indian Charlie into posing for some art ses-

sions with local amateur painters. Probably it wasn't all that hard.
He gave Charlie a little walking-around money, usually a quarter,
sometimes fifty cents. Ex–hired men don't exactly live off the fat of
the land in their retirement years. Charlie hoarded every cent in a
two-quart fruit jar. After he died the locals used the quarters to pur-
chase a decent, if erroneous, headstone. Pyle's painting of Charlie is
arguably his career-best portrait, departing slightly from the Benton regionalist style that dominated his work. While Pyle painted,
his students finished four very similar portraits and hung them in a
row right above the back booths in Pokorny's soda fountain.

"Looks like Indian Charlie, all right."

"A hundred dollars! That says a hundred dollars! Is that for all of
them? For one painting? Holy crap!"

"Why did they paint Charlie? Been easier to take a picture. Those
folks must not have enough work to do."

"Pyle's crazy, you know. Been sent to Ingleside so many times
they've lost track."

"Bet I can stick this straw paper right on Charlie's nose."

*

Highway 30 ran through the middle of town. That was before the
interstate took away the tourist trade. Wasn't anything to see folks
from California or Pennsylvania picking up some film in Pokorny's,
maybe stopping long enough for a cherry phosphate before tackling the heat of the highway again. And they stared at all those
straws, too dumbfounded to even ask. And some of them saw the
Indian Charlie pictures, but nobody bought. We would have been
shocked if they had. Because those four portraits of Indian Charlie
with the $100 price tags had become part of the Pokorny scene, that
jumbled pile of marshmallow creme–stained merchandise that didn't
have much chance of ever being sold. Hell, we were stealing magazines that were three years old.

Maybe the art students slipped into Pokorny's one day when no
one was looking and retrieved their paintings. Maybe the sight of
Charlie shot full of marshmallow-tipped arrows gave them the fantods. At any rate the portraits disappeared.

Pyle's Indian Charlie picture sold quickly, not to the typical thin-lipped high-society Kansas City art collectress that activated Mrs. Pyle II's jealousy glands, but to a well-heeled, savvy Sandhills ranch woman, the kind of woman bound to drive Mrs. Pyle II *completely* nuts. Not that Aaron Pyle fooled around. No sir. He might have used a dab more Brylcreme than was strictly in good taste; his mustache would be considered more car salesman than artistic today. He hung out in Kansas City, where bored rich women are likely to do about anything they want, and he was quiet and unassuming, a sure sign of explosive repressed lust. But the unvarnished truth of it, in spite of anyone's suspicions, was that Aaron Pyle was a goody-goody two-shoes. Didn't drink, didn't cuss, didn't chase collectresses. Mostly he painted and made a whole pile of money, which, if appearances mean anything, he never spent.

But Mrs. Pyle II had her doubts. So when the Indian Charlie painting changed hands once or twice, in each instance for what was a small fortune in those humble times, she may have seized the notion that she'd been ripped off by some floozy in a couple of painful ways. On the other hand, it could have been a simple honest cleaning accident. Someone soaked the painting with ammonia water, accidentally or otherwise, and damn near cooked it. By 1981, when it was successfully restored, part of Indian Charlie's hat and most of his jaw had flaked off.

Ward Newcomb, retired Chappell dentist and full-time raconteur, tells of working in the Montana hayfields as a youth and on a rare trip to town stopping by pure chance at an art show where he could have purchased a Charlie Russell painting for ten dollars. "And I had the ten dollars," he said, "and I didn't do it."

Well, I had the hundred dollars and didn't do it. I could have never paid the freight on Pyle's portrait of Charlie, of course. Certainly that picture has never sold for less than $1,500. But a study of a Hereford wandering around the windmills would have been well within a kid entrepreneur's budget. My somewhat desultory *Omaha World-Herald* paper route paid three dollars a week, and my mother made me bank two. Spending a dollar a week wasn't as easy as it might sound to a child of the Nixon-Ford-Carter years. In the fifties a dollar was twenty cherry Cokes, ten ice-cream sodas, ten tin roofs, six ice-cream sundaes, or twenty Hershey bars. A young man could raise a dandy crop of pimples and thoroughly ruin a decent set of teeth on what a buck would buy, and have money left over for a trip to the movies with popcorn. I had the hundred in the bank, and another hundred just like it if I cashed my war bonds. Of course, no one would have let me touch *that* money. War bonds were sacred college dough, money that was supposed to buy me a serious education, pave my path to leather-elbowed history professorville, money that lasted approximately five seconds into my first encounter with a college registrar. Occasionally I harbor the wildly optimistic whim that the money was spent in the best possible cause.

*

Like I said, Charlie, even if he was a nice guy, was no sissy. Hugh O'Brien, on the other hand, was a pansy of the worst sort. Our new TV could only pull in one fuzzy channel, the one that carried "Gun-smoke" and "Wyatt Earp." Nothing wrong with the theme song, "Wyatt Earp, Wyatt Earp, brave, courageous, and bold," but then Hugh O'Brien strolled into the picture with those tight black pants and that lantern-jawed face. Danged if he didn't wear lace shirts once in a while. Matt Dillon, on the other hand, was a man. Wouldn't catch Matt Dillon wearing any lace.

Had our library possessed any Matt Dillon books, this last little Indian Charlie mystery would never have surfaced. It did have a Wyatt Earp book, though, and I read it. Didn't want to, but in the recently-put-on-television-western-folk-hero genre, that one book constituted the total supply. I followed Earp from Kansas, which was a place so in need of sissifying that Hugh O'Brien never left, to Tombstone, Arizona, the town too tough to die. Shortly after the unpleasantness at the OK Corral, what was left of the Clanton faction started bumping off Earps. Morgan, the most congenial of the irascible Earp family, standing with his back to a plate-glass window, took a fatal charge of lead while playing a game of pool. *Indian Charlie* and two other gunmen were seen running from the scene, but Indian Charlie *was never found*. That's what it said right there in a real book borrowed from the Chappell public library. Didn't take a genius to add this one up. Couldn't be more than one Indian Charlie from Arizona.

*

Tobacco was our drug of choice in those days, and supply was a constant worry. No merchant would sell cigarettes to a little kid, and they kept them behind the counter to discourage shoplifting. Careless parents occasionally left an odd pack on a kitchen counter or in a glove box, but those were undependable sources. Indian tobacco, a shirt-tail relation of the sage family, grew profusely in the canyons north of town. Collected and dried, it served fairly well as a substitute, with the added attraction of being mildly hallucinogenic. But it was basically without risk. There were tons of the stuff free for the taking, and nobody seemed to be interested in keeping it away from audacious boys. Had there been a law against Indian tobacco, we'd have never looked at another Lucky Strike.

I don't know who came up with the idea of collecting cigarette butts from the street in front of the tavern. The price was right, and there were gobs of them. Put nine-year-old dope fiends to work scooping up butts off the street, and it doesn't take long to get several pounds of the filthy things. Take them home, strip off the paper, stuff the mixed-up tobacco in a pipe, and puff away. Everything was cool, except for one vexing mental intrusion—the clear vision of some of the pukey-looking wretches who smoked outside the tavern. We hoped by burning the tobacco, we were killing all the deadly germs pukes were bound to be carrying. But it nagged all the same.

We'd had a good morning, gathering maybe a half-pound of fresh discards, when Indian Charlie rode up on his black-and-white pinto. He was too polite to ask what we were doing. We said hello and started moseying away from the crime scene. Cool, we were cool. What better time to ask Charlie if he'd ever been in Tombstone? Knock him off balance, make him forget all about the minor crime he'd just witnessed.

"Ya, I been in Tombstone lotsa times."

"What did you do there?"

"I worked. Big ranches down there, bigger than here."

"You ever run into any Earps?"

Charlie, the man who smiled as often as he breathed, went slightly berserk. "Bad, Earps bad!" Charlie spat and yanked at the reins, his face rigid with hate. "Earps all crooks," he yelled. He searched our stunned faces for belief. Mistaking our open-mouthed dumbfoundedness for doubt, he spurred his fat horse, who began to amble a little more rapidly.

We followed.

"We heard Wyatt Earp was the greatest lawman that ever lived."

No response.

"We heard the Clantons were all a bunch of jerks."

No response.

"We heard that Morgan Earp was a nice man. Some skunk shot him in the back. You know about that, Charlie?"

"You kids don't know nuthin'. You think you know, but you don't. Earps do bad things. Nobody catch them, but they steal."

"What about Morgan Earp, Charlie? Did he steal too?"

"You kids don't know nuthin'," he grumbled, all at once giving it up. And we let him go then, let him ride off, all the fight gone, slumped down on that impossibly round pony. We never spoke to him again. He'd have probably spoken, but our much-belated guilt held us back. We let him be, and he let us be. And we never told. It perhaps was as honorable a bargain as a bunch of brainless boys were capable of making.

*

To most of us, Charlie's last years looked a little lonesome. An illiterate man with no electricity didn't have a television or a newspaper to keep him company. But he had a certain amount of local fame, even before the portrait business, and everybody liked him, kids especially. He had his fat horse, his parades. Taken together it might have seemed like a pretty agreeable life. Sheepherders, after all, aren't used to much human contact.

One rainy Halloween night Gary Steele and I were beating on doors for UNICEF, our shivering discomfort nothing compared to that of all those starving zillions around the world. The last doorbell had been rung, the last dime stuffed in our official UNICEF donation canister. We were headed back through the wind and wet to the local Methodist church for some dishwatery cocoa. A yellow-orange glow off to our left streamed from Charlie's window. We eased up to his house, not thinking of levying a UNICEF charge on poor old Indian Charlie, a man we'd been avoiding since the Earp set-to, but merely to confirm his miraculous aquisition of electricity. Even if we had known about Charlie's secret burial fund we wouldn't have bothered the shrunken old cowboy sitting at a rough wooden table, staring blankly into a sooty kerosene lamp. While we watched he gave no indication he ever did anything with his wakeful nighttime hours but sit hypnotized by a smoky old lamp. It would have been spooky even if it weren't Halloween.

*

The modern tourist-trap version of Tombstone, Arizona, has all the transient ambience of mining camps immemorial. Raw-lumber sidewalks covered with raw-lumber porches tacked onto raw-lumber storefronts run for several blocks on both sides of the street. On the edge of town, out where the desert expanse of rocks and sagebrush begins in earnest, a supremely tacky souvenir shop guards the entrance to Boothill Cemetery. The cemetery contains most of what little genuine history remains in Tombstone. Full of rocky hillocks and meandering walks, Boothill is the equal-opportunity home to both outlaw scum and genteel shopkeeps. A thinly stocked book-rack inside the souvenir shack, on the far wall opposite the rubber rattlesnake bins, offers a small selection of local histories. Indian Charlie makes token appearances in most of them. Of particular interest to me was a collection of *Tombstone Epitaph* news articles covering the events surrounding the assassinations we now call "The Gunfight at the OK Corral."

According to the *Epitaph*, Wyatt Earp rode down his brother's killer in the hills outside of Tombstone and swiftly dispatched him.

There were many witnesses, a very official coroner's inquiry. Local history books give muddled accounts. Most agree with the *Epitaph*; a couple say Indian Charlie got clean away, probably to Mexico. Hard to imagine a notorious killer like Wyatt Earp resting until his brother's murder was thoroughly avenged, especially since he executed not only the three men deemed directly responsible for brother Morgan's death, but somewhere between six and twelve other guys who might have once spoken a friendly hello to the evil threesome. The actual non–Hugh O'Brien Wyatt Earp was not someone given to kidding around when he was pissed off. Chances are good that he "sieved" the Indian Charlie responsible for Morgan's death, just like he "sieved" anyone else that looked at him crossways. Chances are good that the Indian Charlie I knew just happened to grow up in a countryside teeming with rabid Earp-haters, and thoroughly absorbed the Tombstone-area prejudices before he moved on to Texas and Nebraska. Chances are good, but as I said, accounts are muddled.

∗

What used to be called the Lisco Ranch still spreads over 160,000 acres on both sides of the North Platte River. In place of the archetypical bachelor cowboys and bunkhouses of the early 1900s, numerous hired men and their families live in houses scattered around the ranch. Many of them own some livestock and receive fringe benefits—retirement plans, health insurance, that sort of thing. Large herds of cattle still graze the rough pastures in the breaks above the river, not so many Herefords now, more Angus and exotic breeds. Ranch hands fix several hundred miles of fence every spring; creaking windmills pump all summer; skillful ropers still catch and treat pink-eyed calves. The sheep are gone, replaced by a modern fish farm.

The village of Lodgepole lies a few miles south of the mammoth Lisco spread, strung out along Highway 30 just north of Lodgepole Creek. Aaron Pyle's Indian Charlie portrait, nicely patched up from its ammonia bath, hung in the Lodgepole State Bank lobby for several years. The owner, a rancher from north of town who grew up knowing Charlie, had once swapped houses near Alliance, Nebraska, and made sure the picture above the mantle in the new house was included in the deal. Recently the nail holding Charlie to the bank wall gave way, dropping the picture across some office furniture, leaving a deep gouge across one corner. Charlie is back in the painting hospital, and as soon as he's fixed up he'll hang in the new Museum of Nebraska Art in Kearney. Any fair-minded person who studies that picture will notice that underneath the superficially serious appearance, in the eye crinkles, in the upward tug at the corners of his mouth, in the friendly amusement in his brown eyes, it's all Indian Charlie can do to keep from smiling.

Hall of Science

Not only did his massive white head sprout a prickly military flattop, but his entire mountainous body radiated icy professorial distance. We'd seen his yellow horsey teeth, meticulously picked clean after every noon hour, but no one had seen him laugh. The idea of Mr. Hall, our science cum civics teacher, taking some buddies down to the tavern for a casual beer or perhaps swapping jokes and schnapps in a cold, dark duck blind at five in the morning was patently ridiculous. His one lame gesture at casual public behavior was a weekly Sunday afternoon tour around town with his grumpy fat wife in their saggy-sprung ten-year-old Pontiac. It was the cheapest model, of course, sporting a nifty column-mounted three-speed manual transmission and less than thirteen ounces of decorative chrome. The Halls, old-fashioned teaching gypsies, moved from town to town in search of fatter paychecks. The single most important factor in a teacher's success in the 1990s, sucking up to students, was pretty much unknown in Hall's day. If a teacher got fired in one place, snagging a job somewhere else wasn't particularly difficult. "Good disciplinarians" were always in demand.

A guy who stood six-foot three and tickled three hundred pounds should have, at the very least, a nice rumbly chuckle, one of those hearty bowl-full-of-jelly models. Old Man Hall rumbled all right, but usually he was chewing Harold Boxbender's ass right down to the bone.

"Harold?"

"Huh?"

"Why are you making a paper airplane instead of doing your assignment?"

"I dunno."

"When is the last time you had a passing grade?"

"I dunno."

"What is your mother going to say when she sees your report card?"

"I dunno."

"Do you think Thomas Edison and Alexander Graham Bell spent their valuable class time making paper airplanes?"

"We-e-ll, maybe. Maybe they would've if they'd knowed what they was. Maybe, just maybe they would of. You can't say they wouldn't. Maybe they coulda been making paper pigeons 'er paper locomotives 'er paper-covered wagons by the bushel basket. You don't know. They coulda, coulda easy, guys as bright as them two. Maybe made paper telephones and paper light bulbs for all you know."

KKKRRRRRRWHAPPP! Old Man Hall's palm smacked Harold flat on the cheek, lifting him clear of his desk to sprawl against the mopboard.

"Young man, you're going to run me out of patience one of these days. Then what do you suppose will happen to you?"

Harold, dignity shot to hell, sat on the floor glaring, his face neatly imprinted with Hall's finger marks. He was snuffling some, but he was angry, you could see that, not scared like the rest of us. Maybe he was so surprised he wasn't dead, he thought he was ten feet tall and bulletproof. You take a three-hundred-pound guy's best shot and live, and a certain confidence factor creeps in there. He was stomping to his desk when Old Man Hall yelled, "Well? Why don't you answer me?"

And Harold, shaking mad and probably not hearing the question, stuck out his tongue and gave Old Man Hall the biggest, spittiest PHHHHHHHHHHHHHHLLLLLLLLLLLGGGGGGGGGG you ever heard before he marched back to sit rigidly in his desk, glaring at Hall all the while with his deranged watery blue eyes.

We knew Hall would dismember Harold on the spot, throw his skinny freckled arms and legs in the trash, leave Harold's redheaded skull on the lectern as an object lesson. The important question was, would he stop at Harold? Wouldn't surprise anyone if this guy was mad enough to kill and eat half of us before it was over. Hall sprang to Harold's desk. He grabbed Harold's arm and lifted him until his toes dangled, lifted Harold's desk too, and started for the door. Maybe Old Man Hall intended to butcher Harold out of sight of the squeamish. But the desk wouldn't go through the doorway sideways, and Harold wouldn't turn loose for anything.

BULL-AAAANGGG! That old metal desk hit the doorjamb. BULL-AAANGGGG! BULL-AAAAAANGGGGG! BULL-AAAAANGGG! BULL-AAAAANNNGGGG! And Harold is holding on to save his soul and Old Man Hall is sucking air like a used Hoover. AHHH HUH, AHHH HUH, BULL-AAANGGG, AHH HUH, AHH HUH, BULL-AAANGG! And out popped the desk, with Harold hanging on for dear life, popped up and out through the doorway, and there wasn't a kid in the room who wasn't busy imagining himself being stiff-lipped and strong at Harold Boxbender's closed-casket funeral.

Birdlegs Carlson, who never needed an excuse to bawl, started sniveling. Pretty soon half-a-dozen of the worst sort of hysterical girls had their dang mouths wide open, snot and tears running every which way. They yowled right up to the moment Old Man Hall came back to the room. Where was all the gore? He ought to be painted with the stuff. Must have washed up, the sneaky old fart. Well, he could scrub himself buck-naked with Clorox and a bushel of corncobs for all we cared. We knew Harold Boxbender had been murdered in cold blood.

Hall's thick-soled shoes squeaked as he marched up to the front. He fussed around picking out the perfect piece of yellow chalk and cranked up the porcupine lecture. Anytime things got slack, or he'd run out of facts on frogs or leaves or stars or some other fool scientific thing, Hall blah, blah, blahed porcupines. Come to think of it, he sort of resembled a giant porcupine, one with a military flattop.

"Why do porcupines go into barns and chew up harnesses?"

Nobody, not even that droopy-drawered brown-noser Margaret Christiansen, was stupid enough to risk a casual guess, not five min-

utes after Hall had slaughtered Harold Boxbender. Most of us had
limited horse-harness experience. No one in western Nebraska had
seriously farmed with horses for twenty years. Hall had apparently
suffered some sort of massive harness loss in the dimmy past and
was still steamed up about it.

"You've all seen that, haven't you? Chewed-up harness that isn't
good for anything? Haven't you ever wondered why that happened? Class? Margaret? Haven't you ever wondered?"

"no-o-o"

"No? You never possessed the simple child's curiosity as to why
the devious nocturnal porcupine feasts on the horse harnesses of
hard-working American farmers?"

"no-o-o"

"Well, think about it, class. Haven't you ever had a craving for salt?
Don't you ever think about a bowl of steaming popcorn, just dripping with salt and fresh creamery butter? Haven't you ever, sitting
here in this period before lunch, wondered if the lunchroom staff
has used sufficient salt on the day's menu to bring out the flavor?
No? Class? Anyone? Margaret?"

"well, m-maybe"

"I should think so. If we think about our own body's craving for
salt, our own biological need for salt, when we get to eat salt every
day on our meat and potatoes and peas and beans and eggs and
on our gravy, we can only imagine what the poor porcupine goes
through to get enough salt. Not much salt in tree bark, is there,
Margaret?

"no-o-o"

"I should think not. But horse harness is a different matter entirely, isn't it? Why, class, is the harness of a horse rich in salt? Can
you think of a reason? No? Anyone? Margaret?"

"I'm not sure"

"SWEAT! Horses SWEAT! And the SWEAT soaks the harness, and
the salt in the SWEAT clings to the harness long after the SWEAT is
dried up and gone. Then along comes the clever nocturnal porcu-

pine, completely starved for salt, and gobbles that harness just as fast as he can chew. Now the farmer could lock the harness up in a porcupine-proof room, or he could leave a little cattle salt around the barn and the porcupine would leave his harness alone. But most of them don't. Do you know why? Anyone? Margaret?"

"no-o-o"

"IGNORANCE! Ignorance of the porcupine and his habits, ignorance of nature, ignorance of scientific facts. So there you are."

*

We were surprised to run into Harold on the playground after lunch. He was moving right spritely for a dead guy. Outside of a little extra color in one cheek, Harold didn't have a mark on him. He said the principal, a pencil-necked bald guy we called Chrome Dome, had given him a "talking to" and turned him loose.

"Chrome Dome told me next time he'd take me down to the furnace room and give me a swat with the Board of Education. Big deal. That wienie arm don't scare me none."

"Yeah, big deal," we all agreed, even though nobody in recent memory had actually been taken to the furnace room and swatted, and even though there wasn't a kid standing on that playground, including Harold Boxbender, who didn't think a trip to the furnace room would result in serious, and invariably fatal, bleeding wounds to the bottom.

*

Closed-casket funerals were much on our minds. The inferno resulting from a semi ramming a California car the previous summer fried the unfortunate tourist family so thoroughly that Zimmer, the undertaker, hauled them to the mortuary in his farm truck. That dreadful business had been closed-casket all the way. Not even Allen, the undertaker's kid, could get close enough for a peek at the remains. We were left with the truck, parked behind the mortuary, still littered with black pieces of what we took to be Californians. Allen conducted grisly truck-box viewings for a month after the wreck. If we took that long scary walk to the furnace room with Chrome Dome, our folks would be closing our caskets, no doubt in anybody's mind. Our little butts would be shredded beyond recognition. Have to put our bloody carcasses in plastic bags to keep us from dripping all over Zimmer's truck box. Certain parents would deeply regret they hadn't promptly fired Chrome Dome after our first warnings. Too late now. We knew he was a menace. Goldang aluminum tooth right in front of his mouth. Too goldang cheap to buy gold. Goldang swatboard hanging behind his desk. Goldang board covered with varnish. Shiny thing. Looked hard. Had those goldang holes drilled in it. Made it sting more, according to Chrome Dome. Harold said he wasn't worried.

Harold didn't do anything the next morning. He didn't do anything really bad for the whole next week. Hall called him down for talking a few times, but Harold acted meek, kissed Hall's ass something terrible. We pegged Harold a blowhard and forgot about it. Margaret went back to answering all of Hall's rhetorical questions.

*

Shortly after Christmas vacation Hall hung up his porcupine picture, a real artsy Audubon Society–style watercolor deal, with a couple of cuddly-looking porcupines staring out at the world with beady black eyeballs. You never saw a more innocent pair of salt-hungry little bastards in your life. Old Man Hall was proud of that picture. Once his lecture was over and we were pretending to do our homework, he graded papers or cleaned his teeth or picked his nose or, indulging his very favorite pastime, massaged the living crap out of his gigantic balls. He'd knead or pick the appropriate body part while gazing beatifically at his stupid porcupines. Sometimes, when he was staring away, there'd dang near be a smile on his homely face. That was before he made the mistake of coming to class five minutes late.

"Pssst. Where's Hall?"

"Bet he's layin' a big fat turd."

"Shhh. He's comin'."

"That's Miss Mason in the library, you ding dong."

"Shhh."

"You give that back."

"I don't have it."

"You do too. I saw you."

"Well, what you gonna do about it, Little Miss Pink Panties?"

"I do not!"

"We seen you sit down."

"Shhh."

"Hey, Harold, what you doing chewin' up a whole sheet of tablet paper?"

Harold let fly, throwing that glunky glob with neat economy. SPERLLATT! There was just enough mush to cover both porcupines with a precisely even coating of gunk. We sat like drunken guppies, transfixed by the perfect awfulness. No way we were going to all live through this one. Hall's heavy tread sounded on the old warped stairs. Harold jimmied open his science book, setting off a mad scramble for books and homework papers.

"AHHHUH, AHHHUH, AHHHUH." Hall stood at the doorway, catching his breath while he surveyed the room for criminal activity, a room now frozen in studious tableau. We felt him staring at Harold. He shoved off the doorframe, huffing his way up to his desk. We prayed for a miracle. Maybe this one time he wouldn't look up. But he did, just like always.

"WHAT THE? HUH? HAROLD!" Hall veered off toward Harold's desk. "HAROLD BOXBENDER! YOU, YOU, YOU LITTLE . . .! HUH! OOF! UH! YOU! MMMM! UH!" And Old Man Hall, clutching his chest, stopped in his tracks, then staggered backward toward the door. He swayed in the doorway, one hand on the jamb, his eyes bugged hugely like a giant mad toad, staring in Harold's general direction. "Uh, mmmm, y-you," he mumbled, and reeled on out the door. A second later we heard the KER-THUD of Hall's three hundred-and-some-odd pounds falling dead on the smooth worn boards of our junior high school's main hallway. When we finally mustered the nerve to look up, we could see the bottoms of Hall's black shoes lying accusingly in the doorway. He was wearing loud argyle socks.

"Now you've done it, Harold!"

"They'll whack all of us for this."

"Wa-a-a-a-a-h."

"Shut up, Birdlegs."

"Sniff."

"He ain't movin'."

"That's because he's dead, you pea-brain."

"Wa-sniff."

"Birdlegs! Stuff it."

"Somebody go get somebody."

"Harold, go get Chrome Dome."

"Get him yourself."

"Well, you did it."

"Tough titty"

"Shhh. Someone's coming."

"Margaret, go talk to them."

"Read your books. Maybe they won't notice."

"He's moving. I saw him move!"

"Naw, that's rigor mortis, you dork. They always move when they're getting stiff."

"They do not."

"Do too."

"Do not."

"Sniff."

"Birdlegs!"

"They'll tell our folks, sniff, and we'll all get grounded!"

"Maybe you'll get grounded, Birdlegs. But if you don't quit blubbering I'm gonna punch ya."

"You do and I'll tell."

"You tell and I'll kill you in your sleep with a gun."

"You two morons shut up!"

"Harold, go get Chrome Dome."

"Eat it, Margaret."

"Well, aren't we crude today."

"Eat it double."

"Shhh. Someone's coming."

And someone was. Poor Miss Mason, who lived with her hypo-chondriac stepmother and loved to talk about infections, spotted Mr. Hall on her way back from her daily 11:32 A.M. trip to the rest room.

"EEEEEEEEEEEK!" she said.

"Read your books," said Margaret. And we did. We read like troopers, read right through the shouts and great scurryings in the hall, read through the wailing siren of Zimmer's ambulance/hearse, through the scuffling of feet and equipment on the stairs, through the soft official-sounding mumblings outside our door. And even when Old Man Zimmer and some volunteers first tried to pick up the stretcher, loaded with three hundred pounds of comatose schoolteacher, and there was much grunting and cussing, cussing right there in junior high school, and they had to set him back down pretty goldang hard, and there was a big crash that made us all jump, even Harold, we all read like crazy, read as if our science book's explanation of the annual cycle of the deciduous tree was the most fascinating information we'd ever encountered. We were hop-ing against hope that should some official person stick his head in the door, he would find our diligence reason enough for a full par-don. A full pardon could not, of course, include Harold, no matter how hard he read this book.

"ZZZZZZZZT. You're going to fry, Harold."

"Yeah, sure."

"ZZZZZZZZT. They say your eyes burn first."

"Dork!"

"ZZZZZZZZTTT, ZZZZZZZZTTT."

"Don't push it."

"ZZZZZZZZTTT, ZZZZZZZZTT, ZZZZZZZZTTT, ZZZZZZZZTTT!"

"Why don't you kids go to lunch? Didn't you hear the bell?" Chrome Dome, his aluminum tooth flashing, stood in the door. Leave it to Harold to ask the right question:

"When's the funeral?"

"Mr. Hall's not dead, at least not yet. Don't you count him out. He'll be back before you know it. You kids get going; lunch hour is almost over."

We got going all right. Dang near ran over Chrome Dome bailing out of there. Even old Margaret, that brown-nosing little bookworm, kind of jostled him on the way by. But not Harold Boxbender, no sir. He didn't come out. Missed lunch altogether that day. Took him that long to make sure there wasn't a particle of spitwad left on those porcupines.

*

Mrs. Jacobs substituted for the next four glorious months. No fainthearted normal-school ingenue, she'd taught country school several years before raising a family. Hall's books on deciduous trees immediately disappeared into our desks, replaced by little experiments with pond water and bug collections. We collected so many moths, butterflies, crickets, pinch bugs, sow bugs, ants, wasps, bees, and lightning bugs that half the birds in town had to go on short rations. Hall's civics lectures, comprised entirely of rhetorical questions to Margaret Christiansen, were transformed into free-for-all political debates over the contents of our *Weekly Readers*.

Gary Jensen, a recently imported wise-guy Democrat, who produced so much mucus his folks should have installed two hoses from his nostrils directly into the nearest wastebasket, made the stupidly audacious argument that Alaska should be a state. Why, shoot. You'd have to be a goldanged communist lackey not to see where that would lead. The Bering Sea is about ten yards wide. We weren't eyeball-to-eyeball with any chump-change pseudo-capitalists back then. No sir. These were the same bloodthirsty red hordes that had just kicked the living bejesus out of Hungary and were liable to invade anything anywhere at any time. We needed lots of Alaskan bases; we needed airfields; we needed maneuvering room for our tanks. Most of all we needed a place to drop atomic bombs if those slavering red bastards managed to jump across that ten-yard ditch and get the best of us. You make Alaska a state, and the next thing you know, those Alaskans will be crying about tanks in their back yards, be writing their senators about noisy fighter planes. You drop an atomic bomb up there, even if it's the only possible way to stop the Russians, and you'd have the entire Alaskan congressional delegation on your ass. Leave 'em the hell a territory so they can't get in the way of a sound national defense. Naturally, the Jensen kid, that fountain of snot, that phlegmatic little pea-brain, couldn't see it. Before Mrs. Jacobs could stop us, we were pushing and shoving, yelling all kinds of choice political insults. To top it off, my side lost the class vote on the Alaska statehood issue. I'm still sore about it.

About two weeks into Mrs. Jacobs's tenure, she arranged for the entire class to observe a criminal trial at the county courthouse. A transient simpleton stood accused of burglarizing the local grocery store. He had the vein-damaged face of a chronic boozer and a good case of the shakes from two cold-turkey weeks in the county jail. They'd caught him with a Deuel County State Bank change bag on him and way too many quarters. The sleepy old coot of a judge automatically denied every single defense motion, unless he forgot and the county attorney had to remind him. The two defense lawyers, who composed a good percentage of the community's Democrat population, became more and more frustrated with each detail. They presented four or five character witnesses, former employers mostly, who made the accused sound like a harmless, semidependable drunk. Then the county attorney woke up the judge, and two hours of character testimony were thrown out as irrelevant. The defense team went nuts, throwing papers, jumping up and roaring. Not that it bothered the judge any. He lapsed into his customary semiconscious state until it was time to sentence the drifter to a zillion years in the clink. That poor old crook should have thanked the fates burglary wasn't a hanging offense in Deuel County.

*

Harold stayed below the firing line in Mrs. Jacobs's classroom. Maybe almost killing Old Man Hall had postponed his straight path to career criminality. Maybe Mrs. Jacobs didn't pull his chain. But we discovered something else was going on. Harold had become a loner, declining our invitations to baseball games or trips to

Pokorny's soda fountain. His clothes were a little shabbier than usual. Those notorious Boxbender nosebleeds, something he had always used to escape hours of boring class time, increased in frequency. Rumors began to circulate that a few high-spirited boys from exceptionally "good" families had snatched Harold's pretty older sister off the street and done terrible things. None of the boys kept his mouth shut. Harold's sister, painfully shy even before her recent troubles, was an unlikely candidate to complain. With a father killed in a railroad accident ten years ago and a mother happily remarried to Jim Beam, the Boxbender family was not in any position to make trouble. Lawyer Bob, in his official role of county attorney, declined to prosecute. Harold kept his mouth shut, and so did we, but it must have been eating on him.

The porcupine picture remained free of the smallest dust mote. No custodian in that decrepit building had ever been as meticulous with his job as Harold Boxbender was in keeping Old Man Hall's stupid porcupines clean. And it was a good thing he did, because Old Man Hall came back, just like Chrome Dome said he would—came back two weeks before summer vacation. He'd shrunk, that's the first thing we noticed. His shiny-pantsed gray suit hung all over him. He wasn't moving too lively either, using a cheap black cane to shuffle grimly up to the front of the room. I was already missing Mrs. Jacobs. Naturally, the first thing Hall checked was his porcupine picture, his now-spotless, mirror-finished porcupine picture. He glanced over at Harold, who was drawing like crazy on his Big Chief tablet, and he nodded, very solemnly.

*

We always played a big-deal softball game on the last day of school. Hall chose the sides, leaving me off Gary Fanoele's team. Goldang his gigantic balls to hell. My team got stuck with Birdlegs Carlson, who couldn't catch her ass with a grapple fork, for first baseman. Margaret stood in the shortstop hole, aimlessly picking sandburrs out of her saddle oxfords. Hairy Harris, the shiest girl who ever lived, perched flamingo-like on one leg out in right field. We knew implicitly that any ball hit to right was an automatic inside-the-park home run. Most depressing was Harold Boxbender's presence be-hind the plate, where Hall, for some sadistic reason, insisted we play him. Harold was too weak and clumsy to catch a ball, much less hit one. Catcher, arguably the most important defensive position, was not something we would have assigned to Harold. Short of hand-ing him over to Fanoele's team as a gift, our first preference, we might have chosen him to chase down bats or haul us drinking water. Nonetheless, there was room for limited optimism. Darryl "Darrylybelly" Houk, the best athlete in our class next to Fanoele, was no slouch as a drop-ball pitcher. Jackrabbit Vincent roamed center field and might be counted on to assist in left and right. Jack-rabbit's hitting was sporadic at best, poor guy couldn't see diddly-squat, but once in a while he'd get hold of a pitch by pure accident and hit it as far as anyone. Zimmer thought he could handle third and back up Margaret, which meant Margaret was under orders never to touch a ground ball. I found myself assigned to second base, determined to make up for Birdlegs's inevitable miscues with moves only Bobby Richardson could imitate.

Fanoele hit like crazy; he always did. But Darrylybelly's drop pitches made the rest of them look stupid. Harold threw himself in front of almost everything he couldn't catch, and by the fourth inning had torn the knees out of a pair of nosebleed-seasoned jeans. Hall called strikes on anything within a foot of the plate. Gary "Vol-cano of Snot" Jensen nearly got himself thrown out of the game for arguing a third strike.

"That was a mile outside."

"You are forbidden to argue with the umpire."

"Yeah," said Harold, "arguing with the umpire is against the rules."

"But it landed in front of the plate!"

"You've had your last warning, young man. Now go sit down!"

"Yeah," said Harold, "show a little respect."

Zimmer homered twice, sending balls rolling far out into the Mexican sandburrs, where girl outfielders had the good sense to leave them be. I covered myself with glory by baiting the snot-driz-

zling pitcher with calls of "Booger Breath! Mr. Mucus! We want a
pitcher, not a nose-picker! Look out, he's loading up another one of
his famous snot balls!" And these immortal lines from Longfellow,
recited with enthusiastic help from my entire team:

He shot some snot into the air:
It fell to earth, he knew not where.

After watching four overheated Jensen blazers sail over my head, I
trotted down to first and scored on a series of pitiful infield errors.
We led three-to-zip going into the bottom of the seventh, the last
inning.

Darrylybelly struck out two girls before he weakened and walked
Sharon Munson. Nobody blamed him for that. Wasn't a boy in that
whole school wouldn't have lovingly walked the fabulous, golden-
tressed Sharon Munson on the off-chance she'd remember this
minor act of kindness sometime in the next two hundred and fifty
years. Fanoele scalded a drive that nearly beaned Hairy Harris, busy
dreaming her own brand of hirsute fantasies in right field. The ball
gathered up a nice selection of sandburrs until it came to rest, re-
sembling nothing less than a sleeping hedgehog, flush against the
retaining wall. Jackrabbit ran it down, but two runs had scored and
Mr. Dripping Mucus Democrat was hugging Sharon Munson in a
close and completely revolting manner. It was a sight guaranteed to
upset the strongest stomach of any unfortunate American-patriot
witnesses in the vicinity. Made me ashamed of the entire human
race.

Ashamed and mad, which is why when I fielded Booger Head
Jensen's wussy little grounder, I didn't run over and step on first but
fired a strike in the general direction of Birdlegs Carlson's waify figure over near first base. Naturally Birdlegs ducked. The ball rattled
around the playground swing sets and merry-go-rounds fifty feet
beyond first base. By the time I corralled the ball and threw a rain-
bow to Darrylybelly, Snot-for-Brains was loping for home with the
tying run, grinning like an adenoidal raccoon, probably already
counting on some disgusting mush with that traitorous Munson

girl. Harold caught Darrylybelly's throw cleanly, astounding everyone. Like the legendary Horatius at the bridge, who waited for those snot-nosed Democrat Etruscans to just try it, Harold closed his eyes, steeling his scrawny body against the inevitable collision. Jensen came in feet-high, slamming his tennis shoes hard into Harold's mitt. The softball, still nicely embroidered with Mexican sandburrs, dribbled out between Harold's legs to rest accusingly on home plate. Booger Breath jumped high in the air, ready to start a victory hug-a-thon with the sort of Judas girl a more discriminating guy would have sense enough to ignore.

"You're out!" Hall yelled. Mr. Mucus was incredulous.

"He dropped the ball! He dropped the ball!"

"You deliberately slud into him to make him drop the ball."

"So what? I was *trying* to make him drop the ball."

"You made me drop the ball," said Harold, his freshly unstoppered nose pouring blood down his front. "You kicked me."

"What you did was against the rules, young man."

Huh? Say what? Hall must be thinking of some obscure nineteenth-century rule, perhaps some nineteenth-century rule from Neptune.

"What rule?"

"One more word and you're out of the game!"

That fixed Jensen. No Booger-Brained, Krushchev-loving Democrat Snot Machine was brave enough to risk being tossed out of our big-deal softball game, even if the game was over, even if this was the last day of school, even if we were lucky enough never to see Mr. Hall and his humongous testicles again. Jensen pouted off in lonely ignominy; his stock had never been lower.

We pulled Harold along on our victory walk back to the schoolhouse, as smug a bunch of little conquering bastards as ever irritated a losing side. Our eminently forgettable report cards were waiting, along with a year's worth of truck in our overflowing desks. Nobody much cared about report cards. Well, maybe Margaret cared. That afternoon Harold was our guy. Dropping a ball and still getting the putout takes more than luck. Not even a Yogi Berra/

Roy Campanella kind of catcher could pull it off. Somehow, and nobody was quite certain just how this had all worked, Harold Boxbender had papier-mâchéd our team to victory.

"Nice game, Mr. Hall!" Harold yelled.

Mr. Hall, huffing ponderously behind us, his white shirt clinging wetly to his prowlike belly, didn't say anything. But he did look up, and spotting Harold, gave him a nifty three-fingered salute.

Baseball

My father was never much of a Yankees fan. During the fifties, when the Yankees appeared in seven out of nine World Series, he rooted for the Dodgers and the Braves, who were competitive, and the Giants, who weren't. He even rooted for the Whiz Kid Phillies, who lost in four games straight. But then Dad was always a sucker for the underdog. Any bum with a hang-dog expression and a halfway plausible tale of woe could empty Dad's pockets. Our parsonages must have been red-marked on every hobo map in the country. It was a rare week in the summers when Mom didn't feed one or two vagabonds, who usually looked and smelled like the last survivors of the last ride of Casey Jones. They ate the same as we did, oatmeal bread and one hell of a lot of baked beans, always on the back step, where we'd find nothing but slicked-up plates and stinking cigarette butts by the time my sisters and I muscled up the courage to go back and spy on them.

The Yankees were my team. They won. Kids just naturally suck up to winners. How many kids wearing dog-assed Mets hats have you seen lately? But without Mickey Mantle the Yankees would have been just another team. He didn't just hit home runs; he hit them off light standards. Even when he struck out, the power of his swing almost undressed the pitcher. He was hurt much of the time, and we hurt with him. I'm sure I wasn't the only kid in America who imitated The Mick's stance, limp and all. We prayed he'd stop carousing with Whitey and Billy long enough to heal up good. Of course, we didn't know then that Casey would have played him with a broken leg if he could have. We didn't know that Mickey was scared that if he didn't play hurt he'd be sent down to the minors or traded to Kansas City. Maybe fewer nights at Toots Shore's would have extended his career for a few years; it's hard to say. But when he played he was as good as anyone in the game, Teddy Ballgame Williams included, and there wasn't a boy in my town who wouldn't have traded everything he owned for five minutes in a major-league game as Mickey Mantle.

If there hadn't been a Mickey Mantle I would have been the only Philadelphia Phillies fan in a five-hundred-mile radius. Richie Ashburn came to Neligh in the winter of 1950, shortly after the Whiz Kids had been pounded by the Yankees in four straight Series games. Ashburn, before he became a broadcaster, spent his winters in his hometown of Tilden, Nebraska. He had a little property there, earned some winter money refereeing basketball games. Ashburn was in town for some sort of Boy Scout function—baseball player shows up at the movie theater with a highlights film, signs some autographs, pats a few heads. Dad took me along, even though I was only five years old, too young to qualify even as a lowly Cub Scout. I don't remember much about the film, a grainy collection of pitching and hitting exploits, but I remember looking up into Richie Ashburn's kindly smile and knowing intuitively that he was not only the blondest but the largest human being I'd ever seen in my life.

He wasn't the largest, of course. Uncle Burt, who ate entire pies after Sunday dinner, was much larger. But neither Uncle Burt nor any other person who ever played baseball was as fine a defensive outfielder as Richie Ashburn. He made over five hundred putouts six times during his career. Add together the careers of every other outfielder who ever played baseball, including Mays, Cobb, Mantle, Aaron, Speaker, Snyder, DiMaggio, Doby, Clemente, the whole shooting match, and you can come up with only five seasons of five hundred putouts. Named by the *Sporting News* as Rookie of the Year in 1948, Ashburn went on to lead the league in hits three times, walks four times, on-base percentage four times, *and* he won two batting crowns. Teddy Ballgame, getting his first look at Ashburn in an exhibition game, nicknamed him "Putt-Putt" because he ran like he had a pair of motors in his pants. And Ashburn could run, stealing twenty-five to thirty bases a year at a time when the

stolen base was out of favor. This is a Hall of Fame player who cost
the Phillies all of $3,500 to sign.

*

Like most young baseball players, I was interested in cranking out
tape-measure home runs. And there was no better model for homer
cranking than The Mick. I could use a Mickey Mantle–model
Louisville Slugger; I could get into a Mickey Mantle stance; I could
even take some mighty Mick-like cuts, but the bitter truth was I was
too puny to hit anything louder than a few weak singles. Not until I
adopted Richie Ashburn's bottle bat and choked-up hitting style
did I experience much success.

We played baseball almost every summer morning, right after I
finished my paper route. Sometimes we mustered a dozen players,
usually only five or six. The diamond was laid out on the recess
grounds below the school, and by midsummer it was a solid mat of
dusty green Mexican sandburrs. Left-handed hitters had to hit a fly
ball only 180 feet to reach the friendly cement retaining wall in right
field. Our left-field bleachers were marked by a sidewalk running 250
feet from home plate. Anyone strong enough to hit it out in dead
center field had to muscle a ball 295 feet, the exact measured distance
Mickey Mantle had to clear in the shortest part of Yankee Stadium.

There were never any adults, of course. We had no uniforms, no
rule book, no umpires. Whatever kid was pitching called balls and
strikes, and if the batter argued too much, the pitcher hit him with
the baseball. It was a remarkably efficient system. Gary Fanoele, a
gifted athlete who had once actually witnessed a major-league exhibition game, could hit home runs at will from any stance from both
sides of the plate. He favored an exaggerated Stan Musial stance
from the left side, and took advantage of the short wall in right two
or three times a day. Gary, naturally, was always chosen first. Darryl
"Darrylybelly" Houk, a round brown Indian kid, whimsically
named after Hollywood bigwig Darryl F. Zanuck, either struck out
or cranked whistling line drives over the right-field wall. He was
never much for legging out hits. Usually the Wertz brothers joined
us. Both threw decent curve balls but hit like Democrats. Those

were the regulars, but almost anyone could show up for a game. High school kids came to watch Fanoele hit, and stayed to play. Immediately after being low-bridged for arguing a strike call with a high school senior, I adopted the Willie Mays "hit-the-ground-fast-and-look-for-the-ball later" theory of bean-ball ducking.

Hitting a pitched baseball is arguably the single most difficult feat in all of sport. Major-league players who do it successfully two-and-a-half times out of ten are considered average. Hitters who hit in three out of ten at-bats, a 70 percent failure rate, make more money than the entire gross national product of Poland. Today's Little Leaguers are lucky to get six at-bats a week and, if they aren't pitching specialists, almost never pitch. Not counting our usual half-hour of batting practice, each of us got in fifteen to twenty at-bats and pitched a couple of innings every day. But our big edge on any organized adult-supervised league was that we played for the fun of it. We made our own rules, settled our own arguments, sometimes without bloodshed. If we struck out, no dipstick adults stood around making us miserable with criticism or helpful batting tips. We cheered any kid who got a hit after a long slump, even if he was on the wrong team. Mostly we tried to keep the teams even, and if Fanoele's team got too far ahead, which it most always did, he might volunteer to switch with me or one of the Wertz boys to even things up. We chose drama over winning. Most kids do.

What kid would ever fantasize about coming to the plate with his team ahead fifteen runs? Well, okay, maybe a dog-assed Mets fan, but most kids want center stage, want the game to be in the balance:

> It's the bottom of the ninth, the score is tied, the seventh game of the World Series, two out, Jones is the Yankees' final hope. He's small, but the kid is mighty strong, mighty strong. He reminds me of a young Mickey Mantle. Look at the muscles on that guy. The count is full. Podres winds. He delivers. And there she goes! It's going, it's going, it's gone! A home run! It's over the roof! Holy Cow! Jones hit a tremendous blast completely out of Yankee stadium! The first player to do it!

How about that? They're mobbing him at home plate. Yanks win! Yanks win!

We dreaded the days Charlie Adams wandered into our games. A rawboned redhead well over six feet tall, he was old enough to drive and was borderline mean. His dad, a paunchy Texan who drilled water wells over half of creation, read Louis L'Amour books in his spare time. Mr. Adams kept a jolly wife and five or six carrot-topped, well-freckled kids stuffed into a hot two-bedroom trailer parked just south of our ball diamond. Summers, the Adams kids mostly roamed around town, and who could blame them? The old man had the only air conditioner in his bedroom, and he kept the door closed so he could read his westerns in peace. Later we wondered if those westerns affected the old man's mind, maybe made him think he was one of those steely-eyed lawman hero types. Right after they returned to Texas, he was elected sheriff and got himself killed trying to disarm a bank robber. We wished he'd stayed in Chappell drilling water wells, even if it meant we had to put up with Charlie's temper.

I was in a terrible slump, hitting about a buck fifty for the past two weeks. Darrylybelly and Johnny Wertz had scratched out enough hits to keep my team in the game, but we were down a half-dozen runs when Charlie decided to pitch. He threw a fastball ten feet over Johnny's head and called it a strike. Johnny wasn't a lawyer's kid for nothing. He really let Charlie have it, called him a blind Texas shithead. Naturally, Charlie planted the next fastball right between Johnny's shoulder blades. Johnny snuffled a little as he walked to first, but he was still giving Charlie the business:

"My dad's gonna commit you, you crazy turd. You hit me again, he'll send you straight to Ingleside."

"Oh yeah? Him and who else, Wertz. You maybe?"

"Get the straitjacket. Charlie's cracked. Call the funny farm. He's crazy wild, Darryl. Watch him, he couldn't hit the plate if his life depended on it."

"You better just shut up." Johnny shut up.

Darrylybelly didn't wait to get plunked, but swung at the first pitch and knocked a solid double off the base of the right-field wall. I didn't want to bat. Charlie was working up a serious mad, which he always did when a little kid got a hit off him. I gave him a minute while I choked up a couple of extra inches on my Richie Ashburn bottle bat. I stepped in gingerly, at least three feet from the plate.

"Duck!" Johnny yelled from third.

Charlie glared at him and threw the first pitch right past my ear. I never saw it, although my eyes might have been pretty well closed.

"Strike!" Charlie bawled.

I was alive. That was good, but it meant I had to pick myself out of the sandburrs and stand in there again. He threw the next two pitches in the dirt at my feet. Mad as he was, Charlie was honest enough not to call them strikes. Then he aimed one, not that it wasn't a legitimate fastball. No sir. That baby was humming, boring inside. I had to swing in self-defense. The ball was up in my wheelhouse, and I got around on it, got the meat of that Richie Ashburn bottle bat solidly on the ball. I'll never in my life hit a ball any better. It went straight over Charlie, straight over Darryl at second base, over the sidewalk in center field, cleared the road, and landed on the porch of the county sheriff's house. We stepped it off later at three hundred twenty-seven feet. In all the games we played on that diamond, no one ever hit one further. And while no one knows or cares who won that game, I got enough drama from that one hit off Charlie Adams to keep me warm on a hundred frumpy middle-aged nights.

*

About once a summer someone's dad would get a bee up his Jockey shorts and organize a baseball practice. We'd spend a couple of hours chasing grounders through the sandburrs, while some big-feeling cretin instructed us in the mysteries of "proper" baseball:

"Don't swing at bad pitches."

"Just make contact."

"Get your glove down."

"Don't close your eyes when you swing."

"Run it out!"

"Good eye! Good eye!"

"Don't hold the ball!"

"Don't swing unless I give you the sign."

"Don't steal unless I give you the sign."

"Don't take a pitch unless I give you the sign."

These guys didn't know their asses from third base, but they had more signs than Harold Warp. I never knew one of them that was half as good a baseball strategist as his own kid. No kid, of course, would have the stupid audacity to think he ought to direct every single action of every boy on the team. Leave it to grown-ups to screw up a perfect sport.

The reason we were practicing, it always turned out, was this same half-wit parent had scheduled a game with another town and we needed to "get ready" for the big game. The most important item on the agenda, way more important than teaching us the mysterious finer points of the game, was choosing the starting team. This neatly divided us into "starters" and "scrubs." A dozen kids without the slightest inkling they weren't good enough to play were immediately classified as second-rate.

No self-appointed coach's kid ever sat on the bench, but Darrylybelly did. The second-best natural hitter in the confines of that little town, and he sat on the bench. He was fat; he was Indian; his dad drove a truck and wasn't around much. I had mixed feelings. It was wrong, all right, but having someone as good as Darryl to sit beside made my own humiliation a little more bearable. He was good company. Mostly he sang Little Richard songs. He'd start "Tutti Frutti," and the whole bench got into it, sometimes standing up to wiggle our scrawny butts. When he launched into "Good Golly, Miss Molly" we'd go completely nuts, prancing around, laying down some serious moves. The kid wasn't a bad singer, but even a deaf-mute couldn't butcher a song as fine as "Good Golly, Miss Molly." Makes my tired old feet excited just to think about it. Why our Neanderthal coach, directing the game from his third-base coaching box, never put a stop to this foolishness remains a great mystery. Maybe he thought we were cheering the starting team. Maybe he was too deep into serious sign-giving to notice.

*

The first one of these "big games" was at Lodgepole, a hamlet just down the road. Losing to Lodgepole, a town smaller and therefore punier than Chappell, was unthinkable, in much the same way that it would be unthinkable for any self-respecting major-league baseball team to lose to the dog-assed Mets. Lodgepole flat kicked the hell out of us, going up by fifteen runs in the fourth inning, in spite of two Fanoele home runs. Our coach did his best, bellowing each instruction several times in case we'd missed one of his clever signs. Our fielders kicked every other ball they reached, and threw most of what they caught in the general direction of Iowa. Lodgepole guys ran around the bases like they were on fire.

To celebrate Lodgepole's victory, Darrylybelly lit a fart with his brother's Zippo. The fart sort of sang on the way out, a "Toodle-Doodle-Doo" kind of song, and then it ignited, shooting a narrow blue-green flame straight out between Darryl's chubby legs. It was the stuff of legends, identified forever in schoolboy lore as "the time Darryl blew his ass off with a singing fart." None of us had ever heard a musical fart, much less set one on fire. We immediately begged him to do it again, but in spite of several impressive blazers, a true melodious fart never emerged. The fortunate ones, those of us who actually witnessed the miraculous feat, were subjected to a certain amount of ignorant scoffing, not unlike the abuse suffered by the honest citizen who reports a UFO carrying off his Pekinese.

As the score mounted, our coach, quite overcome with the bitter disappointment of certain defeat, ordered the scrubs into the game.

"You kids go on out there. Let's see what you peewees can do."

Peewees? Don't be calling us peewees, Jack. While you were busy directing our *first* team to total mortifying disaster, your *scrubs* just witnessed a flaming musical fart, one of the most singular acts of pure biological genius in the history of Western Civilization. Peewees? Come on. You wouldn't know a baseball player from a bird turd.

Darrylybelly promptly bounced a rocket off the Lodgepole pitcher's noggin, sending him to the bench. We scuffed up two relief pitches for a few meaningless but nonetheless ego-boosting runs. We still lost, but it helped some. I played two miserable innings in right field, the position usually occupied by a team's worst player. This particular right field was situated in the middle of a fair-sized slough. Swarms of mosquitoes attacked. In my only at-bat, I struck out ignominiously, flailing at three straight pitches above my head.

"Good cut," the coach yelled.

As I took my position in the right-field swamp, the mosquitoes bored in. Those few of the bloodthirsty little bastards that didn't congregate in my ears decided to fly up my nose. I ducked and weaved, took off my cap and beat the air. Nothing worked. I heard Johnny yell and looked up in time to see a ground ball rolling lazily past his reach. I got my glove down, but not far enough. The ball skidded under and on into the swamp for an inside-the-park home run. On the way home, with Harry Caray's broadcast of a St. Louis game crackling faintly over the radio, I asked Dad to buy me a bigger glove. He said I had played a great game.

*

The next year our big contest was across the border in Ovid, Colorado. Even though Ovid was twice the size of Lodgepole and had an impressive sugar-beet plant, we sneered at its relative clodhopperness. The village, nestled down on the South Platte River, had all the associations we put on river towns everywhere. We made particular fun of the town's Mexicans, who we thought might be peaceable as individuals but highly excitable in bunches. Wade Adams, Charlie's little brother, claimed all the Mexicans in Texas carried knives, that getting your throat slit was as simple as calling any Mexican a greaser. We risked getting our throats slit a half-dozen times, but the worst thing we ever got out of it was the finger. Ovid Mexicans, it seemed, were not as warlike as the Texas variety.

We played the game in the semidarkness of two working floodlights. When we weren't fighting mosquitoes, we worried about getting brained by an errant ball descending out of the gloom. The infielders had a little light, but the outfield was completely hopeless. The trick for a hitter was getting a fly ball to the outfield. Hit the ball up in that inky sky, and anything could happen. We hit more fly balls than Ovid did. Fanoele homered on first pitches in four straight at-bats, none of them much more than infield pop-ups. Darrylybelly hit a couple once he got in the game. They never did find one of them. I played my two-inning stint, taking a walk on a three-and-one pitch in the top of the seventh. I made it all the way around to third, and when Wade hit a pop fly to shallow left field, the coach sent me home. Shoot. I could have scored running backward. I could have scored crawling in there on my hands and knees. A guy as fast as I was, a guy who ran at least as fast as Mickey Mantle, could go from third to home in a blink of an eye. Even so, I didn't dawdle, sliding niftily across the plate as the catcher strained for a high throw. I lay there on the plate, safe as a bug, taking the catcher's perfunctory tag as the automatic afterthought it was.

"You're out," said the umpire.

"You're a crook," I said.

"You'd better get out of here, or I'll have you suspended!"

Suspended? Holy crap! It sounded darned serious and very permanent, but what exactly did it mean? Back on the bench I asked Johnny Wertz, who, as the son of an actual lawyer, had deep knowledge of these matters. Never one to be hasty, Johnny mulled it over carefully.

"I think," he said, "that the umpire is full of shit. Number one, you were safe. Number two, he's from Ovid. Number three, we're not in any league to be suspended from. Therefore, he can't do nothin'."

No criminal anywhere could have asked for a more favorable judicial ruling. With total impunity we spent the rest of the game merrily blistering the umpire.

"Homer!"

"Helen Keller!"

"Bat Man!"

"Dingleberry!"

"Sugar-beet breath!"

"Dinkphod!"

Dinkphod! Holy cow! Fanoele actually called the umpire a dink-phod! Nobody had the slightest idea what a dinkphod was, of course, but we knew it was bad, much worse than any cuss word we'd ever heard. Fanoele was really going to get it this time. But when the umpire stayed in his crouch behind the plate, making one bad call after another, we regained our sense of adventure.

"Dinkphod!"

"Dimple dinkphod!"

"Double dimple dinkphod!"

"Triple dimple dinkphod!"

"Ovid dinkphod!"

Ovid dinkphod! Brilliant! What a completely devastating home shot! *Ovid dinkphod* gained immediate currency as the awfulest epithet we could yell at another human being. We used it to good advantage on the umpire for the rest of the game, and on our ene-mies and sisters for months afterward. Anyone labeled on Ovid dinkphod was honor-bound to stop whatever he was doing and go to war. I once gave Harold Boxbender a bloody nose for tearing my spelling book. When he foolishly called me an Ovid dinkphod, I hit him a couple of good whacks on the head with a fence post. You have to nip that sort of thing in the bud.

*

The brilliance of the best of the Whiz Kids—Ashburn, Roberts, Ennis, and Simmons—was frittered away for eight long pennant-less summers on weak supporting casts and grumpy Philadelphia fans. By 1959 the Phillies had deteriorated from mediocrity to some-thing much worse. They traded Richie Ashburn to the Cubs for three very pedestrian players. Ashburn had a pretty good year in 1960; Wrigley Field often has that effect on incoming veterans. In a hitter's paradise, they blossom at the plate; the fans love them again, inspiring has-been bodies to one or two more decent years.

On the golden day in 1960 when I finally saw Richie Ashburn play baseball, he was already a relatively ancient thirty-three years old.

My father took me to the game. He was a die-hard Cubs fan, having served as an usher in the thirties when he and my mom were working his way through seminary. He'd seen Babe Ruth in his last sad tour as a Boston Brave. The Babe, he said, hadn't looked too healthy.

The Milwaukee Braves, between stints in Boston and Atlanta, were in town, still wearing the bloom of their two recent National League flags. Cocky bastards. Joe Adcock hit ten home runs in batting practice, most of them out on Waveland Avenue. Early in the game both Aaron and Mathews homered, and the contest was pretty well over. Bob Buhl started for Milwaukee and, except for Ashburn, handled the Cubs easily. Ashburn wore his pants higher than anyone, ending at the knee. He looked sort of old-fashioned, but maybe he wanted the umpire to know exactly where his knees were. He walked in the first inning, bunted safely in the third, swiped second base, walked in the sixth, and, when he came up in the last of the ninth, he pretty well represented the entire Cub offense for the day.

Buhl was long gone by then. Some young fireballer was on the mound throwing straight heat. Ashburn worked the count to three-and-two, and then started fouling off pitches. He must have fouled off a half-dozen before the crowd woke up to what was really going on. The kid would rear back and fire, and "Crack," Ashburn fouled it down the left-field line where we were sitting. Next pitch, "Crack," he sent it down the right-field line. Then he'd foul it straight back and start over. The kid wouldn't walk him, but he couldn't get it past him either. And Ashburn clearly wasn't after a hit. That would have been too easy. The crowd cheered louder with each foul ball. When, after fifteen straight foul balls, the kid finally caved in with ball four, Ashburn trotted down to first to a standing ovation. He was grinning, too. Thirty-three years old, and no hot-throwing kid could strain him.

Ashburn slipped a bit in 1961, and the Cubs, goldang them, let him go to those dreadful, dog-assed 1962 Mets. The Mets lost one hundred and twenty times. Ashburn hit .306 and led the league in on-base percentage. When he became a Phillies broadcaster in 1963, he became the last player to retire after a season as a regular hitting over three hundred.

*

I didn't know it at the time, but that murky game in Ovid was to mark the end of my two-game organized-baseball career. Wade and Charlie Adams moved back to Texas and tragedy. Darrylybelly's family simply disappeared. One day Fanoele and I went to get Darryl for a movie and found the house empty. Maybe they were trying to beat the rent, or maybe they'd had other troubles. We never knew. The next summer, no well-meaning father stepped forward to schedule our one day of practice or a game with an enemy town. We still played our own brand of baseball, of course, but without Darrylybelly it was never quite the same. The next year I moved away, abandoning my one-walk, one-strikeout, one three-base-error baseball accomplishments for the more physical game of football.

I retired from baseball, never having worn a uniform, unless you want to count the generic red baseball caps we wore once a year, never having played a regular schedule of games, never going to more than one rotten official practice a summer. But I had done something much, much finer, something any kid in town would have given his left nut to have done. I had hit a Charlie Adams fastball three hundred and twenty-seven feet.

Mark Twain Made Me Do It

The *Adventures of Tom Sawyer. The Adventures of Huckle-berry Finn.* Mark Twain chose those titles for one simple reason—the books contain adventures. Tom Sawyer had adventures. He "borrowed" a raft, witnessed a murder, uncovered a tidy little treasure, attended his own funeral. Huckleberry Finn survived his own set of fine adventures, faking his own death, borrowing quite a variety of stuff, absconding with a runaway slave, stumbling into a deadly family feud, and helping expose a pair of con men. There is, however, a formidable segment of the lit-crit community that remains stubbornly insistent that Twain's so-called adventures are nothing less than elaborate social criticisms, lead-brick heavy with moral inference. The archetypical American-literature professor who can't spend half a semester enthusiastically pounding social implications into *Huckleberry Finn* might as well hang up his or her PMLA subscription and sell insurance.

The first time I read *The Adventures of Tom Sawyer*, I was ten years old and blissfully ignorant of formal literary criticism. Kids sneaking out of their bedrooms at night, kids borrowing rafts, kids living on an island without a particle of adult supervision. Sure seemed like sound procedure to me.

Getting out of my second-story bedroom was a piece of cake. Just like Tom, I had a handy drainpipe outside my window. Not only could I slide to the ground in a nanosecond, but when my nocturnal ramblings were finished, I could shinny safely back up by that same route.

My bedroom, in the unshaded southwest corner of the house, soaked up heat like a sponge. It also attracted all manner of pesky insect life. Drawn by the blistering room temperature and my late-night reading lamp, box-elder bugs, millers, crickets, red ants, gnats, sweat bees, mosquitoes, June bugs, stinkbugs, and all their cousins and in-laws tramped across my bed, occasionally giving up their familial disagreements for the opportunity to bite me silly. Roaming alleys and darkened back yards in the cooling hours just before dawn promised not only sterling adventure but much-needed relief from my stifling, overpopulated room.

Sneaking out of the house wouldn't have been nearly so much fun if Allen Zimmer, the undertaker's boy, hadn't been up to the challenge. He slept in a ground-level sleeping porch, and the act of merely crawling out his window, while not as romantic as my per-ilous descent down the drainpipe, had the marked advantage of be-ing virtually noiseless. This was an important feature because Zim-mer's eldest sister, a bona fide bookworm of the worst sort, stayed up to all hours reading "serious" books.

If we tired of our diligent searches in neighborhood gardens for ripe strawberries and cantaloupe, we could usually "borrow" Zim-mer's grandmother's immaculate 1951 green Chevrolet coupe. We pushed it down the long circular driveway and, when we were clear of vigilant bookworms, started the well-muffled engine. We visited towns for miles around—Sidney, Sunol, Oshkosh, Lodgepole, and Big Springs in Nebraska, and Julesburg, Ovid, and Sedgewick just over the border in Colorado. Those towns, it was widely rumored, were full to the brim with fabulous, willing babes eager to get their lust-starved hooks into two precocious ten-year-old smoothies. Al-though it was forty miles away, we visited Sidney on a regular basis. Sidney women, we were told, were so exceedingly immoral that they seldom bothered to put on clothing after dark. Although these loose women proved to be danged hard to find, it wasn't for lack of effort. We spent a good part of our lives, it seemed, peering vainly out of that green coupe at blocks of deserted sidewalks. Man-hungry babes, we discovered, went to bed early.

Whenever we met a Sidney police car, we scrunched down low in the seat so that no cop could identify us. An old lady's immaculate coupe, driven by no one, sailing sedately down the street, should have excited some polite curiosity. We were never stopped, either because of incompetence or benign indifference. But we sweated plenty of blood.

Chappell's night constabulary consisted of two good-natured oafs known to everyone as Eagle-Eye Ernie and Fearless Frank. Fearless Frank once concluded that he could gain a terrific edge in his late-night war on crime by driving with his lights off on the wrong side of the street. No hot-rodding kid, he reasoned, would spot his police car until it was much too late. And it might have worked out just like Frank had hoped, but before he could arrest any kids, he collided with the mayor, totaling both the squad car and the mayor's rather limited sang-froid.

The July night all hell broke loose, Zimmer and I had scheduled a midnight rendezvous. Wheat harvest in the Nebraska Panhandle wasn't yet underway, but several local combine crews, made up mostly of high school boys, were back from Texas and Oklahoma, well-armed with cherry bombs and M-80s. The trouble started innocently enough, with the boys driving by and throwing a few cherry bombs at the light plant, where Ernie and Frank typically whiled away their shift. Ernie and Frank jumped in their car and set off in hot pursuit. I'd been hearing firecracker explosions and sirens for a full hour before I clambered down the drainpipe. Zimmer was expecting me, and I've always been a little obsessive about schedules.

Zimmer's house cornered an intersection bathed in the lights of the Chappell Memorial Library. Even on quiet nights, crossing the street meant hugging the sheltered east side of the Methodist church until I reached the end of a lilac hedge, checking for cars and late-night pedestrians, then zipping across to the Zimmer property. Old Man Zimmer owned a full quarter of a block. The Zimmer residence and the old man's funeral home were surrounded by what once had been elaborate grounds, now an overgrown jungle of ornamental trees and creepers hiding an assortment of vine-covered gazebos. The yard was pockmarked with crumbling cement fishponds, presently devoted to full-scale production of pond scum and mosquito larvae. Over several summers Zimmer and I worked like badgers creating a vast network of hidden trails and secret tunnels.

If I made it onto the Zimmer estate unseen, I was safer than in my own bedroom.

I had to wait by the church while a couple of open-throated hot rods thundered by. Once the coast was clear, I ran across the street, burrowing deep into the spirea bushes that surrounded Zimmer's sleeping porch. I had no time to settle in before a series of explosions walked toward me from Main Street. Cars careened through the intersection, leaving a carpet of deafening blasts in their wake. A full beer bottle shattered on Zimmer's sidewalk, showering me with glass and beer. Where was Zimmer? I scratched on the screen. Nothing. I whapped the screen with my open hand. Nothing. A spotlight tracked across the lawn toward my hiding place. Eagle-Eye Ernie! I dove for the dirt at the base of the porch. The spotlight probed my hiding place, then covered the sleeping porch in harsh whiteness. The cops knew everything! Someone had tipped them off! My sister Miriam, darn her nosy hide, must have heard me climbing down the drainpipe and called the cops. Geez, what if they've already arrested Zimmer? Maybe that's why he doesn't come out. I wonder if Zimmer's grandma knows we were going to steal her car? We'll be in jail for years. Where's Frank? Why don't they turn on their siren? Why aren't they chasing those firecracker guys?

The spotlight moved on, skimming lightly over Zimmer's jungle to rest on the corner of the Methodist church. Several glasspack mufflers rumbled toward the intersection. There was a smattering of suppressed laughter. My teeth in my throat, I chanced a peek at the squad car, trapped in the intersection by a circle of snarling cars, fully half of them *de rigueur* late-model Ford convertibles.

"You boys are under arrest." It sounded like Frank.

"Now!"

A firestorm of M-80s, cherry bombs, and Silver Salutes rained down on Ernie and Frank's luckless police car. Each convertible had three or four passengers, all lighting and throwing firecrackers. The boys driving Ford coupes stood outside their cars, reaching in the open doors to get more ammunition. Fireworks debris rattled the sleeping-porch screens like summer hail. Incandescent explosions strobed the intersection. With no possible way to escape unseen, I snuggled deeper into the moist earth. Hot cardboard spun into the bushes overhead. Ernie started out of the car, gun drawn. Someone, quite possibly the dorky little preacher's kid in the spirea bushes, was about to get shot. A cherry bomb sailed in the open squad-car door, landing neatly beside Fearless Frank. Frank bailed out.

"KER-BLAM!" The squad car's interior blossomed orange. Outside, a fresh rain of cherry bombs landed all around the cringing policemen.

"WHAM! BLANG! KER-BLAM! BOOM!" Ernie and Frank began to run. I could see guns waiving above their heads, and a pair of broad-beamed butts scuttling hemorrhoidally down the street. "BOOM-BOOM-KER-BOOM-BOOM-BULANNG!" Laughter.

"Let's take their car!"

The revelers lobbed occasional firecrackers at the retiring policemen, who were now a half-block away, scurrying for the light plant and, for all I knew, a couple of machine guns. The squad car roared to life and disappeared up the street, streaming smoke from open windows. Car doors slammed, engines hummed, tires howled, leaving long black streaks of burned rubber as the boys dispersed into the night. Except for some tire tracks and considerable fireworks debris, the intersection was as empty as Fearless Frank's head. And apart from the ringing in my ears, the only sounds were the singing night bugs and the snores floating out of Zimmer's bedroom.

*

This adventure was officially over. Those overheated Sidney babes would just have to wait. I'd had my fill of exploding police cars, cops waving guns around. Time to take this half-deaf boy back to the safety of his bedroom. Nobody on fire could have run faster.

The trip home was nearly uneventful. I made it halfway up the drainpipe before I spotted the squad car creeping down the alley. Ernie and Frank sure had gotten remounted in a hurry. I dove for the lilac bush. Flashlight beams poked all around me.

"I thought I saw someone."

"You sure, Frank?"

"He ran over here. Dadgummed numskull! See him?"

"No, I don't see nothin'. Nobody's gonna be on foot, Frank. All them kids have cars. Come on, let's go look for my car. Them kids musta left it someplace."

No wonder they showed up so fast. They'd run down to the light plant to get Frank's new squad car, the one the city bought after he crashed into the mayor. They drove up a few more feet, right beside my hiding place.

"Them kids'll come by here, Ernie. We wait here, they're bound to come by sooner 'er later."

"So what if they do, Frank? Last time we caught up to 'em they damn near blew us up while you was sittin' there like a ninny."

"Ninny! At least I wasn't the ninny that opened the dadgummed door an' let a dadgummed cherry bomb in the dadgummed car."

"I was about to make an arrest."

"Sure you was."

"Well, I was. I said I was and I was, just like I said I was."

"Sure you was."

"I want to find my car, Frank. We're just spinnin' our wheels sittin' here."

"Okay, but we're givin' up a golden opportunity."

"Sure we are."

I stayed hidden for a bit after they drove away, lights off. One thing you had to admire about Fearless Frank—he didn't give up on an original law enforcement idea just because it hadn't worked out the first time. Even if driving blind didn't help Frank catch the bombers, it sure was bothersome to me. I lost track of them immediately. Maybe Frank was coming up the alley again. Maybe he was coming down the street. I'd better lie low down here in the bowels of this lilac bush a while longer. Bugs started chewing on me in earnest. When I could stand it no longer, I crawled to the drainpipe and started climbing. I'd just reached the roof when I was bathed in the shaft of a blinding spotlight.

"There's one of 'em!" It came from the alley across the street.

"Come down with your hands up."

These guys were serious. Eyes shut, I jumped, lit smack in the center of the lilac bush. Branches gouged my face and arms as I slid down through to the ground. I was up and running before Frank realized I was missing from the roof. While his beam swung wildly around the yard, I squirreled up my favorite linden tree. Frank's light winged back to the porch, then down the alley. I kept climbing. Good thing, too, because Frank deduced correctly that I must be in that linden tree. It's a rule of mine that just when you decide a cop is too dumb to live, he solves a difficult case against all probability.

If Frank had bothered to drive across the street and poke his spotlight straight up, I'd have been a goner. I kept the trunk between me and the light until I'd gone up twenty-five feet. The spotlight played all around the first set of branches and a couple of planks left over from a tree house that never quite got built. I was hoping Frank wasn't about to drive over.

A laboring engine roared down the hill and on past me. I could just make out the star on the door. I heard a yell from across the street. Doors banged. A set of headlights came on, and Frank's car lurched out of the alley and tore out after Ernie's stolen squad car. After a couple of blocks he turned on his siren. I wondered if Zimmer was still snoring.

None of my harrowing adventures that night discouraged future trips down the drainpipe. After all, like Cortez and his search for the cities of gold, we were convinced if we looked hard enough, we'd find that magical City of the Willing Babes. We weren't going to stop until we found it. We did, however, divert some time and money into the Huck Finn Raft Expedition.

*

The mystery of the universe most resistant to explanation is the phenomenon of otherwise normal people reading *The Adventures of Huckleberry Finn* without immediately stealing a raft on the nearest river and setting sail for New Orleans. What kind of doltish mind could resist the appeal of that kind of adventure? And if you were that doltish, how much more doltish would you have to be to admit it? Okay, so maybe a dog-assed Mets fan would admit it.

Johnny Wertz came over the day after we'd gone public with the plan.

"Your parents are crazy if they let you do this."

"Oh yeah? How come?"

"Well, you could drown. There's quicksand on that river, and water moccasins. If you get in trouble there'd be nobody to help."

"That's right, John. There'd be nobody to help. That's the whole blamed idea!"

"I think your parents are crazy if they let you do this."

Maybe my parents were crazy. After all, these were the same incurable optimists, one of them seriously pregnant, who'd driven out of Nebraska in 1937, headed for two years of seminary in Chicago with twenty bucks in a sock and a few quart jars of tomatoes tied to the running boards. If I were crazy enough to dream up some fool river trip, they were crazy enough to help me do it. Mom got busy on a suitably nutritious menu. Dad was kind of wistful when he said, "Everybody ought to be able to go on a trip like that."

Johnny Wertz wanted to go. His parents had done a superb job of brainwashing him into thinking otherwise, but he wanted to go. He was always asking questions—how was I going to do this, had I thought of that. He was half hoping his folks would relent, and half hoping my folks would call it off so he wouldn't feel so bad. Fanoele wanted to go too, but his folks agreed with John's. Only Zimmer was game. But then he hadn't asked yet.

Zimmer helped me bring home two used tractor inner tubes from the Farmer's Co-op. They were six feet across and cost two dollars apiece. We built two rough wooden platforms and lashed each one to a tube. The platforms weren't easy on bony little asses. By the time we'd finished constructing, most of the boards contained three or four dozen bent-over nails.

Dad sprung for two mail-order Sears and Roebuck canoe paddles, one red, one blue, five dollars and fifty-three cents with shipping. Using paddles was a deviation from the text, of course. Huck would have poled the raft in shallow water and used a large sweep to steer when out in the belly of the Mississippi. We were faced, however, with a very different sort of river.

Our chosen river, an eighty-mile stretch of the South Platte from Julesburg, Colorado, to North Platte, Nebraska, met most of our requirements. We could resupply from any of the several towns we would pass; no other folks were likely to be on or near the river with us; each mile of river would reveal uncharted territory, reputed to be full of treacherous quicksand and evil-tempered cottonmouths; we would be the first kids from Chappell to tackle that river. All the South Platte lacked for our purposes was water. A dependable little stream in the years before the Denver Water Board and the big-feeling irrigators of eastern Colorado got their mitts on it, by midcentury the South Platte could manage high water for only a few weeks in early spring. Once the mountain snowmelt was over, and the big upstream users started diverting the water in earnest, the river shrank to a meandering set of shallow creeks, occasionally combining into a central current which might reach a foot or more in depth. Zimmer designed our tractor-tube rafts expressly for shallow water. Fully loaded with gear, the trailing raft drew only three inches.

We debated the relative merits of tents and tarps. Sawyer/Finn protocol dictated we either find a pirate cave or sleep under the stars. Caves, pirate or otherwise, are nonexistent in the South Platte River bottom. I argued for starlight. Zimmer, ever the inventor, said we could lean the two rafts against each other, drape the resulting inverted V with a tarp, and have a dandy tent at negligible cost. He generously volunteered to supply a heavy canvas tarp, but I insisted on an old plastic one from our clubhouse roof. The previous summer Old Man Zimmer had used that canvas tarp to haul the pitiful remains of a California family burned up in a fiery car-truck accident. I didn't let on, but the idea of inadvertently brushing up against some of that human charcoal gave me a severe case of the heebie-jeebies.

We picked up gear and supplies from some surprising sources. Jim Wertz lent an official Boy Scout compass. Mr. Turner gave me a crude road map left behind by a guest in his hotel. The mapmaker had drawn the South Platte River in red. Mom contributed cans of beef stew and cornmeal mush. Dad let us rob his tackle box. Sawyer/Finn theology dictated a diet of freshly caught fish, and we wanted plenty of hooks and sinkers. The manager of the local movie theater donated the four one-gallon popcorn-oil tins we planned to use for drinking water.

*

As March warmed into April, the cottonwoods and Siberian elms of the High Plains sprouted with the faint promise of spring. Word filtered up from Julesburg that the South Platte was running bankfull. Zimmer and I rolled the tubes up out of the parsonage basement, practiced packing our supply raft. We figured on spending at least a week on the river. If fishing was poor, our food wouldn't last long. We wished for a rifle. Shooting a couple of deer and turning them into jerky would certainly ease the food situation. Zimmer bragged up some revolutionary compound bow he was thinking of inventing. Ten-year-old swashbucklers could shoot plenty of deer with this baby. Arrows, Zimmer claimed, were cheaper than bullets because they were reusable.

A couple of days later Zimmer finally asked his father about the raft trip. Old Man Zimmer was pure de Kraut and brooked no argument. Allen took his chances over the dinner table after his old man had inhaled the better parts of two chickens and was working on a third. The old man discouraged dinner conversation, and usually the only sounds around that groaning kitchen table were the munchings and crunchings of the seven substantial Zimmers. As the meal wore on, the old man emitted increasingly gratified grunts. Once he'd worked his way through a fourth helping of mashed potatoes and was making the motions for a last pre-dessert cup of coffee, it was time for an enterprising child to plead his case. Zimmer's dad said no.

"Why don't you ask him again? Maybe he'll change his mind."

"He won't."

"Maybe he would. You won't know until you ask."

"He won't. He never does."

"Did he say why?"

"He never does. Doesn't have to. Just says no."

"What the heck are we gonna do?"

"I've been working on this robot lawnmower. It's gonna have a little map of the lawn inside and will tool around following the map. All I'll have to do is turn it on, sit on the porch, and watch it do all the work. Beautiful. Pops won't know whether to shit or go blind."

*

I needed a partner crazy enough to run a hundred miles of snake-invested river. But even if I were fortunate enough to find a guy like that, he'd have to own a couple of parents as crazy as mine. I moped around, kicked the furniture, generally made a festering pustule of myself, did everything short of asking out loud for help. I don't know who came up with the idea of taking Cousin Dick. I'd like to claim credit for a stroke like that, but I suspect Mom suggested it.

Dick would tell you that he wasn't all that crazy. For one thing he was one of the smartest Tupper cousins, a crew sporadically blessed with considerable brains. A natural-born entrepreneur, he always had some kind of lucrative scam going. During the winters when he lived on the farm down in Franklin County, he fooled around with a trap line. Made more money with his furs in a couple of months than I made on my newspaper route in a whole year. After his family moved to Colorado in the early fifties, he picked up high-paying odd jobs. The Air Force Academy was under construction, and he'd nose out work from contractors, do a good job, and get some more work. If Dick showed any incipient craziness, it was in his sense of humor, which was excellent, in his ownership of an actual accordion, and in his ownership of a magnificent three-story tree house. The tree house, built in a towering cottonwood, served as headquarters for his gang and had double walls filled with razor-sharp chunks of obsidian. Each lodge member owned at least one Wrist Rocket slingshot, a deadly blend of steel and surgical rubber. During their hotly contested slingshot battles with rival fraternities, Cousin Dick's band had several hundred pounds of lethal ammo always at their fingertips. If the rules of war dictated BB guns, the gun ports in the walls commanded an open field of fire over the nearby yard and bordering dry creek. It was a credit to Cousin Dick's architectural genius that during all the bloody warring, no enemy force ever got within twenty feet of his fort. His foes, sore from all their defeats, waited until he and his family were in church one fine Sunday morning, slunk into his yard, and torched his wonderful tree house. He could have rebuilt, but he said his heart wasn't in it.

Dick's romanticism might best have been compared to Sancho Panza's, particularly before he (Dick) tackled a mostly dry South Platte River on a couple of leaky tractor tubes. His parents, however, were another matter. Aunt Doris, whose usual worried expression broke into a dancing smile whenever Dick was around, possessed a noticeable weakness for direct-marketing organizations. Shaklee. Neolife. Amway. Not to mention the humble aloe vera cactus under all its brandnames and incarnations. Doris heartily approved of the thousands of aloe vera vitamin pills, facial cremes, and doggie hemorrhoid salves any marketing whizz with a bathtub and seventeen cents worth of ingredients could concoct in a couple of long afternoons.

Uncle Clinton's flamboyance generally ran to spectacular feats of athleticism. He wanted to be the boy who could run faster, pitch more hay. If he fought, he won. As a kid he held onto the reins when a team of runaway workhorses dragged him down a road for a quarter of a mile.

"I'm glad they stopped running when they did," he said later. "The bib of my overalls was about gone, and the gravel was starting to bite into my hide. Wouldn't have been long I might've had to let go."

Clinton wasn't immune to the occasional hot business opportunity. While farming in Nebraska he once tried chinchilla ranching, an economic activity limited to the quintessentially romantic. After two years and a couple of thousand bucks in cages and breeding stock, Clinton had one minuscule chinchilla pelt, the hide of a puny pneumonia victim. I could never figure out why the skins of such ineffectual critters were worth so much. The chinchillas were ambitious little bastards when it came to calisthenics, running their doofy brains out inside their personal little exercise wheels. However, in the reproductive arena, Clinton's chinchillas exhibited a stubborn gender neutrality, never once adopting the rigid sexual roles that lead to victims, degradation, and lots of brainless chinchilla offspring. He sold out, took his licking, had enough class to laugh about what must have been considerable damage to his finances.

In the early fifties Doris's always-fragile health began to deteriorate. The doctors recommended a more arid climate. Clinton, defying my grandfather's wishes by turning down the offer of a better spread close to town, quit farming and took his family west, settling just north of Colorado Springs at Monument, Colorado. He worked every job he could find, putting in terrible hours, steadily building a solid construction business on the side. It wasn't unusual for him to come home for a rushed supper, pull on a clean pair of pants, and head off for a time-and-a-half wage job that might last all night, building cement forms or pumping gas.

When he lost his leg riding a Caterpillar tractor off a sleet-slick Colorado bridge, he strapped on a prosthesis less than a month later and unloaded enough ninety-pound bags of cement to keep his concrete business going. The family's decision to let Cousin Dick go to Nebraska for a wild-haired river trip couldn't have made Uncle Clinton lose much sleep; Doris either.

*

A round-trip Continental Trailways bus ride from Monument, Colorado, to Chappell, Nebraska, cost a shade over twelve dollars and, with tedious layovers at Denver and Cheyenne, killed most of twenty-four hours. A slightly frazzled Cousin Dick crawled off the distinctive red-and-silver bus in front of Mr. Trump's Plainsman Hotel. He carried a small suitcase in one hand and his BB gun in the other. Maybe we weren't going to have real rifles on this trip, or even a fancy Zimmer-invented compound-complex bow and arrow set, but at least we'd be armed.

Cousin Dick enjoyed a close and very personal relationship with his BB gun. He always bought at the top end of Daisy's lever-action line. The pump models packed more power, but they cost twice as much and were much slower to cock. Worse, from Cousin Dick's skinflint perspective, pumps wore out three times as fast. Lever actions shot well enough. Uncle Clinton used to astound unbelievers by wedging kitchen matches in the gate post and having Cousin Dick step off twenty paces. From that distance, Cousin Dick could shoot BBs with such improbable accuracy that he lit the matches. If Uncle Clinton had been a betting man, he could have made a fortune.

I could never shoot as well as Cousin Dick, but my Daisy Defender was the Cadillac of lever-action BB guns. Not only did it have an adjustable peep sight but a secret BB storage area in the stock and a sturdy canvas sling, just the thing for long forced marches against the enemy. The barrel magazine held over five hundred BBs. On a good shooting day I'd fill that barrel twenty times. If any man or beast along the South Platte River had any troublesome ideas, they'd better be prepared to get their asses shot clean off.

I don't remember sleeping that night. We pitched my parents' Sears and Roebuck umbrella tent in the back yard, fed a small cottonwood-bark fire, and talked of the coming trip. Maybe we wouldn't stop at North Platte. If we caught enough fish, shot enough game, our ten-dollar nest egg might last to Grand Island, maybe Omaha. If we got to Omaha we could make some real money. Talk about your trashy women! Omaha had 'em. One peek at two steely-eyed Daisy-wielding river conquerors, and they'd be throwing money at us. We could make twenty-five dollars a night without half trying, have them begging for mercy. Save our money, buy a fishing boat, go clear to St. Louis. If that worked out, if we enjoyed ourselves on the Missouri, if we could tolerate catching a thirty-pound catfish every time we threw in a line, we might just head for New Orleans. Three whole months until school started.

Wouldn't everyone just croak if we made it all the way to New Orleans? We'd show up just in time for school. Come back swingin' a chain. Be plenty of jealous guys then, wouldn't there? All those gutless weasels too chicken to take on the little old South Platte. Bet just the sight of the Mississippi would make them crap their pants. Sure would hate to be those guys. Dinkphods, nothing but dinkphods, 100-percent Ovid dinkphods.

*

The South Platte Valley of the 1950s more closely resembled the valley as it was in the mid–nineteenth century than it looks today. Empty sere prairie ran up to the riverbanks, dotted occasionally by struggling clumps of young forest. A peculiarly vivid imagination could visualize squat hairy French trappers hauling canoes up the glittering center of that vacuous landscape. Now, thick stands of cottonwood and expansive boring fields of irrigated corn fill the first bottom from Julesburg to North Platte. To a contemporary observer the valley might as well be a sterile Grant Wood rendering of Iowa. We were fortunate to tackle the river before it became civilized.

*

Just east of the Julesburg bridge. We sat Indian-style on our nail-studded platform, paddles eager. Sunlight boiled off the meandering Platte, slitting our eyes under the fitful shade of our official Sawyer-model straw hats. We bobbed against the south bank, where the anarchist current held at its maximum eighteen-inch depth. One thirty-foot clothesline rope, tied in fantastic, highly irregular knots, lashed our supplies to the drunken trailing raft. Dad pushed us off. "Have fun," he said. Not "Be careful" or "Watch out for snakes" or "Don't, for pity's sake, show up drowned." If we looked back I don't remember.

We did more hauling than paddling the first day. The channel wandered capriciously all over the riverbed, disappearing under a sandbar on the south side to reappear magically two hundred yards to the north. Twenty minutes of hard pulling over feet-blistering sandbars might net us a five-minute floating respite until the channel slid underground once again. We learned to read the river like veteran Mississippi riverboat pilots. Dick spied out the longest stretches of channel up ahead, saving us from the most egregious portages. We handled the occasional electric fence with ease, Dick lifting the fence clear of the water with a dry paddle while I floated the rafts under.

A cottontail rabbit watched incuriously as we glided by his small island. Dick reached for the supply raft and his BB gun. I poled backward, trying to hold the rafts close enough for a clean shot at our first big game, not two feet off our starboard bow. Dick drew a bead just as a rattlesnake bit the rabbit square in the ass. The bunny jumped almost as high as we did. Our raft spun lazily down-current as we goggled-eyed the recoiling snake and his twitching victim. The snake looked smug.

Later, after our shrunken hormonally-disadvantaged testicles had a chance to descend a bit, we wished we'd have riddled that sneaky reptile's sorry carcass with hot lead. Teach him to steal game from the big boys. We'd have made a couple of spiffy hatbands from his tanned hide. Any snake could take a full-grown rabbit out that quick had to be thirty feet long. Hell, we could have made hatbands for the whole damned town. Made some meals out of him too. Would almost be worth eating snake just to tell those 100 percent Ovid dinkphods we'd done it. We ever get another chance at a rattler, we'll shoot first, ask questions later. A trip this long we could lay up half a hundred trophy skins by the time we hit North Platte. But even with our snake-killing urges brought to a froth, I don't remember either one of us suggesting we go back and look up the first and last rattlesnake we were to see.

Along toward evening, as the heat began to lift and the frogs and cicadas began to harmonize in earnest, schools of foraging carp brazenly roiled the shallows near the sandbars. They proved not much interested in canned corn or in the well-baked worms we pulled from a foul-smelling coffee can. BBs, even Dick's well-placed shots at their horny black backs, inconvenienced them not at all. Twain's glorious text ordained that we catch, among other things "some handsome bass, a couple of sun perch, and a small catfish." We were wading through dozens of fine five-pound carp, and had nothing to show for our good fortune.

"How about we bonk 'em with a paddle?" Dick was never one to stand on text if it got in the way of results.

"Ye-e-e-e-a-h!"

We hit the water running, bashing carp and water alike with prodigious paddle swats. Given the Rhodes Scholar intelligence of your average carp, it wasn't too surprising we were able to behead a good number in a manner of minutes. If they sensed a threat from behind they just naturally assumed they'd be better off swimming in the opposite direction, even if it meant beaching themselves silly. No suicidal pilot whale could have managed it any better. Maybe in the late twentieth century, two modestly educated youngsters in a similar situation would have shown a bit more bio-sensitivity. Perhaps, with more environmental empathy, we would have been content to commune with our finny friends, learn their disgusting habits, osmotize their wretched piscine souls. All I know is that when we stopped to survey the carp-littered landscape, I was overwhelmed by a certain snakelike smugness.

Among Chappell fishermen, carp carried a reputation for swampy bone-packed flesh and strong, if unimaginative, fighting ability. The community approved of the catching of carp, particularly large carp, but held the eating of carp to be bad form. Some fishermen threw carp on the bank, leaving sightless dessicated carcasses scattered on the sand dunes around area lakes. The thrifty dragged them home to Squanto-ize their gardens. Nobody in our acquaintance, including local master angler Mr. Trump, was known to actually cook and eat carp. Trump once gave me a ten-minute lecture on the evils of carp, how they ruined the habitat for better game fish, how lax fish-and-game officers should be shot for failing to seine Lake McConaughy free of every last carp. This from a man sufficiently hardscrabble to eat all the tasteless white bass he hauled home. As an afterthought he whispered a rumor of pressure-cooked carp which ended up tasting just like salmon. Not that he'd ever stooped to try it.

We had filled our text-mandated fish limit all right, but the contents were suspect. Every 100-percent Ovid dinkphod that heard about it was going to ride us if we ate carp. We owned no frying pan. Possessed no cooking oil. Our official menu, written down by my mother in precise Palmer-method cursive script, dictated a diet rich in the basic seven food groups, but did not include freshly beheaded carp. Tonight's officially sanctioned meal, looming large in both our appetites, including hot chocolate, canned pears, and some sort of cheap beef stew that was supposed to contain every basic seven representative not contained in the first two items. In the end we determined not to stink up our supply raft with a month's stock of headless carp. Dick selected a plump smoke-colored three-pounder with minor enough damage to go on the gill stringer, and we floated him belly-up to our night camp south of Brule.

*

In a short half-hour we established our temporary fortress on a large sandy island in midchannel, the two rafts propped up in a sheltering V, a fire large enough to roast a full-grown hippopotamus. A rough boma fashioned of heavy deadfall cottonwood limbs and water-smoothed driftwood circled the camp; two Daisy air rifles were propped within easy reach inside the shelter. Any foolish coyote who braved the boma would find a warm welcome. There was some idle talk of cougars. Wild tales of large cat tracks in the South Platte Valley had filtered up from Julesburg in recent years. Dick, living in the heart of bloodthirsty cougar range, contributed expert opinion on their behavior. Dogs and an occasional baby had been carried off, it seemed, but attacks on well-armed rafters like ourselves weren't likely. Slavering knife-armed Mexican immigrants, making their wily way north through this valley, constituted a much graver threat.

"They'll be hungry if they come," I said. "They're always hungry. Mom feeds 'em all the time. Puts the food on the back step. They eat everything, even beets. A man that'll eat beets has got to be starving. They sneak in here, it'll be for our food. They wouldn't think nothin' of slitting our throats for a can of beans."

"We'd have to blast 'em."

"I deliver the paper to this Rivera family. Mrs. Rivera and about thirteen kids live in this crappy basement house just east of downtown. I must've beat up Julian Rivera at least six times. He's bigger than me, but he's weak from eatin' beans. He quits once I give him a bloody nose. He always says he's going to get him a big knife and kill me, but he never has. All they eat is beans. Got a big pot sits on the stove all day. Every time I go collect it takes 'em an hour to round up the money. One time I'd been in the kitchen so long they probably forgot I was there. Julian's big sister shows up with a plate. She's naked as a jaybird. Got more of everything showing than I could get sized up all at once. She didn't run out. Just called her ma in Spanish and helped herself to the beans. Mrs. Rivera came in and told me she didn't have the money that week. Sis was eating beans and staring at me, like she was daring me to do something about it."

"What did you do?"

"I left. Stupid, huh?"

"I dunno. You said there was lots of kids around."

"Yeah. Maybe next time. Then there's this other lady on my route answers her door naked pretty regular, but she's old. Must be at least twenty-five."

"No foolin'?"

"No foolin'. I can't figure it out. She's beautiful. Blonde. Got knockers on her that would choke a horse. She always asks me in. When I stay on the porch it kind of pisses her off."

"Why don't you go in next time?"

"I think maybe I will." But I wouldn't. No use lying about it. Mrs. Wampler scared me half to death. Big talk about servicing half the women in Omaha aside, the idea of actual physical contact with a mature woman shrunk me up like a spider on a hot stove. Not that I minded staring at her, or that I didn't fantasize like crazy within the teeny limits of my personal experience.

"I think I should get a paper route."

"The money ain't bad either."

*

The carp was a disaster. We spitted him and subjected him to a thorough roasting. Dick and I managed to lose most of our eyebrows and eyelashes in the process. That was some fire. Black on the outside, raw on the inside, one bite was plenty. If we were hungry enough to cook and eat mud, there was always lots of it around. We ate pears while the watery stew cooked in the can. Nobody had explained the physics of heating unopened cans on a roaring fire. After the explosion we fished out the remains, two charred carrots and a tablespoon of stringy beef apiece. Hot chocolate partially repaired our spirits. We must have drunk a half-gallon of the stuff.

A steady southerly breeze, which had kept our camp fairly free of mosquitoes all evening, suddenly dropped to nothing. The air became oppressive. The mosquitoes went nuts. They filled our ears with ravenous humming, flew in our noses, bit the living crap out of every exposed patch of skin. My personal pack, a World War II vintage gas mask satchel, contained one stick of GI insect repellant. It must have been mislabeled insect bait, for it only encouraged the little bastards. We finally hid in our sleeping bags. If the Mexicans were able to brave the mosquitoes to rob our momentarily undefended food supply, they were welcome to it.

*

Two well-chewed boys were now sweating like a couple of barbecued carp. We tried to pass the time telling jokes, but told through the side of a sleeping bag even the best stories became so garbled we gave up. The awful heat and our intermittent thoughts of cougars and hungry Mexicans kept sleep at bay. Finally, after what seemed an eternity, a smattering of distant thunder promised cooling rain. Maybe in a few minutes those damned mosquitoes would be drowning, and we could watch. Teach them to attack the camp of the toughest explorers ever to run this river. About then a humongous cold wind swooped down out of the southern sky, scattering our fire into the north channel. The next icy blast carried our raft shelter clear over the river into the blackness. Torrential rain soaked us and our sleeping bags in an instant. Large chunks of hail began bouncing off our skulls. We ran. Sprinting pell-mell across the north channel, unmindful of tennis shoes full of sand and water. Running in mindless panic. Running vaguely toward Brule and some kind of succoring civilization. It was, without doubt, the most gutless performance of my entire childhood. Lightning crashed all around, revealing bending trees and falling branches. Wind-driven hail stung our backs, urging us on. We expected at any moment to be blasted by the bolts hitting all around us, electrocuted into unrecognizable smoldering corpses. A half-mile north of the river we hit a cornfield, scampered down parallel rows, calling out to make sure we were still together. By the time we arrived at Highway 30, the storm had settled down to a steady pounding rain, filling the road ditches waist-deep. A lone motel on the west edge of Brule sported a partially burned-out vacancy sign. A suspicious woman in curlers refused to let us in the lobby. She stuck a register card out through the screen and snatched eight wet dollar bills out of Dick's hand. I never could figure out why she never turned us in as runaways.

We squished our way back to a narrow stinking cabin. The bed, a lumpy ruin, was at least dry. Before long the monotonous rain rattling the roof and the snugness of our situation began to rejuvenate our dampened courage. Not that what we'd done wasn't awful. At no time in the text had Tom and Huck rented themselves any prissy motel room. Hadn't the Black Avenger of the Spanish Main and Huck the Red-Handed ridden out a storm on Jackson's Island at least as bad as this one? Dick, ever the practical, pointed out that without a cave or some equivalent sort of shelter, there hadn't been much of a choice. Besides, what kid did we know with balls enough to rent himself a motel room? He had a point.

"We can't ever tell, Dick. Our folks would kill us if they knew we'd spent eight bucks on a crummy motel room." Now that we were dry, the rain didn't seem like so much. Who could admit running from a little rainstorm? Sure, no Ovid dinkphod would have stuck it out. But they'd laugh at us just the same. "We tell nobody, I mean it."

"Sure." Dick didn't care one way or another. He hadn't ever been a kid for telling other folks his business.

A clear early-morning sky greeted us as we eased away from the motel. That old harridan might still call the police. It was high time we got on down the river. Surely we'd find our rafts in good enough shape for the trip. So far they'd proved impervious to the many snags we'd run into. Dick found his straw hat impaled on a cottonwood limb at the north edge of the river timber. We followed a trail of scattered possessions back to camp, gathering as we went. Our rafts, still securely lashed together with trusty clothesline, lay upside down on the north channel bank. We stepped off two hundred yards from our soggy sleeping bags, soaking in a puddle where we had abandoned them. I got a fire going while Dick hung our wet stuff on bushes to dry in the warming sun. After a few rushed cups of sugary hot chocolate and some cornmeal mush, we packed the supply raft with partially dried gear and shoved off in some haste. The river bridge overlooked our camp and snoopy police were much on our minds.

*

Ogallala, the next town, lay a scant ten miles downstream as the crow flew. By nightfall we should be well past there, nearer Roscoe, and if the river gods smiled on us and we didn't hit too much shallow water, we might get clean to Paxton, well within a good day's float of North Platte. The river, ever contrary, widened and promptly split into dozens of meandering shallow channels. The sun, blazing out of storm-cleared skies, blistered our backs as we sweated the rafts over one sandbar after another. Sandflies took great hungry bites out of our legs. By noon we'd exhausted our canteens, and it took some mighty discipline to wait until we stopped for lunch to open the reserve stock in the popcorn-oil cans on the supply raft. I probably hadn't washed them out well enough after a winter stored in our damp basement. At any rate, each can was full of scummy green water that smelled like it came straight from the Ovid sewer system. Less fastidious adventurers as thirsty as we were would have drunk it in a heartbeat. Or at least boiled it and tried it on for size. We just didn't have the sand. It smelled too bad.

After a hard-swallowing dry lunch we attacked the river with a new urgency. Our thirst, magnified a hillion jillion times by the fact that WE HAD NO WATER, drove us downstream at a trot. Sure, we could have safely drunk boiled river water, but we'd floated through too many feedlot crossings littered with cowpies, and we'd passed beside the flowing outlet pipes for the municipal sewers of both Julesburg and Brule. Even boiled, that water would still be full of cow shit and people shit, and we weren't having any. By midafternoon, halfway to Ogallala and near self-induced delirium, we'd reached a state of stone-faced wretchedness, afraid to open our mouths for fear we'd lose the scant cottony moisture. No telling how long we would have gone on that way. Probably until we dropped. I don't remember anyone talking of giving up, heading for the highway and help. We'd burned that chance by taking a cowardly motel room. Self-respect demanded we work our way out of this one, even if it killed us.

Dick, sharp-eyed as ever, spotted a windmill just over the lip of the south bank. Laden with canteens and two of the suspect oil cans, we clambered up to the first bottom and set off across a quarter-mile of grass and soapweed. A large feedlot full of thousand-pound fat cattle surrounded the windmill, which pumped into an iron-bound wooden tank. The cattle watched us with some alarm as we scampered through them up to a galvanized pipe spouting the most delicious water I ever drank in my life. Loath to leave, we sat for a good while, taking turns at the pipe, until we were gorged to the gills. Brown hills of arid grassland stretched to the southern and western horizons. North lay the damnable river, beyond that parched wheatfields and a particularly bleak stretch of Highway 30. Far to the east, rising out of the dusty green of the river bottom, Ogallala's silver water tower shone bright with welcome.

We returned to the river with full tummies and a noticeably lighter step, despite the weight of sloshing water cans. Nothing like conquering disaster to boost the spirit. The river obliged us by narrowing into a single free-flowing channel. For the first time on the entire journey, we floated down easy miles, paddling only to stay fixed in the current. But the river was tricky. Its sinuous twists increased our distance by a factor of three. Not that we cared much at that point. Everything was under control. We surprised a doe drinking in midchannel. She stared unblinking for a long time before fear overcame curiosity and she bolted into the trees. Probably had never seen a Zimmer raft design up close.

At a spot along the south bank where a small creek spilled into the river, creating a rare pool of relatively deep water, we pulled over onto a wide sandbar to scout for fish. We'd lost interest in carp, and improbably hoped the fresh creek water would attract a better grade of game fish, perhaps trout or even catfish. Twenty minutes of desultory fishing failed to yield a decent nibble. When the sandfleas got around to us we decided to give it up as a bad cause. I volunteered to push us off. Dick was on the lead raft paddling furiously, trying to pull us clear. I lifted and pushed, gaining a little with every shove. Just as the supply raft floated free, the sand gave way, and I was stuck fast, up to my waist in clinging quicksand.

"Quicksand! I'm caught!"

"Grab that stringer!"

The last foot of our trailing yellow fish stringer slithered just within reach. I latched on, making quick wrap around my wrist. The first jerk pulled me flat. Sand filled my mouth. Dick, yelling like a madman for me to hold tight, jumped off and gave the raft a mighty yank. I popped out into the river like a champagne cork. Spitting sand, I ran to catch up. There hadn't been time to get scared. Afterward we wondered why everyone made such a big deal about quicksand. Heck, quicksand wasn't anything two cool-headed river masters couldn't handle. Not that we would in good conscience, recommend it to the average slow-witted Ovid dinkphod.

*

Mom had planned an unusually full meal for this second night out. We ate our way through a couple kinds of canned vegetables and some ersatz beef hash made by the same experts who'd concocted last night's abbreviated stew. This time we made careful steam holes in the can. One exploding stew can was enough. Dick, who was allowed to drink milky coffee at home, had hidden a small can in our larder. Sipping hot boiled coffee, made especially piquant by the day's hardships, filled us with an enormous sense of well-being.

"This is a blast." For Dick there was no higher level of experience than "a blast."

"I'll bet none of those puny dinkphods back home could have done it."

"They'd have been crying for their mamas."

"They'd have shit their pants."

"We should probably have shot that deer. Been eating venison tonight instead of hash."

"Nah, she probably had a fawn hid somewhere. Besides, a BB would have probably just wounded her."

"Yeah, you gotta hit 'em in a vital spot."

We pondered on that one. Where the heck did you hit a deer with one dinky BB that would do more than piss her off?

Dick picked up his Daisy and sighted on a red-wing blackbird chirping in a nearby willow. "When we were on the farm Dad made the mistake of offering me a dime for every sparrow I shot."

"How many did you get?"

"Got a hundred the first day. You should have seen his face when he saw all those stupid dang sparrows laid out in the haymow. He paid me my ten bucks all right, but said I was going to bankrupt him if he didn't call it off. Man, that was easy money."

"Bet those Ogallala women will pay us plenty. They all work at Goodall's you know. Some of 'em make a buck an hour."

"That'd be a blast."

Camping within sight of Ogallala considerably eased our fears of ghostly cougars and starving Mexicans. A persistent southern breeze cleared our treeless island bare of mosquitoes. Driftwood burned cheerily in a small firepit. Loaded with hot chocolate and cheap-assed hash, we slept the sleep of the just, two loaded Daisy rifles within arm's length.

*

The Ogallala river bridge hove into view just before noon. We hauled the rafts up under the bridge onto the shaded riprap. It was time for two chain-swinging river runners to saunter down Main Street. Unfortunately, all the loose women were in hiding. Must have heard about us. To the timid, a man can sometimes have a little too much of a good thing. We homed in on a drugstore soda fountain. Thirty minutes and five icy Green Rivers later, talk turned from loose women to our prospects downriver.

Dick worried about our cash. "Two bucks won't get us enough food to make it to North Platte. It's twice as far as we've come, and it took five dollars worth to get here. We have to keep some cash to call your dad to come after us. I don't figure we can make it much past Roscoe on what we've got."

"There's two cans of mush and some beans. Maybe we could stretch it. There's bound to be more rabbits and fish than we've seen so far."

"I looked in those dang water cans we filled at the windmill. That water's already green, got weird things floating in it."

"We look around here, we can find something better for water."

"I think we oughta call your dad while we're in town. We've got the money to call him. We buy food, maybe we'd be so short of change we'd never get home."

"That'd be given' up. The plan said we were going clear to North Platte. We get down to where the North Platte hits the South Platte, it'll be easier sailing. Got to be more water. We'll make better time."

"Yeah, but what if the river twists and turns like it did the last ten miles? Could take us a week to get down there. We'd be out of food, and maybe out of water in two days. I don't want to go through that water business again."

"I don't either. Okay. I'll call Dad. He won't like it. The plan said North Platte, and that's what he expects."

He didn't like it. Uncharacteristically brusque when he told me he was jammed up with church activities for a couple of hours. Said we were to be packed up and ready to go when he got to Ogallala. He was on a tight schedule.

The call put me in a blue funk. We were bailing out. Chickens. Everyone had counted on us to do what we said we'd do. Now a little droughty stretch of river and a mere lack of beans had us pissing our pants. Might as well call ourselves dinkphods and commit suicide. How many chances does a kid get to run a river? Dick was already talking of working full-time on Academy construction next summer. I was looking at church camps. We blew this shot by quitting; maybe no one would trust us with any future adventures.

Not admitting for a New York minute to my niggling feelings of relief to be leaving the river, I turned on Dick. Called him awful names. Tried to shame him into going on. Dick gave me a look of stolid disappointment. Who could blame him? I'd changed without warning from bosom buddy to low-rent traitor. Waiting under the bridge for Dad, we sat sulking, backs studiously aimed at each other. I'd been a fourteen-caret jerk, no question, but was too stiff-necked to own up.

Just when matters descended below miserable I remembered something. Old Man Zimmer sold his customers little brass cylinders for messages of endearment to be dropped into their loved ones' caskets. These five-dollar items were guaranteed to keep messages in pristine shape for a hundred years. When Zimmer was still part of the expedition he'd donated one of these handsome brass cylinders to the cause. The plan was to bury an account of our trip under the North Platte bridge or the Missouri River bridge or the Mississippi River bridge at New Orleans, if we got that far. Any pilgrims stumbling upon that cylinder in a century or so would be knocked flat on their asses by the wonderfulness of what we'd done. Maybe Dick and I weren't going to make it to the North Platte bridge, but the sturdy cement structure at Ogallala would serve just fine.

The process of dredging up three days of high adventure lifted the doldrums. We cobbled together three pages of highly embroi-

dered tales. I'm not sure how long our favorite rattlesnake was supposed to be, but it certainly was a world's record. We signed our
names with John Hancock audacity, slipped the pages into the
velvet-lined cylinder, and buried it beside the south abutment,
knowing beyond doubt some historian in the dimmy future was
going to immortalize us, probably in several volumes. Maybe some
brave lads would attempt to duplicate our mighty deeds. Pity the
fool who tried. Stand unbowed to the force of an all-night tornado?
Go days without water? Survive giant rattlesnakes and innumerable
beds of sucking quicksand? Hold off wave after wave of slavering
cougars and knife-wielding Mexicans? Seduce half the female population of Ogallala and get paid for it? Not likely.

By the time Dad showed up, not even his prickly mood could
dampen our revived humor. We babbled all the way back to Chappell, covering everything—the water near-disaster, the quicksand,
not even sparing the Brule motel embarrassment. Halfway home
Dad's eyes began to twinkle. His chuckles inspired further torrents
of half-baked fable. Maybe he was thinking of his own childhood,
isolated on those northeast Nebraska hardscrabble farms. I knew in
my bones he'd have jumped at a river trip if his parents had given
him the choice. For as I looked at his shining eyes, I could see he was
right there with us, floating on that twisting river, searching downstream for the one swift channel to carry us far beyond the tugging
sand.

Jackrabbit Vincent

Jackrabbit didn't come to town school until third grade. That's when his neighborhood one-room school closed, and Jackrabbit and his two sisters began to make the fifteen-mile trip every day. The one thing the town kids noticed right off was how good-natured the new boy was. We ragged him plenty, usually about his shoes, which were the kind of heavy plow shoes we called clodhoppers. Sometimes we teased him about his bib overalls, which often stank of manure. Jackrabbit had to milk cows in the mornings before he came to school, and the Vincents didn't have the money to buy him many changes of clothes. He accepted his chores as a fact of life, just as he accepted our cruelty. He was, after all, a new boy.

New boys, even if their clothes were perfect, had a rough time at our school. Usually we beat them up, left them bleeding and sniveling in some alley. But Jackrabbit was always big, much bigger than most of us, and strong from all those farm chores. Once an eighth grade bully grabbed Jackrabbit's cap and held it high out of reach over his head. Jackrabbit laughed right along with everyone else. He could see a joke as well as the next fellow. Then he asked for his hat. When the older boy jeered, Jackrabbit grabbed his testicles with those teat-hardened fingers and tried very hard to twist them off.

After that, nobody in our class ever punched Jackrabbit, even in play. We didn't pinch him, trip him, or ever, ever steal his cap. But we found that regular childish ribbing rolled off him like nothing, that he seemed to get some pleasure out of it, even though his own tries at humor were lame and way too foolish for our third grade minds. He had a place, much below our town-boy station to be sure, but a firm place. And when, in fourth grade, he became the only boy with spectacles, we barely took the time to tease him.

By sixth grade Jackrabbit had a single-shot .22 rifle, the J. C. Higgins model Sears sold for twelve dollars and fifty cents. In those simple times bullets could be had for a half-cent apiece, and Jackrabbit treated them like diamonds. On his way out to hunt he'd take only one bullet from the box on the shelf. Dead jackrabbits were worth fifteen cents each at the mink farm in town, and he didn't intend to reap less than a fourteen-and-a-half cent profit on each rabbit.

He collected lots of fourteen-and-a-half-cent profits over the years. What a sight all those dead jacks made, piled level-full in the back of his dad's pickup when he brought Jackrabbit to school on Monday mornings. It was the kind of awful carnage that's particularly fascinating to children. We'd stare at the stacked-up rabbits, all stiff and gory, each with a neat bullet hole between the ears. We couldn't imagine how a boy with such poor eyes was so deadly with a rifle.

I found out his secret the one time he took me hunting. I don't remember why I condescended to visit his house. I'm sure I didn't tell anyone else I'd done it. Perhaps I just wanted to pile up some rabbits, wanted to take advantage of all those square miles of soapweed pasture that surrounded Jackrabbit's farmyard.

Once we crossed the pasture fence, he loaded his rifle with his precious single cartridge. Jackrabbit proved to be very particular about this. I always crawled under and over fences packing a loaded gun, never thought anything about it. Jackrabbit stopped every time, unchambered his bullet. "Dad said I should," was all he would say.

We hadn't gone ten steps when a young jack exploded out of a pair of soapweeds. I blasted away, working my bolt-action .22, jerking the trigger. The rabbit ducked and juked this way and that, all the time windmilling his ears like crazy, until he ran over the crest of the hill, completely unmarked. Jackrabbit was disgusted. "That's no way to do. You wasted half a box of shells. "Where'd you learn to hunt anyhow?"

So we did it Jackrabbit's way. Kick a rabbit out of the soapweed and let him run, that was Jackrabbit's theory. Wait for the rabbit to stop, and they always do stop, because a jack is full of curiosity and he wants to know if anyone's still chasing him. When he stops, run after him, make him move, tire him out.

We hounded that rabbit through ten miles of the roughest canyons and hills I'd ever seen. Jackrabbit Vincent didn't run particularly fast. He had a heavy, pounding run, made worse by those clodhopper shoes. But he ran to a steady, plodding rhythm, up hills and down, carrying his rifle at arm's length. Each time we spooked the rabbit it was for a shorter distance. I was grateful, could easily have quit if there were a face-saving way to do it, but Jackrabbit was still fresh, not even breathing hard. When the rabbit paused to take his last long look at us, he was only ten feet away. He must have thought we were the most curious creatures he'd ever run into. Jackrabbit took his time with the shot, put it between the ears like usual. "There," he said, "that's how you're supposed to do it."

*

In our little town most everyone went out for sports. There were a fair number of sissies that passed on junior high football, and one or two who played no sports at all, even baseball, which was considered mandatory. But Jackrabbit participated in nothing beyond his required hours in school. "Dad wants me home," was all he'd say.

*

By the end of our freshman year, Jackrabbit had almost passed from our lives, consigned to agriculture courses in faraway buildings, studying welding and auto mechanics and cattle feeding, stuff in which aspiring doctors and lawyers had little interest. The track coach was interested in Jackrabbit, however. He'd heard stories from somewhere about his legendary endurance. He had a track meet coming up and no one to run the mile. So he talked to Jackrabbit, pleaded with Jackrabbit's dad, sold and cajoled, all the time doing the best imitation he could muster of a real human being. What he got for all his trouble was a one-shot deal: Jackrabbit could run in the meet if it would help the school, but he couldn't practice, and he wouldn't be available again. Surely a coach this persuasive could talk someone else into running the mile for the rest of the season.

Julesburg was always a tough opponent. It was a river town and had kids that weren't afraid to scrap and claw, kids with a little hunger in their bellies. When they filed off the bus that fine spring afternoon in their bright Kelly green and gold track clothes, they looked unconquerable. Not only were they bigger and older, but they had more muscles, longer legs. Maybe the rumors about twenty-year-olds masquerading as high school kids were true.

Somehow our puny team held its own during the sprints and the hurdles. We lost ground in the field events. Those Julesburg guys could throw anything farther than most. They murdered us in the relays. By the time the sun was down to the horizon and Jackrabbit Vincent was setting up at the start of the mile run, we had been as soundly thrashed as we had expected. No victory hung in the balance. The thing was over.

Someone had loaned Jackrabbit a pair of black high-top sneakers. He wore his white gym shorts, yellowed now from so many washings. His track shirt was brand-new, deep orange with a black satin slash across the front. For the first time in his life he was sporting the school colors of the Chappell Buffaloes. He looked uncomfortable.

After the first lap Jackrabbit ran them all into the ground. It was that same rabbit-killing pace, pounding up on one green Julesburg runner after another, his thick legs, already grown fleshy, quivering with each heavy step. By the start of the fourth circuit, he'd lapped the field, and beaten runners were giving up, now trying only to finish the race.

He ran that last lap the same as the first. Maybe his feet were a bit heavier, his stride a little shorter. When he pounded down to the finish line he was sweating. I remember being amazed by that. Everybody yelled, the coach most of all. We jumped and pounded each other, hugged, rolled on the ground. It might as well have been the state basketball tournament as an early-season track meet on our humble cinder track.

Jackrabbit broke the school record. Smashed it to smithereens. His name inscribed on that brass plaque that hung by the gym door.

He never ran again. His dad kept his word and worked Jackrabbit at his nightly chores.

A year or so later things started to go bad. Jackrabbit took up with some tough kids, kids who smoked cigarettes, kids who swiped cars. Sometime along in there he quit going home to do chores. He stopped going to school altogether, finally drifting off to work in other states without leaving a track anyone has been able to follow. He's out there somewhere, old and fat and bald, like the rest of us.

But for me he'll always be pounding up to that finish line, running straight into a golden sunset, his weak eyes squinting against the glare. The whole world was gold at that moment, the track, the crowd, the grass of the infield. I hope it was gold for him too.

Back to the Basics

Mrs. Keister had a temper. And when she lost control, as she usually did if one of her junior high students mistook a verb for an adjective, she didn't fight it. She didn't take a deep breath, didn't grit her teeth and try a different tack. She shrieked. Shrieked long ear-splitting one-note screeches so high up the scale they threatened every window in the room. "EEEEEEEEEEEEEEEEEEEEEEEEEEEEEEEEEEEEEEEEEEEYOOOO OOOOOOOOOOOOOOOOOOSTOOOOOOOOOOOOOOOOOOOOOO OOOOOOOOOOOOOOOOPID IDJIT!!!" Her face, blood-puffed and twitchy, radiated a physical, searing heat. She always threw her grammar book. Usually it knocked over the trash can, spilling papers and wet gum. "EEEEEEEEEEEEEEEEEEEEEEEEEEEEEEEEEE YOOOOOOOOOOOOOOOOOOOOOOOOOOOOOOOOOOMORRRRRR RRRRRRRRON, PICK THAT UP!!!" And the poor wretch who had started the whole fuss, knees banging together like cymbals, had to clean up the mess. Had to clean up the mess while she stormed back and forth across the room shrieking and kicking the walls, stopping only to hurl erasers and odd bits of chalk. Long white strings of drool flew out of her mouth onto our faces and notebooks. We sat, frozen and witless, little lumps of protoplasmic dough, quite ready for embalming, too scared to wipe off the spit.

Mrs. Keister, always capricious, operated free of any recognizable restraint. We never knew when she'd blow, or for how long. She could scream for an hour one day and smile benevolently for an hour the next. No one had a clue as to what terrible things she'd do to us if we misdiagrammed a sentence. We just knew it would be awful.

New Keister horror stories floated around school every week. She slapped kids, grabbed ears and hair, banged heads against the blackboard. When a big eighth grade boy said, "We was" twice in one class period, she raked his cheeks with her red nails, leaving long welts that branded him for days.

But after Mrs. Keister hit the Swartz boy with the unabridged dictionary, some kids started missing school. I think it was because she tricked him that frightened us most.

*

Elmo Swartz was a nice kid, dumber than a box of rocks, but nice. Minded his own business. He plugged away, did the best he could. Too bad he couldn't read French. Our reading book had a long story about a young French war widow raising Parisian versions of Dick and Jane in the harsh milieu of postwar Europe. To celebrate one of the earnest little tots' birthdays, the widow scraped together their last francs and bought enough eggs and milk to make crepes.

Mrs. Keister had us reading aloud, taking turns. Margaret was batting along in good shape:

"Monique opened the apartment door. She placed her packages on the table. 'Simone. Jean-Claude. Come quick. I have a surprise for you!'"

Mrs. Keister interrupted. "Elmo, see if you can read today. Start where Monique calls the children. What? You weren't paying attention? Someone help him find his place. What were you doing, Elmo? Picking your nose again? Find it? Hurry up, we're waiting. Help him, someone. That's right, the fourth paragraph where it says 'Come quick.' Do you have it, Elmo? Good, it's about time."

And Elmo, bless his heart, started out strong, like the trouper he was, stumbling only a little.

"'C-c-c-ome quick. I ha-have a su-uh-prise for y-y-you.'"
"'Wha-What is it?'" the ch-children a-asked."

Right there, most of us started holding our breath. We had skipped ahead to the next sentence. There was no way Elmo was going to get through it.

"'I h-have eggs and m-milk. Tonight we will make ca-ca-ca-reepies.'"

"CA-REEEEPIES? CA-REEPIES? CA-REEPIES!!!" Mrs. Keister threw her book. Elmo ducked. "EEEEEEEEEEEEEEEEEEEYOOOO OOOOOOOOOOOOOOOOOOSTOOOOOOOOOOOOOOOOOPID IDJIT!!" Then she stopped. Maybe it was over. I peeked. She was in the back row, standing over poor Elmo, hands on hips, her face scarlet and jumpy. Elmo had his book straight out in official reading position, gripping it for all he was worth. She tore the book out of his hands and slammed it to the floor.

"Pick up the book, Elmo."

Elmo never blinked. And when he obediently leaned over, Mrs. Keister hoisted the big yellow unabridged dictionary from the stand, lifting it high above her head.

"Nobody said, "Look out, Elmo!" or "Watch out!" or "Duck!" We just sat, quiet as thieves, watching that huge book take its terrible ride downward. It hit him smack behind the head, drove him straight onto the floor. He lay on his side, unmoving except for one leg, which stuck out at an odd angle, quivering. His eyes were open. A little blood welled up in his ear, until it was full, then rolled down his neck in a steady stream. Some fool girl started crying.

Then he was gone, snatched from the floor and carried out in a blur of red fingernails, overalls, a dragging foot, a white shirt, a tie. Somebody said the principal was there. Someone else wondered what he'd do. Then Mrs. Keister was back, white-faced for once. I remember that. Margaret started reading again. She read for a long time, and when she was done, Mrs. Keister beamed and said she was proud of us all.

When we left school Elmo's parents were getting out of their pickup truck. We stepped off the walk to let them by. Mrs. Swartz didn't look up, but Elmo's dad was angry. He stared at us. We looked at our feet.

*

A cold, lightless parsonage provided scant succor from a bad day. Sister Judith in college at Lincoln, Miriam off doing her big-cheese cheerleader stuff, Mom at her country school digging out from under papers and gradebooks, Dad ministering somewhere. I slid my

J. C. Higgins .22 rifle from its slick imitation-leather case, fed exactly twenty-eight cartridges down the tubular magazine. Pooch, our Dumbo-eared mongrel, trotted loyally behind as I made my way to the vast soapweed-dotted pasture north of the school. The air turned milky-blue as an unusually wet snow fell limply on the somnolent landscape. Only the faint squeak of my combat boots and Pooch's irregular panting sounded through my heavy stocking cap. No jackrabbits exploded from the soapweeds. Hunkered down, waiting for the storm to get worse before it passed, they knew, as I did, that no Panhandle storm that began with little wind and a batch of heavy wet flakes could end in anything less than a fifty-mile-an-hour howler. Pooch found the end of a culvert sticking out of a dry pasture dam. Probably full of sleepy rattlesnakes. Wedge myself in there like a goldanged badger, they could bite me twenty times before I flinched. Better wing a shot through there, about an inch off the bottom. Make any dopey snakes or hungry coyotes know I mean business. Pooch barked at the shot. No slitherings or furtive paddings echoed from the tunnel.

I cleared tumbleweeds from the culvert's mouth. A partially buried snakeskin, sloughed off months before, dissolved under a full-bore Pooch attack. A long-abandoned assortment of bones and hair, some critter's interrupted dinner, lay scattered down the culvert floor. A second blast, guaranteed to clear out any remaining biting creatures, rolled down the culvert. I backed into the entrance, scootching Pooch in beside me. My rifle commanded a clear field of fire. No goldanged coyotes could get me from the front. Pooch would warn me if they came from behind. Snug as clams, we heard the rising wind, saw it curl the first small drifts across the far side of the dam. I squinted down the rifle barrel, now flecked with juicy flakes. Come out, you shrieking hell-bitch, stomp your way into my sights, throw every goldang unabridged dictionary you can haul out of that goldang school, turn yourself purple, yell your loudest, foam at the goldang mouth. Because if I screw up and don't blow your sorry ass to Kingdom Come, then Pooch here will sure as hell make up the difference. We waited, my finger tight on the trigger. Blurry threatening shapes loomed near, then retreated. Pooch and I, undoubtedly the deadliest combination in the known universe, faced them all down.

The wind began an intermittent howling, sneaking little stinging flurries into our cubbyhole. Pooch shivered and shoved his nose under my arm. He whined and licked my ear. I wondered if Mom and her old balky Chevy had made it back through the storm.

We sailed home through the blackening dusk, a roaring thirty-mile-an-hour wind pushing us south. I worried we would miss Chappell entirely and end up frozen in some dirty snowbank halfway to Ovid. The spectral hulk of the school reared up in the gloom. Pooch and I scooted past and on down into the sheltering town. The parsonage lights were on.

Miriam, who was in high school and knew everything, reported that Mrs. Keister had denied any crime, said Elmo was an epileptic, said he was always having fits. The principal asked Margaret about that, with Mrs. Keister sitting right there, listening to everything. Margaret couldn't remember any previous fits, but sort of remembered this last one. Mrs. Keister was back in her room the next day, smothering us with manic cheerfulness.

Elmo stayed out of school for a month. When he came back, sporting a pink hearing aid in each ear, Mrs. Keister called on him just like always. He made the same mistakes he always made, but Mrs. Keister never screamed at Elmo. Screamed at the rest of us, made the windows rattle, but not at Elmo. She smiled at Elmo. Elmo was safe.

Growing Up Methodist

Mr. Hockersmith had his faults. Always grumpy when we cut across his vegetable garden, he'd somehow lever his tall old bones out of his chair and onto his porch before we quite got out of earshot. "Yoo-hoo, boys, yoo-hoo. The sidewalk is over there." One summer he called my parents with a pointed inquiry about a particularly toothsome watermelon we'd borrowed from his garden the night before. But in any season hardly a week passed without Mr. Hockersmith interrupting one of our lighthearted boyish pranks with a self-righteous lecture on the joys of being good. We hated him. Hated him with all the thorough simplicity only the pure in heart can muster.

Your basic turtledove is a stupid, trusting creature that has nothing better to do than sit on power lines all day cooing boastful laziness at the entire countryside. Naturally, we slaughtered them by the hundreds. Phhttt, plink, thud, phhttt, plink, thud—sweet BB-gun music to any child. We'd often have a stack of twenty-five doves before noon.

We were heading back with some fresh additions for the dead pile when we ran into an ambush—Hockersmith and Eagle-Eye Ernie, one of our town cops. Mr. Hockersmith, dumbfounded, stared through his thick spectacles at the huge stack of cordwooded doves for the longest time. "Murderers," he said. "You boys are nothing but murderers." If the truth be known, we might have been feeling a tad bit sheepish before Eagle-Eye confiscated our priceless weapons "for illegal discharge of a firearm in the city limits." That broke it. You don't take a man's gun. It's the first law of the West.

John was in the seventh grade, a year younger than we were, but he had the baritone voice and vocabulary of a grown man. He could impersonate a mysterious out-of-town admirer to a credulous high school girl and after five minutes on the phone be practically going steady. Mostly he adopted the persona of the generic stud duck from Julesburg. John always set up a public meeting place, a movie theater or maybe the Dairy King. The girls showed up, of course, all made up and no place to go. Our last victim started crying in the movie theater. We had to give it up. Not much fun in crying girls.

John listened to our current problems with Mr. Hockersmith. He made a proposal. We accepted. I dialed. John never messed with dialing his own calls. He was, after all, something of an artiste by then.

"Mr. Hockersmith, this is Milt Peterson, your utilities superintendent. That's right, Mr. Hockersmith, I like singing in the choir very much. Yes, Mr. Hockersmith, I'm sure you do too. Yes, I'll be sure to tell her. That's kind of you to say, Mr. Hockersmith. The reason I called, Mr. Hockersmith, is that we're going to be installing a new pump in a few hours, and we don't know for sure how long it will take. That's right, Mr. Hockersmith, the water will be off. If things go the way we want, it could be only a day or so before we're back to normal. This is a new kind of pump, and there's a chance we could be out for three or four days. Yes, Mr. Hockersmith, that would be a hardship on older people. Yes, Mr. Hockersmith, I'm sure you do pay taxes like anybody else. What we'd like you to do, Mr. Hockersmith, is to store water in case things go wrong. Well, Mr. Hockersmith, I think buckets actually. Cream cans would be fine. No, nothing wrong with jelly glasses either. And fill the tub, if you have one. Handier to get water to flush the toilet that way. Yes, Mr. Hockersmith, all the receptacles you have around there should be filled, especially your trash barrel. A town truck will come by this afternoon to pick it up. We'll need everyone to pitch in if we're going to meet our industrial needs."

This last bit of genius struck us as being particularly funny since our little village had about as much industry as Antarctica. John had to cover the receiver until we could smother our giggles.

"Yes, Mr. Hockersmith, Art will most likely be driving. Yes, Mr. Hockersmith, I'll tell him to be careful backing in. Thank you for your cooperation. And, Mr. Hockersmith, would you please contact every household on your block and inform them of the city's needs? Yes, Mr. Hockersmith, each and every one. If we spend our whole day on the phone, we can't be hauling those barrels, can we? that's great, Mr. Hockersmith, you're a real good citizen."

After some gleeful backslapping, we all headed downtown to Pokorny's drug store for a congratulatory tin-roof sundae, and added a few more straw wrappers to the hundreds hanging above our heads.

On the way home we passed by the Hockersmith place. Mrs. Hockersmith, fully as bony and humorless as her husband, was filling the birdbath from a two-quart fruit jar. The old man was out in the alley, ramrod straight, sun helmet clapped on his head, topping off his shiny green trash barrel. We waved.

My home had become a motley sea of brimming vases, china cups, jelly glasses, and heavy cooking pots that stretched from the front hall through the living room to the dining room at the rear of the house. I had to go around to the alley door. My sister was at the kitchen sink with ten dusty boxes of empty fruit jars hauled up from the cellar. I could hear water running in the tub upstairs. The phone rang. It was John. Houses all over town were overflowing with re-cycled jelly glasses. Better to call it off early, he said, than to have certain fathers and mothers find out the truth after two days of soggy turmoil. Tell Hockersmith to phone everyone he'd contacted earlier. That way, if anyone checked with the water department, the onus would be on Hockersmith. He looked crazy enough to fit the part of town nut. John had already called Hockersmith with the good news. The great water shortage was over. Citizens' trash bar-rels could be returned from industrial assignment. Mr. Hocker-smith, John reported, sounded almost disappointed.

*

Eagle-Eye Ernie brought our BB guns around after a few days. He thought the whole affair was no big deal. "Why don't you boys shoot the turtledoves in my end of town for a while? Hockersmith's been kind of grouchy since that little stroke a few months back."

Stroke? No foolin'? Maybe that's why that one eye droops. We just thought he was so old his face had started falling off.

I'd like to be able to say the stroke news caused our prepubescent hearts to bubble over with remorse, that we left Hockersmith alone out of a proper sense of atonement. Truth was, with the stroke and all, we didn't figure he stood out as a worthy opponent. We preferred our enemies mean and capable. When the high school boys drove over to eat lunch in our cafeteria, we mostly ignored the nice guys and threw our snowballs at the low-slung automobiles of certified bad-asses, who could be counted on to pound us to slush if they caught us. Hockersmith was a sanctimonious, interfering old scudder, but he was too frail and gullible to be much of an adversary. We gave him a pass.

*

I saw Hockersmith in church every Sunday, of course. Saw him and his wife, two stiff-jointed piles of bones, sailing in and out of their pew like elderly egrets. Saw everyone in church. Commit some obscure minor crime, liberate a small neighborhood cantaloupe, decorate a passing car with a well-thrown egg, feed a certain banker's yappy poodle the scant contents of a discarded vodka bottle, any of the hundreds of forgettable transgressions of a normal human development, and come Sunday, the happy victims would be in church, singing lusty Methodist hymns and reciting theologically oxymoronic Methodist responsive readings. Almost without exception these vacuous martyrs beamed goodwill at criminal and innocent alike. To a more feckless set of young adventurers this beaming might have proven disarming. Redemption and reform might have reared their ugly heads. Happily for us there was always a blessed handful of permanent scoundrels on hand to keep the game interesting.

There was, for instance, Mr. "Shorty" Churtedeprich, bullet-headed church treasurer, moronic Napoleon, character assassin *par excellence*. Unlike most of the Chappell congregation, which was as genial a set of folks as I ever encountered, Shorty was the evil-tempered patriarch of a large family of poverty-advantaged Bible-thumpers and the most frequently unemployed guy in that prosperous town.

Every year or so Shorty's short fuse and penchant for covetous gossip greased his own skids. Dad begged new bookkeeping jobs for him. There was, after all, a passle of innocent kids involved. Churtedeprich was as grateful as you'd expect. And though he tried his best to bring Dad down, muttering dark things in anybody's ears, in typical Shorty fashion, he had chosen the very hardest row. In a small place where folks know everybody's history, people occasionally discount a source as sour as Shorty. Then Dad just never was much of a hand at making enemies. He was too self-effacing, too much fun to be around, too genuinely caring, too charismatic, too much of all the things Shorty wasn't to make a very good target. Undeterred by his lack of success, Shorty kept it up.

Give him credit, the man took some pride in his avocation. It takes no great imagination to feel the glee Shorty felt when the fates delivered him one small but useful brick to use against my father. Shorty must have thought all the meanness and poverty and Bible-belching he'd inflicted on his family had finally earned him the Holy Grail. For the brick he found lying on the street was me. In Shorty I acquired a personal publicist, one who, over the years, broadcast my misadventures, no matter how trivial. And if I failed to produce the kind of richly embellished copy he wanted, as happened during my occasional bouts with childhood illness, he was delighted to supply it free of charge. I like to think if I had known the scope of Shorty's war of attrition on me and my family, I would have settled his hash on the spot. There should be no doubt in anybody's mind I would have tried.

My father was as open-minded as the next guy, probably more so, but he stubbornly resisted my superb arguments in favor of exterminating life's enemies. You wipe out an enemy, there's no way he can do any more harm. Seems perfectly logical to the Serbs and the Sicilians and to me. Dad, on the other hand, was of the "Don't get bogged down in the concerns of idiots, be nice to 'em, and, if that doesn't work, just ignore 'em" school of diplomacy. And, most of the time, against all odds, it didn't work that badly for him. I didn't guess the full meaning of the maniacal gleam in Shorty's eyes. I don't think Dad knew either, although he may have suspected. We wouldn't learn most of it for years, long after Shorty burned his final local job, long after Dad prevailed on a smug church college in the eastern part of the state to reward Shorty for his own peculiar strain of self-sanctifying Methodism with a minor bookkeeping job. After all, the man who barely made half an income, who kept his brood in hand-me-downs and lived in an unpainted hovel that bleakly advertised his asceticism to all creation, was the same guy who gave forty percent of his meager earnings to various church causes, not the least of which was a certain third-rate Methodist college.

Blissfully ignorant of Shorty's obsession, I nonetheless sensed his disapproval and retaliated in kind. After services he marched on stubby legs up to the altar to officiously bag the collection money. If a few boys, while he was up there laboring over his sums, happened into the sanctuary, perhaps to enjoy the cooling mist of a water pistol or the sedate sport of church-bulletin paper-airplane flying, he'd scowl at us so violently his jowls shook. Naturally, this didn't discourage us much.

*

Mrs. Churtedeprich, who looked exactly like a vampire bat, beady-eyed and extravagantly canined, was shorter and scrawnier than her diminutive husband. Daughter of a successful minister, she assumed the elevated circumstances of her birth, and the gaunt nature of her adult life granted her the inside track on the keys to the kingdom. She periodically descended from her strange tree, like an avenging raptor, on our Sunday school or vacation Bible school classes, where she carried out obscurely conceived missionary actions, invariably leaving anger and confusion in her wake. No church my father served suffered from any abiding ministerial interest in creating a fearsome, sin-punishing supreme being. Dad was more interested in feeding sheep than in drawing up lists of transgressions and allocating suitable penalties. Shorty and his wife took

Dad's benign philosophy as a personal insult and worked like a pair of unhinged carpenter ants to offset its corrosive influence.

The first time I remember Mrs. Churtedeprich in her teaching role was early in our Chappell years during vacation church school. My class was young enough to be using brightly colored glops of modeling clay to fashion little *objets d'Holy Land*: camels, donkeys, Ten Commandment tablets, Holy Sepulchers, unleavened bread, Arks of the Covenant, Sea of Galilee fishing boats.

Jackrabbit Vincent, whose family never came to our church, had nonetheless been hornswoggled into giving up a week of his summer's freedom for Mrs. Churtedeprich's addled tutelage. Oblivious to the religious instruction being dished out with our clay, he was industriously rolling a hunk of brown clay into a large fat cylinder.

"Don't you know Jesus rode a donkey [no giggle-inspiring references to asses from this shrewd Bible-thumper] on Palm Sunday? Don't you remember he rolled the stone away from the grave? That's a very pretty stone, Margaret. Don't we all remember the wise men traveled on camels to and from Bethlehem? Master Vincent, what Bible story are you going to illustrate with your sculpture?"

Jackrabbit, locked into a fog of Michelangelan endeavor, hadn't heard a word.

"I say, what are you making? This wouldn't be Lot's wife? She disobeyed the Lord, didn't she? And was turned into a pillar of salt for her foolishness. One look at sin and she was salt forever and ever. All you children remember that, don't you?"

No answer from Jackrabbit; a couple of ignorant shrugs from the rest of us. The brown cylinder, still perfectly symmetrical, grew ever longer and narrower. Jackrabbit, squinting, tongue sticking earnestly out the side of his mouth, paused to take a table-level reading of his sculpture's elevation. Mrs. Churtedeprich's control snapped. Slamming the table with her palm, she hissed in Jackrabbit's face, "What-is-it-you-are-making?"

Jackrabbit, as if meeting her for the first time in his life, gave her a big loopy grin. "I'm making a turd," he said.

As you might expect, our little group of vacation Bible-school scholars dissolved into your basic unrestrained gaiety. Legendary incidents like this were what made vacation Bible study tolerable. Mrs. Churtedeprich's expression may have activated that teeny corner of my consciousness where a red warning light blinked sporadically, but it warned only for Jackrabbit, and not with any real urgency. After all, she'd been the one doing the badgering. And, truth be told, what fair-minded person could argue against the historical presence of turds in the Holy Land?

Mrs. Churtedeprich attacked, not Jackrabbit, our conscientious turdmaker, but yours truly, busy playing the easy role of amused spectator. "This is all your doing, Mister Smart Aleck! You planned the whole thing, didn't you?" She sank her talons into my biceps, one of which was hotly swollen from a recent tetanus shot, and began to shake me for all she was worth. "Didn't you? Didn't you? Didn't you? You're always bad. You're bad, you're bad. You just wait, you, you. You'll get what's coming to you. You'll get it too, don't you worry."

That day I learned that crazy people, no matter how small and ugly, can possess incredible strength. I tried to deny my guilt with a negative jerk of the head, but her vigorous shaking made my head bob a hundred agreements. My attempts to worm out of her grasp were foiled by her steely grip, vising my arms to jelly. A small implosion of sharp pain in my lockjaw-free right arm finally let me slip away, passing out cold on the basement floor.

I roused to another Churtedeprich tirade, this one on the subject of what a malingerer I'd become. "He's got everyone fooled with his sick-acting ways. He misses school for weeks on end for no reason but laziness, just plain idle-bones laziness." For a kid who seldom missed a day of school, this was quite a bulletin. "I know this boy, know all of his slick, sneaky tricks. He doesn't fool us for one second. He's going to pay for what he is. Believe it."

I summoned enough composure to get through the rest of that sullen session. Public opinion, if it were ever undecided, swung solidly behind me and bitterly against the witch. We mysteriously got a new teacher the next day, who finished out the week without further unpleasantness. I concluded, on scant evidence, that I'd been victimized by a vendetta. Allen Zimmer and I swore, with draconian seriousness, to someday even the score with Mrs. Churtedeprich. Opportunities came to boys who kept their eyes and ears open. Nothing indictable. We weren't completely stupid. No, this would be the niggling kind of stuff designed to irritate, inflame, disable. Mrs. Churtedeprich's emaciated ass was, as they say in Texas, grass. The entire biblical sculpture affair resulted in only one immediate casualty: Jackrabbit refused to return for more Bible/art class. He said he'd had enough Christianity to hold him for a while.

*

We eventually passed through a wide assortment of Sunday school teachers, some mediocre, some dreadful, some laidback social-gospel types like my father, some throwback thumpers eager to scratch out Satan's eyes. Mr. Steele, our favorite thumper, who filled in wherever he was needed, had been a pretty fair high school football lineman. The right question, if properly timed during a lull in his standard sermon, could launch him into an elaborate detour into proper rolling-thunder side-body blocking techniques, the flying wedge, Statue of Liberty plays, all the arcane terminology of the single-wing offense he'd played twenty years before.

Much more comfortable with football than religion, Mr. Steele nonetheless had an all-purpose theological question in his quiver, one he never failed to use during his emergency substitutions: "What would you do if Jesus came to your house?" This jewel never failed to promote serious brow-wrinkling among the fidgety multitudes. Sometimes a naive new kid would venture a lame guess:

"Give him cookies?"

"Call the minister?"

"Offer him a chair?"

"Ask him about Heaven?"

"Wash his feet?" That from Margaret, who was hardly a rookie but could never resist showing off, even if it meant mustering the stupid audacity to answer a purely rhetorical question. Mr. Steele, of course, had his own ideas.

"Would you want to explain to Jesus exactly what you were doin' just before you opened the door? No? I wouldn't think so. How about cussin'? And by that I don't just mean taking the Lord's name in vain. I'm talkin' about a *hell* here and a *damn* there. I'm talkin' about *bastard*, *bitch*, and *Judas Priest*. You want to tell Jesus about that kind of cussin'?" No one volunteered to enlighten Jesus on the subject of cussing, least of all Margaret, whose mouth had inelegantly fallen wide-open. "How about lyin' to your parents? Any of you ever do that? You want to tell Jesus about all the times you fibbed to your mother?" I decided right then, if Jesus, against all probability, stopped by for a serious interrogation, I would keep mum. Maybe he'd get bored and move on to the next house.

"How about pride? You know what Jesus thinks of pride. You think he wants you wearin' those fancy clothes you think make you so much better than everyone else? You think he wants you ridin' around in those shiny new cars with your noses up in the air? Jesus says pride goeth before the fall. Remember what happened to Adam and Eve? They thought they knew just about everything before the devil sicced that evil serpent onto 'em. Then they was mighty sorry they was so prideful, wasn't they? Wanderin' around in the desert naked as jaybirds pluckin' thorns out of their feet. Like Jesus said, 'Ye who eat the forbidden fruit will feel my thorns.' You want to get throwed out of the garden, just keep eatin' them wicked pride apples like you're doin.'"

I had the bothersome thought that perhaps Mr. Steele wasn't as fond of his dusty ten-year-old Ford as he always claimed to be.

"Have you been mean to your little sisters and brothers? Jesus won't stand for it. Didn't he say, 'Suffer the little children to come unto me?' That means if he finds out you've been whuppin' up on your little brothers an' sisters, throwin' 'em down the stairs, tearin' up their stuff just to be ornery, beatin' on 'em with your fists, lyin' to your folks about what you've done, why, Jesus is gonna be merciless, and I *do* mean merciless. You won't have no more chance than a snowball in Hades."

As Mr. Steele's agitation increased, generous sweat beads bubbled up on the crown of his bald head, moisture darkened the armpits of his modest black suit. I wondered if he had grown up as a youngest child in a family of sadistic older siblings. If he had, I could certainly empathize.

"What would you say if Jesus walked up and asked you, 'Are you sinning in your heart right now?' What would you say to that? Would you tell Jesus you hadn't never hit your thumb with a hammer and cussed to yourself, even if you didn't cuss out loud? It's not easy to go face-to-face with the Lord, is it? And what about smokin' cigarettes and drinkin' that whiskey? Are you gonna tell Jesus you never wanted to try those things?"

Margaret's blank look testified that maybe one of us hadn't thought too hard on the cigarette-and-whiskey question.

"And what about that covetin'? Don't people always look over the fence and see their neighbor's stuff and wish it was theirs? It's greed is what it is, just plain greed, greed for thy neighbor's gold, greed for thy neighbor's new car, even greed for thy neighbor's wife."

We could go along with coveting gold and cars, but who would be dumb enough to want a wife? All the married women we knew were at least thirty and were always nagging us to eat this and clean that. A guy who coveted that kind of grief needed his head examined.

"Remember it was Jesus who said, 'He that covets his neighbor's ass shall go straight to hell.'"

For some reason this struck us as funny. But Mr. Steele had the bit too firmly in his teeth to be interrupted by a few furtive giggles.

"What Jesus means is that covetin' other people's stuff is about as bad a thing as you can do. And if he shows up at your door, and you'll never know he's comin' 'cause Jesus don't call ahead for no appointments, you don't want to be covetin' nothin'. Don't be lookin' over there in your neighbor's driveway to see what's sittin' there. Just be satisfied with what you've already got. Because Jesus keeps a special place in Hell, right next to the liars and the cussers, for the coveters. And the fires down there burn mighty hot, believe you me."

*

The challenge to Mr. Steele's covet bone might not have been nearly as threatening if the Ford dealer, Mr. Cormer, hadn't sold so many new cars in those years. Wheat prices, buoyed by the Korean War, allowed most farm families to trade cars whenever they wanted. Some even traveled to Denver to bring home new Cadillacs. Spacious brick houses went up all over the community. Local life-insurance salesmen racked up permanent fortunes in a couple of years. Money rained down so plentifully that the new Methodist sanctuary and the remodeled education wing were paid off almost before they were finished. Our own well-traveled Ford disappeared into the GM dealer's garage one day and came out, courtesy of a generous congregation, a shiny new green-and-white Pontiac. They also gave us our first television, a classy Dumont. Poor TV reception limited the novelty. About 30 percent of the time we could tune in a snowy version of the inimitable Mo Milliken. On Saturday nights the ghostly images of "Tom & Jerry's Furniture Showcase" midget wrestling flickered intermittently. We watched anyway, hoping to catch a glimpse of anything, even the half-hour sofa commercials. Our barnlike residence got a remodeled kitchen, a second bathroom, and a coat of paint. There was serious talk of building an entirely new parsonage.

Perhaps all the wheat money rolling in his door allowed Mr. Cormer to endure Shorty's savage tongue. Mr. Cormer, quiet and unassuming, was as decent a guy as lived in that little town. Maybe all the mouths Shorty was supposed to feed weighed on his thinking. At any rate, he kept Shorty employed for a record stretch, some three years. It couldn't have been easy. One hot June afternoon, coming out of the Hested store with a sack of fifty dozen brightly colored balloons, I spotted Cormer and Shorty across the street locking up the garage for the day. They parted in silence, Shorty's back stiff, his walk typically angry as he marched to his car. He paused beside the open car door and blistered Cormer's back with a thirty-second broadside. Cormer, neck bent, shoulders slumped, took the shots and kept going, shambling dispiritedly down the street toward the cafe and the late coffee crowd. Difficult to believe this Shorty-deflated version was the same Cormer who was selling ten new Fords a month, the same man who'd just paid cash for a half-section of wheat land on the north table.

*

Early on in the summer, Zimmer had discovered a secret ladderless route to the church roof involving a concrete banister, a couple of protruding facing stones, and a short length of drainpipe. We planned to fill a good supply of water balloons before supper. Long after our official bedtime, we would be running a military operation from the church roof, winging water balloons down into the cruising covertibles of the certified bad-asses and their dates. The true genius of the setup was that no bad-ass, even in the unlikely case that he figured out where the balloons were coming from, would be able to reach us. My Daisy Defender would keep any ladders well away from the building. We'd be thirty feet up in the air, totally invincible. Zimmer was bringing a sack of peanut-butter sandwiches and a water jug, in case the natives became over-anxious and we had to wait out an all-night siege.

A setup that looked this sweet was bound to have some hidden flaws. We knew any mistakes with this particular set of targets would likely result in severe and protracted retribution. If the balloon throwers were identified, we might not, for instance, be able to go near the local swimming pool, a bad-ass hangout, for the rest of the summer. As it turned out, our only serious miscalculation was the number of water balloons we would use up in a two-hour period of constant bombardment. When one of the Castle boys took the first hit, centered neatly into the dashboard, it was as if we had shot the lead crow. Enraged bad-asses circled the block, running the gauntlet, hoping to catch sight of their tormentors. We had enough elevation to get three or four shots at every car. We hit most of them at least once. In desperation they sent out a foot patrol of dateless aspiring bad-asses, who had to retreat in complete disarray under a barrage of high-arcing mortar rounds. If our ammo had lasted and we hadn't been interrupted, we might still be up there, soaking laughing high school girls and their snarling dates.

About two in the morning, when we were down to our last dozen balloons and the vituperation from below had reached an unseemly level, a bitter wind swooped down from the black southwestern heavens. In typical Panhandle fashion, the temperature dropped twenty degrees in five minutes; dust devils veered crazily up and down the streets. No one had to be told that one of the brutal hailstorms that hit somewhere in the area two or three times a summer was on its way. Bad-ass cars roared for home and safe garages. Lightning bolts slammed through the black air over our heads. Zimmer and I slid down to the base of the church and sprinted for our respective homes. I watched from the safety of my bedroom window as sporadic blizzards of wind-driven ice denuded every tree in sight. Haphazard windrows of leaves and hail drifted against the curbs and out across the church lawn. The nagging question to any Chappell resident awake at that dim hour in late June was how much of the wheat crop would be lost. Was the swath so wide it crossed both the north and south tables? Every wheatland owner, whether it was the struggling farm family living on the north table or the newly prosperous Ford dealer, tried to acquire land on both tables. The prevailing wisdom held that hail rarely wiped out a crop on both tables in the same year. Since getting even half a crop might ensure survival, land was regularly swapped to get respective owners the desired geographic balance. The longer this storm raged, the more likely that some folks would go without any crop this year.

The eastern horizon was barely pink before the county roads were crawling with slow-moving vehicles. Concerned landowners, laden with equal burdens of dread and hope, wanted any bad news early and firsthand. Mr. Trump, the innkeeper who sponsored much of my fishing and hunting, had the latest damage summary by the time I brought his *Omaha World-Herald* at 7:30.

"Mostly it pounded the town. I would guess most of the roofs will need replacing. This flat roof didn't get hurt much. Most of the gravel's still on from last year's re-do. I'll have the adjuster look at it, but I doubt he'll find anything serious. The boys at the coffee shop say after it got done working us over here in town, the storm skipped off to the northeast. Nobody up there got it like we did, just some scattered narrow strips. The only guy that got hurt much was Churtedeprich. Peterson said it looked like someone had one-wayed the whole place. Pounded the wheat so far in the ground there's just little bits of green and gold showing through the dirt. Didn't hurt the house. 'Course, not much short of a merciful fire could damage that house."

*

Not long after Shorty and all of his favorite charities lost a year's crop, our car eased down the driveway headed for my first church camp. Mr. Hockersmith, wearing his perpetual sun helmet, stood stiffly in his hail-shattered garden listlessly hoeing decimated weeds. Life is, after all, just a bunch of habits. I waved. He waved back.

My father and the other district ministers had donated countless hours constructing Norwesca, as it was called, near Chadron. They once spent an entire week on a well, chipping through thirty feet of blue shale with pick and shovel. Located in the heart of Nebraska's Pine Ridge country, the camp sprawled over forty timbered acres of prime sandstone bluffs and winding canyons. It was, at first glance, the finest cougar habitat I had ever seen.

Except for irregular scrutiny from Margaret and the assorted Churtedeprich children, who, of course, attended en masse, I was free of small-town shackles for one glorious week. My assigned tent was populated by lighthearted lads who all enjoyed a bit of fun and weren't overly intimidated by camp regulations. Gordie McConnell, a minister's kid from nearby Oshkosh, assumed the reins of leadership by virtue of his willingness to lead and a suitcase full of Wings cigarettes. Wings cigarettes sold for pennies a pack and contained mostly tobacco stems. Harsh in the extreme, smelling like burning tires, Wings worked as well as any more upscale brand when it came to marking us as serious guys who weren't to be messed with. In reality, except for some stealthy sessions out in the trees when everyone puffed scorching smoke like coal-fired chimneys, we pretty much did what we were supposed to do. The rotund camp director was a relaxed country reverend from Cherry County. Mostly he wanted everyone to have a good time. Hard to undermine a guy like that.

Late on the first day, just before supper, our pudgy little camp counselor arrived. Our tent had sorted itself out with minimal adult supervision and established a blossoming esprit de corps. Guys with a couple of packs of Wings stashed here and there aren't apt to meekly accept the late-arriving dictatorial regime of one of the world's most ridiculous self-promoting gasbags. The Reverend Bat C. Henry, he of the middle-aged shining head and ferocious windpipe, wrote the book on gasbags. We might have tolerated his fake Scottish burr, his selfabsorbed mega-decibel hymn singing, his lame excuses for chronic tardiness and broken promises. But he had to see us bow. Made us move our bedding to the bunks he chose. Made us march to the dining room in the order he established. Made us sit at assigned plates. Made us sing the obscure hymns he picked just so he'd have an excuse to listen to his own tremulous singing voice. Nothing we wanted counted with him. Every kid in camp might be playing in an after-supper softball game, but nothing would do except we trudge out to the woods, sit worshipfully in a circle around Reverend Henry while he emptied his vacuous head of whatever religious blather was temporarily stored there.

The next afternoon, when we were scheduled with the rest of the camp for a trip to the state-park swimming pool down the road, a pool reputed to be populated with hundreds of sleazy, half-naked women, Reverend Henry sent us to our bunks for an extended nap. We needed the nap, he claimed, because we'd been restless the night before. The real reason soon became apparent. Reverend Henry wanted his charges sound asleep so he could write next Sunday's sermon. If we weren't allowed to swim, we felt it only fair that Reverend Henry feel our pain. When he opened his Interpreter's Bible and started scratching wisdom on a fresh writing pad, we launched the usual cacophony of annoying clucks, coughs, sneezes, bunk rattles, armpit-generated farting noises, fake hiccups, and muffled obscenities. He yelled at us, threatened to call our fathers, said we wouldn't eat for the rest of the day if we didn't "stop that racket this minute." When we didn't stop but instead increased the volume, he picked up his sermon-making stuff and personal toilet kit and stomped off to the parking lot. We found a short note on his bunk.

To whom it may concern:
I have been called away by an emergency at
home. I will return as soon as humanly possible.
Your obedient servant in Christ,
Rev. Bat C. Henry

We, of course, did not advertise our supervisor-free status. For three days our little outlaw group continued to attend meals, softball games, square dancing in the dining hall, nature hikes with friendly girls. Any questions about Reverend Henry's whereabouts we brushed off with "He's working on his sermon" or "He's had some stomach trouble, and he's been spending lots of time in the outhouse." It was a mark of Reverend Bat C. Henry's general obnoxiousness that no one missed him enough to look for him. Some of the more adventurous lads arranged for late-night rendezvous with similarly inclined lasses from neighboring tents. Mostly we walked cross-country through prime cougar territory to the state park, where we swam in the ancient pool, rented leaky rowboats, ate bad hot dogs, all the while keeping a vigilant lookout for loose women. Loose women proved to be in short supply that week. Gordie McConnell struck up an actual conversation with a shy broomstick from Scottsbluff. Gordie, always glib, made a couple of reasonable suggestions, but the girl failed the reliability test miserably by running screaming for her parents.

After supper on our last night of Henry-free existence, the camp director announced that in honor of the predicted full moon everyone was going on a moonlight hike. "Most of you will probably like to pair off." Huh? Say what? Is he suggesting we secure an actual date? What kind of crazy church camp is this anyhow? There was a mad scramble for dates.

A guy under five feet tall has painfully limited choices. All the cute short girls were snapped up before I got around to asking. That left me the unpleasant decision between a bucktoothed stubby waif from Lewellen and a mannish sawed-off ranch child from Valentine who chewed tobacco and had a voice several octaves below mine. Long in the lower lip, I was facing a night of strict celibacy with not a little bitterness. Then fate struck me a stupendous blow between the shoulder blades. A wide-eyed blouseful, effervescing an invincible strain of estrogen, asked me to walk with her. Janelle, who hailed from Chadron and had actually read *Catcher in the Rye*, was the almost-perfect incarnation of my most improbable fantasies. She was, undeniably, a scant two inches taller than I. If the height difference bothered her, she never let on. Insatiably curious, she impatiently bombarded me with questions. She was excited about school, wanted to know everything I had studied. The novelty of the question struck me dumb. She tried again.

"Well, do you have a chemistry set?"

"No, but I've made some rockets from scratch that shook up the neighborhood pretty good."

"What did you use for fuel?"

"Sulfur and powdered aluminum."

"Where did you ever get hold of powdered aluminum?"

"It wasn't easy. I could send you some if you want."

"Yes, do. I've wanted to try sulfur and powdered aluminum for years and years. Do you use electrical detonators?"

"Not yet, but I'm working on it."

"Have you read *Huckleberry Finn*?"

"You betcha, several times."

"Don't you like the way he ridicules slavery?"

"I think so."

"I read *God's Little Acre* this winter. Have you tried Caldwell yet? No? Oh, you'd love him. He's so earthy, a lot of people think he's crude. He does write about sex quite a bit, but it's all such a big satire I'm surprised people take him seriously."

Crude writer? Earthy sex? Sounded like my kind of book. Sounded like my kind of reader. I was a smitten pigeon, even before we set off on that enchanted moonlight hike, thoroughly smooshed by one of life's romantic semitrailer rigs.

Not so smitten I could afford any precipitous moves. I fully intended to play it cool, to maneuver with the masterful intelligence guaranteed to drive women, no matter how naturally chaste, into unbridled sexual frenzy. People were supposed to walk side-by-side for a suitable distance, allowing arms and hands to brush accidently. Only after an hour or so of completely deniable physical contact could the really suave guy risk taking a tentative grip on a girl's hand. Two steps into the hike Janelle cut through hours of diplomatic red tape by grabbing my hand and holding on. Who would have thought of such a thing? With one lightning impetuosity Janelle moved our relationship beyond hand-holding, an area in which I had solid experience, having once, while waiting to perform in a second grade Christmas program, held the hand of the fabulous Betty Mel Thompson, to the threshold of some stuff I'd heard about only through loose secondhand speculation. It was enough to make the most calloused smoothie a tiny bit lightheaded.

Two hundred rural kids, some hormonally disadvantaged, some bursting with dangerous bubblings, some too dorky to know the difference, shambled along the narrow deer trail, following our jovial camp director through the sparse timber. I could see a pair of Churtedepriches up ahead, brother and sister, walking chastely side-by-side. Periodically one of the adults would start up a lugubrious hymn, which filtered haphazardly down the line until it petered out among the couples walking drag. Just dusk, a large pale moon hung over the eastern horizon, brushing the tops of the spindly lodgepole pines. I knew this because the camp director pointed it out. I was preoccupied with the miracle of Janelle's hand, how alive it was, how it squeezed mine at just the right times, how it promised just the kind of silent sin that sent blood racing around to all sorts of odd places.

Like an extenuated Arkansas chain gang, the long line of paired campers lockstepped its way up and down the moonlit landscape, always bearing south, away from the dining hall. About a half-hour after full dark, our leader called a halt on a grassy ridge. The steep hillside, dotted with soapweed and thin pine groves, sloped away to narrow canyons. Someone spotted the blinking yardlight, far to the north, that stood outside the camp showers.

"Be back here in twenty minutes," the camp director bellowed. "If I have to come looking, you're not going to like what happens after I find you. So show up on time. That's it. Scatter! Go on! Git! Scoot!" Most of us stood still as spotlighted deer, unable to believe our ears. I remember Margaret, standing next to some Lodgepole dope, looking exactly like someone had made her swallow a live box-elder bug. I wondered if someone shouldn't bring up moonlight hikes the next time Mr. Steele taught Sunday school.

Janelle tugged me toward the trees. "He wants us to go make out. C'mon." I went, and we did. If this represented my future in the Methodist Church I was ready to sign up for life. As for kissing, from what I remember, Janelle already knew most of everything important I was ever going to learn on that subject. Wise girl, that Janelle. Nice enough not to comment on my timidity and woeful ignorance. Naughty enough to impart one skull-bending, toe-rattling, ten-thousand-amp kiss after another. On the dreamy long walk back, she listened patiently to my rapid-fire plans for the future, for family visits, a daily correspondence. I even considered proposing marriage. We had, after all, engaged in serious lip-lock for almost twenty straight minutes.

"I always write back," I said. "I'm good about that."

*

Reverend Henry returned from his emergency around 4:30 the next morning. What sort of harebrained thinking went into his reentrance timing is anyone's guess. Perhaps at the moment his emergency resolved itself, duty drove him to return without delay. Perhaps he finally finished his sermon. The reason I know the precise time Reverend Henry crawled into his sleeping bag is that Gordie McConnell had thoughtfully lined the bottom of said bag with sturdy prickly pears. There was a certain amount of noise. The authorities were called in. Suspects were readied for questioning. Gordie saved his mates the embarrassment of ratting on him by owning up right away.

"Sure I did it," Gordie said. "He's a jerk." But Gordie was unwilling to plead to Reverend Henry's charge of premeditated assault and battery. "I put 'em in there all right, but how was I to know he'd ever come back? By the way, why don't you ask him where he's been all week?" Gordie might have had a legal point, but he couldn't dent Henry's nonnegotiable demand that Gordie be sent home immediately, even though camp had only one more day to run. To our eternal disappointment the camp director rolled over. He marched poor Gordie out of our tent and down to the dining hall to wait for his folks to pick him up. Gordie insisted on one private phone call. Twenty minutes later, the director was called away from his breakfast to answer the phone. A short time after that he interrupted Reverend Henry's singing shower and hauled him down to his office for more phone calls and extended consultations. Gordie had his stuff unpacked by noon. "Dad knows this bozo from way back" was all he ever offered in explanation. Reverend Henry, for his part, assiduously ignored us for the next twenty-four hours, paying us precisely the same notice as he did the local tree stumps. A few of our more sensitive tentmates were hurt by this.

This last night of camp promised too much excitement to worry much about pouting gasbags. Janelle was still around, of course, and this was the final chance to make my indelible mark on her affections. I rehearsed my speeches, gave some thought to ultra-suave moves. Gordie, who had gone dippy over a hot number from Gurley, was doing the same. Tuning up in the bathhouse before supper, we used plenty of deodorant and borrowed pink butchwax from Margaret's Lodgepole dope, laying so much gunk on our GI dos that if some passing arsonist had set fire to our heads, we'd have burned for days.

After supper, the director issued a cattle call for a much-rumored impromptu talent contest. My name was called, due entirely to some pre-supper mumblings in the right ears. I'd been wanting to try an Elvis impersonation for quite some time, but had lacked a suitable audience. Maybe I hadn't read Erskine Caldwell, but Janelle hadn't heard this Elvis. If the deal worked, she'd be Putty City. I allowed myself to be begged onto a tabletop. Someone slipped a broom under my arm. If I had paused, even for an instant, stage fright would have frozen me so solid Lot's wife would look like a contortionist in comparison.

"Oh, since my baby left me, I found a new place to dwell, You'll find me wa-a-ay down on lonely street, at He-a-a-a-rtbreak Ho-tel." I remembered to do a little Chuck Berry duckwalk. "And I'm so lonely, baby, so lonely, baby." Banged my knees together a few times. "Ah-ah-ahm so lonely, baby, I could die." Shoot, knocked 'em dead in the aisles. Had to do three goldanged encores. They clapped themselves stupid. Some dopey girls screeched. I was wishing I'd learned one more song. What a supremely appreciative audience for my rock debut. Everyone but Reverend Henry shook my hand and pronounced me wonderful. Janelle gave me a hug right there in front of the entire camp. Made me wish I were taller.

We closed down camp about like you'd expect. Janelle and I made the most of our opportunities, five minutes here, ten minutes there. I learned more about mysterious things. Gordie did too. Margaret mooned over her Lodgepole dope, especially in the parking lot before we got in the car to go home. It was a sickening thing to see. Everyone promised to write. Hardly anyone ever did.

*

I haunted the Chappell post office for two weeks before Janelle's first letter arrived. I'd already mailed her four. Her tone was friendly but reserved. She talked mostly of books and authors, most particularly J. D. Salinger, who had captured her fancy. She made *Catcher in the Rye* sound like the smartest book in the world. The books on my reading list, some Twain, every Edgar Rice Burroughs book in the Chappell Memorial Library, one Zane Grey adventure about jaguar hunting, seemed juvenile and stodgy in comparison. In my books no one ever farted out loud during chapel. No one in my books ever went to New York and tried to hire a hooker. Janelle's literary world was so much bigger than mine, I despaired of ever catching up.

After a couple of distant notes, she stopped writing altogether. No question it was all my fault. I was a dunce. A big literary dog in Chappell, Nebraska, even one who sang a pretty fair "Heartbreak Hotel," didn't cut much of a figure with a well-read Chadron intellectual. I made myself a promise to never again get caught short in the book department. Within three years I had bored through all of Hemingway, Steinbeck, and Erskine Caldwell. One bout with Faulkner taught me I was out of my depth. But I took special care to read everything I could find of J. D. Salinger, most of it several times. If a beautiful smart girl ever asked me to go on a moonlight hike, I intended to have my literary ducks in order.

*

J. Steinway Stoble, when he wasn't living in his permanent basement room at Mr. Trump's Plains Hotel, hitchhiked all around the country. He was an Eagle, an Elk, a Moose, a member in good standing of the VFW, American Legion, Rotary International, and the Odd Fellows. Most months, somewhere in the United States of America, at least one of J. Steinway Stoble's organizations was having itself a convention. J., as he was known around town, loaded up his much-decaled leather grip with William Penn cigars and a box of worn poker chips and headed down Highway 30. He had a little folding one-legged stool, which allowed him to sit in relative comfort on the side of the road thumbing rides. Chappell residents sighted him everywhere—California, Texas, Mexico, Canada, once in the Bahamas. Most had picked him up in some faraway place and deposited him at an equally obscure destination. The mystery to everyone was how an old man as tall and ugly as J. got so many rides from strangers. He claimed, and no one doubted him, that he had never been late to a convention. Eagle-Eye Ernie, who bought J. an occasional morning coffee and sweet roll at the south cafe, said if he didn't know J. from Adam he'd arrest him as a probable escaped mental case.

"Just look at him," Ernie argued. "No teeth, tobacco juice runnin' ever' which way, crazy Legionnaire hat with pins all over it. He smells like the very dickens. If that don't spell ax murderer, I don't know what does."

I slipped the *Omaha World-Herald* under J.'s door the few days a year when he was home. He was a notorious late sleeper when he returned from an expedition, and I seldom saw him. In the few rare instances when I caught up with him and he was in a garrulous mood, he'd talk my leg off. He'd know just about everything there was to know about a town he barely lived in. This early July morning when I approached his room, the door swung open and there stood J. in his pin-striped suit pants and red braces, cadaverous white chest, blue gums clamped into a smelly William Penn cigar. Behind, covering the far wall to a height of four feet, stood J.'s stash of pristinely cellophaned William Penn cigar boxes. Come nuclear war, hell, or high water, J. was prepared.

"Needin' money?" It had been six months since I had collected his *World-Herald* bill. J. was a hard man to find.

"Two dollars and thirty-five cents."

"Take a check?"

"Sure."

"Good. Soon's I git hold a some money I'll write ya one." Skunked again. It wasn't unusual for a third of my customers to be into me for a couple of month's paper bill. "Had yer morning smoke?"

"No."

"Take one a these. It'll put sand in yer craw."

"Thanks." I slipped the cigar in my pants pocket. I'd had one go-round with cigars. No sense in throwing up on Mr. Trump's clean floor. Try it out later in private, see if I'd grown into some tolerance.

"What ya hear from yer buddy Shorty?"

"Don't guess he'll be runnin' up much of a combine bill."

J. cackled. Took a big hit on his cigar. "No, don't s'pose he will. Couldn't happen to a sweeter fella. Some folks downtown say Cormer's finally got himself a bellyful. Guess Shorty told half-a-dozen folks Cormer was turnin' back odometers. Cormer give him more of a chance than I would've. Told Shorty if he went to all those folks and set 'em straight maybe he could stay on. Shorty wasn't havin' any. Told Cormer he was tired a workin' fer a crook. That Shorty ain't got much of a reverse gear on 'im, does he?"

"Not that I've noticed." This set J. off on another smoke-punctuated cackling spree.

"What ya hear from Alvin?" The Alvin in question was Alvin Churtedeprich, Shorty's dumber brother, who fed a sullen brood of cross-eyed children with an occasional truck-driving job. He also supported a wife, a blubberous slattern who sprouted rank outcroppings of moles and coarse facial hair, and had not, according to the town wise men, added many IQ points to the family gene pool.

"Never talk to him."

"Seen his latest kid?"

"I think so. About two years old?"

"Blonde? Blue-eyed? Acts a hair brighter than yer average Churtedeprich?"

"Uh huh."

"Remind ya of anyone? No? Seen Heavy Swanson around lately? Sure ya have. Heavy's always around. Sure was a cute little towheaded bugger when he was a tad."

Heavy Swanson? This was too rich. Debonair sign painter when drunk, smooth pool hustler when sober, Heavy, who weighed one hundred and twenty-five pounds, liked the ladies drunk or sober, and, drunk or sober, the ladies liked him. Eclectic in his romantic interests, Heavy dallied with bankers' wives and stale saloon flowers on a more or less equal basis. But Viola Churtedeprich? Heavy must have been too drunk to see or smell. "Some a the boys was sayin' Shorty's wife is sittin' on a hemorrhoid over the deal. Guess she don't want Viola to be no closer than three hundred miles. Wouldn't surprise anybody if one a them families hit the road. What with Shorty's big wheat crop goin' back in the ground an' him fallin' out with Cormer, my money'd be on Shorty's outfit pullin' stakes. Be a tough break fer you, wouldn't it, Jonesy?"

*

Over the years Mrs. Churtedeprich continued her irregular Sunday school depredations. Whenever she rushed into our classroom, usually five minutes late, we could count on her demanding a memorized Bible verse from each of us. Perhaps she wanted a palpable demonstration for some imagined audience of the total incompetence of all our other teachers. Or maybe it was just her way of hammering us down with our own ignorance. We tried to accommodate her with short, easily remembered verses, engaging in considerable unseemly maneuvering for the rights to "Jesus wept." Zimmer, by virtue of natural advantages in size and stubbornness, usually had hold of that one. The fact that Mrs. Churtedeprich invariably asked us to recite in reverse alphabetical order, forgetting she'd already used that little trick a dozen times, only added to Zimmer's advantage. Zimmer's virtual lock on "Jesus wept" left the rest of us stuck with our wretched memories and some pretty doggoned long verses. It was no good trying to slip by a succinct made-up verse like "Mary walked" or "Moses spoke." She knew her Bible too well. So we did the best we could with the likes of "A happy heart is like good medicine" and "So encourage with these words."

Margaret, of course, was hopeless. "I can't decide," she'd say primly, "if I should do Mark 3:4, 'And he saith unto them, Is it lawful to do good on the sabbath days, or to do evil? To save life, or to kill? But they held their peace,' or if I should do John 20:29, 'Jesus saith unto him, Thomas, because thou hast seen me, thou hast believed: blessed are they that have not seen, and yet have believed.' Which do you like best, Mrs. Churtedeprich?" It was enough to nauseate a hyena.

Mrs. Churtedeprich's last Sunday school class began like any other, five minutes late. She bustled around in typical metallic fury, sending out for chairs we didn't need, hissing at squirmy younger boys, scolding when the collection for missions was short a few nickels from what she judged sufficient. Roughly herded into chaotic rows for our Bible recitations, we hadn't a clue this was the bat's last stab at our salvation. Had we known she was leaving, known for certain the exigencies of hail, illegitimacy, and Shorty's employment status had forced the issue, perhaps we would have summoned a bit of compassion, allowed her vitriol to wash over us unanswered one more time. A class that raised eighty cents for distant Congo missionaries surely could have pooled up one final burst of tolerance. But we didn't know, not for sure. And while we weren't laying for her exactly, a few of us had taken the time since her last visit to memorize some strategic Bible verses. Mostly we were scratching around for some kind of defense, something to make her leave us alone. When she summarily directed the brown-nosing Margaret to lead off, robbing Zimmer of his usual leadoff position, it only confirmed our worst fears that Mrs. Shorty was cooking up a fresh scheme to embarrass the crap out of us.

Margaret took a not-so-gentle swipe at all the substance abusers in the room with John 2:21, "But he spake of the temple of his body." She was such a smug little snip. Mrs. Shorty beamed her approval.

Zimmer volunteered. He couldn't help smirking his way through "Jesus wept." Some wise guy in back clapped.

Gary Steele, no Bible slouch himself, launched our first salvo with a low-key recitation of II Corinthians 6:12, "Ye are not straitened in us, but ye are straitened in your own bowels." Nobody laughed. We were playing this straight all the way. Her mouth tightened a tiny bit before she moved on to her next victim. First blood.

One of the Johnson boys, using Paul, that old lunatic misogynist, laid a little I Timothy on her: "Let the woman learn in silence with all subjection."

Another Johnson, a distant cousin of the first, followed immediately with "But I suffer not a woman to teach, nor to usurp authority over the man, but to be in silence." He fairly yelled the silence part. Oh, she was hot. Would have liked to stone the lot of us, especially one bratty little preacher's kid who was looking straight through her, a faint hint of confidence in his face. My turn. Time to anticipate, and perhaps blunt, the looming onset of hysterics as well as settle some old business.

"And the chief priests accused him of many things: but he answered nothing."

She tried to stare me down but failed to catch my guileless eye. There was a bit of a flutter; cheeks flushed, arms flapped. She started for me, setting off a distinct puckering in my nether regions. At that point her gyroscope cracked, and she veered off to march in mad circles around our bemused ranks, all the while mumbling and massaging her forehead. It was a sure sign of impaired judgment that she waved a distracted finger at Harold Boxbender, anointing the least likely Bible scholar in the entire community to come to her rescue. Harold's interest in things biblical was notoriously sparse, which might explain why she picked him. Our silent hopes for a stunning knockout verse rested uneasily on two things—Harold's anarchistic hatred for all authority and the loyalty he accorded his friends. That he could remember any verse, long or short, lethal or benign, was a miracle to everyone.

"B-b-but was rebu-buked for his ah-ah-iniquity: the d-dumb ass speaking w-with m-man's voice f-f-forbad the m-m-madness of the p-prophet."

The little kids in front threw a predictable hissy fit over the "dumb ass speaking" business. Our tight little group kept a disciplined front, no one evincing anything other than scholarly good will. Our coolness, more than the biblical shots amidships, finally drove her raging incoherently from the room. The door rattled in its frame. We could follow her progress out of the building from the diminishing percussion of crashing doors and shuddering woodwork. Margaret, with the perfect radar of the chronic suck-up, moved a few feet to her left, to stand directly behind the winning side.

*

That August I acquired a new and mysterious pen pal, one Linda Miller from Midwest City, Oklahoma. My name had surfaced among shadowy mutual friends, friends who bragged me up as "a really neat guy." Well, heck, why argue with your friends, even if you don't know them? Linda sent three letters a week whether I wrote or not. Her usual five pages contained vague references to mundane school and summer activities. Mostly she asked questions. She seemed to know more about me than she knew about herself. Asked me several times about my rocket experiments, about how my dog, Pooch, was doing. My own questions deflected off a mirror, turned back with rhetorical answers. Not as quick as I should have been. It wasn't until she revealed for the umpteenth time a remarkable knowledge of my circumstances that I dug some of Janelle's old letters out of my lockbox for a peek at the handwriting. What the heck was she doing in Oklahoma masquerading as Linda Miller? I asked that question, in a roundabout way, possibly afraid she would tell me. She didn't. She wrote instead of a cardboard world of vacuous friends and drive-ins and cheerleading, everything flat and lifeless, as impervious mask of gum-snapping stupidity. Not rich enough to fool anyone, nor was it meant to be. I came to understand that this was where her grief and self-flagellation took her, that elaborate games with a near stranger provided some tenuous solace. So I played along. Did my bit. Hoped that in acting out my role as a gullible audience and writer of hapless drivel I would be of some help to her. Perhaps I was. She kept it up for nearly eight months. Never in the entire correspondence did she pretend to hold any ambition higher than head varsity cheerleader.

*

With my romantic ventures stuck in limbo, I renewed my long-standing interest in outer space. Rival governments had embarked on highly visible rocket programs, each side working mightily for some reliable method of raining nonpeaceful atomic energy down on its enemies. Most of this research was with liquid-fueled rockets, using highly unstable oxygen and hydrogen. The technicalities defeated Zimmer's early attempts at duplication. After a few gasoline/alcohol/paraffin/powdered-matchhead conflagrations, one of which decimated most of a Hockersmith lilac bush, we dedicated our resources to a search for fast-burning solid rocket propellants with enough oomph to send a Zimmer-designed satellite into permanent Earth orbit. We haunted Pokorny's Pharmacy, mystifying the permanently befuddled Mr. Pokorny with requests for massive quantities of saltpeter, sulfur, benzine, and talc. He took our money and reminded us, with the resigned air of a bartender selling two drunks a second bottle of whiskey, to be very careful.

We experienced some minor successes with a saltpeter/powdered-matchhead/gunpowdered/benzine mix packed into an aluminum rocket tube and allowed to dry. One that didn't explode on the launch pad flamed a spectacular path high over the street to buy itself in Elmo Carlson's rose garden. A slight misadventure with some .22 cartridges during the tricky gunpowder-extraction process led us to abandon our crude homemade concoctions for the real stuff.

Dr. Larsen, after digging considerable brass shrapnel out of my face and chest, stalked down to Pokorny's and shut off our local supplies permanently. Larsen was always inclined to be a little heavy-handed, infected as he was with your basic small-town-doctor-as-god virus. Fortunately Zimmer ferreted out a mail-order source in one of his ham radio catalogs. Innocuous brown boxes arrived, stuffed with plastic bags of powdered aluminum, sulfur, and an assortment of other rocket-fuel components beyond the imaginings of even the most brilliant Russian commie scientist. Not long before I departed for church camp and the fair Janelle, we launched our most successful space probe to date, a parachute-equipped aluminum rocket that soared nearly three blocks before floating gently down on the roof of the movie theater. Invigorating climb.

Seasoned rocket scientists like to mix their sulfur and powdered aluminum in a controlled atmosphere free of stray sparks and the unpredictable jottings of electricity. I was standing in the cool depths of our parsonage basement, innocently folding a half-pound of powdered aluminum into a bright yellow pile of sulfur, when some passing electrons with too much time on their hands voted unanimously for mischief. A pillar of fire that might have put Moses on notice shot to the ceiling, where it began to chew through the living-room flooring. Water had no effect. The small unreasonings of total panic began to tickle. Should I run for it? The house would be coming down around my ears in short order. Did I have time to rescue my baseball card collection? My lockbox? Was there any way to blame this inferno on someone else? Maybe a passing hobo sneaked down here and dropped a cigarette? Could I call the fire department without tagging myself as chief culprit? Think hobo, think hobo. Think cigarette. Yeah, it might work. Then, inspired mostly by pure dumb luck, I took a final swat at the blazing pile with an old broom handle, scattering aluminum and sulfur over the cement floor, where it quickly burned out in a hundred benign little fires. It took me a bit longer to soak down the smoldering floorboards ten feet above my head. Left quite a charred mess up there in the floor joists. Nobody ever said anything. I know I didn't.

This near-disaster prompted Zimmer to propose formaldehyde as a possible rocket-fuel ingredient. He figured a thimbleful in each batch would lessen the build-up of static electricity. If we spread the mixture thinly over a tabletop, he predicted, the formaldehyde would dry off, leaving a shelf-stable mixture with plenty of remaining explosive energy. He was wrong about that. Our embalming fluid-laced mixtures refused any sort of enthusiastic ignition. But as Werner Von Braun used to say, "Verst der embalming fluid, den der knowledge."

*

Zimmer was in the bowels of the embalming room digging around for a partially emptied bottle, one his dad might not miss. I was upstairs in the mortuary's only viewing room, now empty of viewees. The fact of the matter was I was too chicken to help Zimmer look. I'd been in that room, seen Old Man Zimmer's crude instruments, seen the dark-stained drainboard. I imagined and dreamed horrible things for months afterward. So I begged off the embalming fluid search, volunteered to serve as a lookout. Zimmer, who by then had become pretty well inured to the spooky nature of his father's business, shrugged off my cowardice as some inexplicable quirk and went about his business.

Just off the main viewing room were two small side rooms, used occasionally for overflow viewings if the trade got backed up, as it seemed to do every spring. Old folks who fought their way through one last tough winter seemed to let go once they felt the first warm days of April and May. A wonderful idea began to stir. What if I duck into one of the side rooms? When Zimmer comes upstairs with his bottle of embalming fluid he'll think I've skipped out. Just when he's good and comfortable with that idea, BAM! Jump out and scare him stupid. Brilliant!

Zimmer's triumphant shout filtered up from the basement. I scurried into the nearest room and closed the door. The heavily shaded room was so deep in gloom, my hand, resting uneasily on the doorknob, was barely visible. Zimmer's feet pounded up the stairs. I could hear him calling. Almost time. Poised to burst through the door, poised to scream like a banshee, I glanced to my right. Lying on a fainting couch, not twelve inches from my shoulder, was the white grinning face of Mrs. Hockersmith. Her freshly washed hair, a dark iron-gray, flowed out over the pillow. I stared dumbstruck. When did she die? I didn't even know she was sick. Whoa, maybe she wasn't dead after all. Wasn't her chest moving a little? Didn't that eye just twitch? It was too dim in there to be certain. No, that grin was a little too skull-like. Didn't Zimmer once say his mother washed out dead ladies' hair in these rooms? Dead ladies? I was in a dinky little black room with a dead lady, one that hadn't been too awfully fond of me when she was alive. I had stolen watermelons from this woman. Probably killed her favorite turtledove. No telling what kind of horrible stuff was going to happen to me in about one second. I fumbled at the door, all thoughts of scaring Zimmer well-dissipated. I botched the opening several times. With one final mighty yank, I stumbled out into the viewing room, a squeal of panic teasing my throat. My head banged into something soft and human. It seemed to be someone's stomach. I looked up into the blood-red, mightily pissed-off face of Old Man Zimmer. He yelled. I yelled louder. I'd been saving up. He grabbed at my shirt, but I was gone, streaking out the front door and up the street like a scalded cat. Deep in the jungled yard, Zimmer waved lazily from his backyard hammock. I didn't stop to visit.

*

Mr. Trump fulfilled a long-standing promise by taking me pheasant hunting that fall. I had acquired a slightly rusty single-shot .20 gauge shotgun for the princely sum of six dollars. Mrs. Wilson, who once campaigned for William Jennings Bryan and sometimes paid her *World-Herald* bill in Indian-head pennies, took pity on me. Or perhaps she needed the six dollars more than her husband needed the shotgun. At any rate, I was now certifiably pheasant-crazy, convinced I would get my limit in ten minutes of uncanny blasting. Trump waited for heavy snow, which he thought forced the birds to bunch up.

The north table lay under an even six-inch blanket of dust-darkened snow. Compared to most road hunters, who roared around section lines hoping to catch herded-up pheasants unaware, a Trump expedition moved at glacial speed. Trump drove at a crawl, scrutinizing every fence post, on the off chance a cottontail was hiding on the lee side. The man had eyes a Comanche could envy. If one puny whisker, one bit of brown fur strayed beyond the sheltering post, Trump unsheathed his Browning .22 automatic and dispatched the poor bugger with one neat hole in the head. On cold days like this one, with twisting snakes of dry snow slithering across the east-west roads, Trump might bag three cottontails on every mile stretch. A consummate meat hunter, he and his wife ate every cottontail, grouse, squirrel, quail, or ringneck pheasant he brought home.

I was only a little surprised when he pulled off the road into the Churtedeprich place. Trump loved abandoned farmsteads. In a flat country with no trees, critters took what shelter was offered. Trump considered it powerful bad luck to walk an old set of buildings without killing at least one edible something or other. Like orphaned farms everywhere, Shorty's place had already begun its gravitational melding with the surrounding earth. The heaps of bare, wind-warped wood, colored a homely camouflage of brown and gray, sat twisted on haphazard foundations, doors sagging open on droopy hinges. Stray bits of scattered window-glass glinted on gray snow. When Trump suggested a tour of the house I could hardly refuse, although I was troubled momentarily by the image of a slavering Mrs. Shorty cleverly hidden in an upstairs closet, waiting patiently for the chance to sink her batty fangs in a certain kid. I shouldered my .20-gauge and stepped up on the listing front porch.

Whatever scraps of living that once furnished this ramshackle affair of rooms tacked onto rooms had been hauled away by the Churtedepriches or thieving hunters. Not a single Churtedeprich button, clothespin, paper clip, coat-hanger, or picture-nail remained. Tea-colored wallpaper hung in long lazy shreds from the dilapidated walls, holed cruelly in places by shotgun blasts. Raccoons had been busy on the roof, and expanses of ceiling plaster had given way, creating menacing black holes, sometimes reaching clear to the attic, covering the floors with mounds of chalky rubble. Only a faintly greasy outline on the wall where the stove once stood identified the bare kitchen, now completely stripped of cabinets. The back door, jammed open to the east wind by a solid wedge of gregarious tumbleweeds, looked out on a foot-hardened path that led to the drunken outhouse.

Ernest Wilcoxson's .08-gauge boomed twice from behind the northern horizon. Trump immediately became twitchy, as he always did when he thought someone else was having better luck than he was. "Maybe we should scout behind the barn and get on up the road. Wilcoxson must've stumbled into something."

We skirted the barn gingerly, as alert for scattered nail-studded boards as for lurking pheasants. An explosive pounding of wings. Two roosters powered out of the tumbleweeds, cackling their way across the barnyard. They were barely settled into a long low glide when I fired, knocking one small feather from the lead pheasant. Trump folded him up with his first shot, swung over and rolled the second cock lazily to the ground with his second. "Model 12 Winchester," he said. "Finest shotgun ever made."

I bird-dogged Trump's pheasants into the car trunk, almost content to bask in the reflected glory. The roosters, iridescent feathers masking the lead pellets that killed them, rested easily beside a large assortment of brainless cottontails. Maybe by the time I was as old as Trump I would shoot as well as he did, maybe have a kid playing stoop-and-fetch for me. If I took a kid along, I'd never send him home empty-handed. No sir. He'd at least have a goldanged rabbit to show for all his hard work.

Trump carefully unloaded his shotgun, pumping the remaining shell onto the front seat. He nodded approvingly at the open breech of my shotgun. Two more Wilcoxson blasts echoed thunderously in the north. "Let's git," Trump said, starting the engine. We rolled out of the yard, an occasional tumbleweed grazing our bumper. Trump poked a careless thumb over his shoulder. "Not much of a place, is it?"

By the time Trump let me out in front of the parsonage the day had dissolved into a dismal collage of gray and white. I carried my shotgun easily in the crook of an arm, as if I'd done it all my life. If I had no game to show my mother, at least I'd acquired some style. Pooch welcomed me with great tail-waggings and excited yips. He coaxed me to the back of the house, where he showed me an empty food bowl.

Across the dusky back yard, teetering around his back porch on stilted legs, was the vague form of Mr. Hockersmith. He appeared to be sweeping. I waved my new shotgun high overhead. He stopped his broom, stared stupidly in my direction, inflicted, no doubt, with disturbing thoughts of murderous shotguns and innocent turtledoves. He lifted a mittened paw, let it flap once, then showed a ramrod back as he broomed his stiff-walked way out of sight behind the lightless house.

Polio

I did not want to be in that automobile. I would much rather have been flat on the ground being pounded to a bloody pulp by one of the bad-asses. I would have preferred reciting long, incomprehensible Bible verses at the sneering behest of Mrs. Churtedeprich. If it meant being spared this car ride, I would have volunteered to wash windows for my mother while she stood inside, as was her habit, helpfully pointing out all the places I'd missed. I might even have traded this trip, which amounted to nothing less than a kidnapping, for the chance to dive behind a tree while the new dinkphod in town plinked at me with his wildly inaccurate zip gun.

*

Zimmer hadn't really meant to wreck the little guy's bicycle. The new kid had drifted into town a couple of weeks before with his fine-boned, highly rouged mother. I never understood why they came or what they lived on. He sure wasn't stupid. He had a quick wit and a sharp tongue. In fact, if the little dork hadn't been so busy questioning our parentage and intelligence and generally exposing the weird wiring in his doofy little red-headed brain, he would have noticed that his pink *girl's* bicycle, now traveling at a high rate of speed, was on a certain collision course with Mr. Thompson's Mercury coupe. Made quite a dent. Bent the crap out of his pink *girl's* bicycle. Knocked the front wheel very nearly square. If we had it to do over, Zimmer and I would probably skip the part where we pointed fingers and laughed like goofs. Nor, when the new kid tried to roll his injured *girl's* bicycle back home, would we choose to go into a fresh round of hysterics every time his geometrically advantaged front wheel kerthumped against the pavement. He took it for half a block before his patience gave out.

Zimmer and I had heard about zip guns, of course. We knew

pretty nearly every citizen of Denver owned at least one. We knew any child with half a brain could make one from a chunk of car aerial, a gun-shaped block of wood, a homemade metal firing pin, rubber bands, and gobs of sticky electrical tape. But we'd never seen one until Mr. Big Shot Bent *Girl's* Bicycle Baron whipped one out of his coat pocket and fired. *Pop!* Sounded like a ladyfinger firecracker. We took the nearest available shelter, two skinny linden trees. We could shield our heads and most of our bodies, but if Mr. Annie *Girl's* Bicycle Oakley got lucky we'd be taking serious flesh wounds to our arms and legs. Goldanged linden trees never grew any healing moss when you needed it. The bark on this pair was as bald as Old Man Thompson's chrome dome. *Pop!* The new kid was taking quite a bit of time reloading. Zimmer, busy figuring trajectories and feet per second, said, as if he'd studied zip guns intimately for years, that extracting the empty .22 casings was a chronic problem for zip gun aficionados, one that no seriously delinquent genius had ever solved. He suggested we engage in strategic retreat, commencing immediately after the next shot. *Pop!* We were off, running in the prescribed weaving patterns favored by the army guys in Audie Murphy movies. After a hundred yards of hard sprinting and tricky maneuvering, I chanced a look over my shoulder. Mr. Big Brave Zip Gun Guy Who Pushes a Bent-up *Girl's* Bicycle was pointing his own gleeful finger in our general direction, apparently content to take our less-than-dignified retreat as a victory of sorts. Or maybe he was out of ammo. As humiliating as the entire bicycle incident became, I'd have chosen to relive it a hundred times rather than make that early-fall automobile trip, the sole purpose of which was to do good.

*

My father did not habitually ask much of me beyond minimal civility to my fellow human beings. He so seldom interfered in the choices I made that when he did I was always surprised, like the time he took note of my contemptible behavior toward Ronnie Borgens. Ronnie was harmless enough. I don't remember him making a cutting remark, or ever trying to assassinate somebody with a zip gun.

Ronnie Borgens should have, at the very least, been a regular recipient of community benevolence. Everyone in town knew that male members of the Borgens clan suffered from a rare, and invariably fatal, genetic predilection for gradual loss of muscular control. Ronnie had an extremely limited chance of living to a ripe old age. For reasons known only to the high school bad-asses, they chose to subject Ronnie to considerable scorn. No Indian leper suffered greater social ostracism than Ronnie Borgens. When they weren't shunning him, they played cruel tricks.

They once proposed a highly imaginative snipe hunt, this one for a rare species of snipe that lived underwater in Lodgepole Creek and could be captured only in the dead of winter. They had Ronnie chop the hole in the ice. He was so grateful for being included, he scarcely noticed he had been assigned all the hard work. He was to stick his hands through the open hole into the freezing water, making a sort of temporary net, while the other boys went upstream to pound on the ice with big sticks. The snipe, startled from their wintry hibernation, would rush downstream, straight into Ronnie's waiting fingers. With luck, the boys said, Ronnie should be able to catch two or three hundred snipe before they got wise and swam in the opposite direction.

In spite of the below-zero temperature, in spite of the quick disappearance of his temporary snipe-hunting buddies, Ronnie stayed at his post, waiting diligently for the deluge of disoriented snipe. After a couple of hours, the bad-asses, back in town and chuckling up their sleeves, began to worry. Why hadn't Ronnie shown up? Maybe he'd lost his way. Nobody intended for the poor guy to freeze to death. The cars that had been leisurely touring Main Street took off across the Union Pacific viaduct for Lodgepole Creek. They found him at his post, hands loyally immersed in icy creek water, nearly paralyzed from cold. Four of them carried Ronnie to the car, settling him gently on the front seat close to the heater. When he did not immediately thaw out but slipped into a state of unresponsiveness, they panicked. Some voted for the hospital, others for the street. In the end they took him home, propping him up on the front porch while someone rang the doorbell. Ronnie survived, though he had a bad time of it for a week or so. Once he returned to school, the bad-asses continued to pretend he was an inanimate object. Perhaps the practical jokes were chosen a little more carefully, although, with that bunch of cherubs, it probably was purely accidental. When they referred to Ronnie at all, which was seldom, they called him "The Spazz." If he wasn't shaking now, the theory went, he'd be shaking before long. It was in the genes.

*

Members of the Methodist Youth Fellowship were in front of the church, loading into cars before heading to Sidney and a showing of the new Martin Luther film at the Fox Theater. Nobody thought to ask the obvious question of why a bunch of Methodist youth were particularly interested in the life story of a guy who, like Paul, was one of the more dyspeptic misogynists in the history of the human race, particularly one who was indisputably of the Lutheran persuasion. Probably thoughts of fragrant Fox Theater popcorn and chance encounters with habitually naked Sidney women outweighed theological considerations. I know they did with me.

Every car but ours had been piled full and had departed for Sidney. Ronnie Borgens, looking a little like last week's laundry, was left standing on the sidewalk. "I'm not sitting with him." I figured I might as well state my position before Mom and Dad and Ronnie got themselves situated.

"Why not?" There was a dangerous tone in Dad's voice.

"He's a spazz. Nobody likes him. He's different." That summed it up perfectly.

"So what if he's different? Does that mean you have a right to be cruel? What harm has Ronnie Borgens ever done to you?"

"Nothing."

"Nothing? Even though you say Ronnie Borgens has done you no harm, even though he has as much right to ride in this car as you do, you choose not to sit next to him? How would you like it if somebody did that to you?"

Most likely I wouldn't like it any too well. So I sat next to Ronnie

Borgens, even deigned to make light conversation. By the time we
got to Sidney, I'd worked the thing around until I became, in my
eyes, the most saintly, self-sacrificing little bird turd since Francis of
Assisi. But that didn't mean I wanted to make a habit of riding with
Ronnie Borgens, or of visiting every sickly kid that showed up in
the neighborhood, even if the kid in question belonged to the
Methodist minister who had recently moved to neighboring Big
Springs. Crippled by polio, the boy was supposedly bedridden after
another in a long series of operations designed to repair the damage. "Ben," Dad said, "will surely appreciate a visit from a boy his
own age. After a month confined to a bed, most anyone would enjoy seeing a fresh face." Dad was doing his best to help me be a
decent person, but I wasn't having any. The truth was I wasn't particularly comfortable being in close proximity to serious polio damage. The Great Polio Epidemic of 1952 was only a couple of summers
past, and I could remember it all too well.

*

We were living in Neligh, in Antelope County, one of the polio hot
spots. In 1952 cases statewide jumped from 435 to 2252, the highest
per-capita polio rate recorded in the United States. My mother became increasingly fearful through the summer as the numbers
mounted and more of our classmates were afflicted. We stayed
home most of that deadly summer, on the advice of our family doctor, spending hours in bed taking forced naps. Mostly we listened
to Judith Ann spin innumerable stories about Susabelle and her
magic Band-Aids. Susabelle's Band-Aids could fix anything. The
Tilden swimming pool, where we usually swam, was ordered
closed, but had it been open we would not have been allowed to
swim. My mother assumed the slightest cold symptom, the smallest
nose drip, the least sign of throat scratchiness, was polio's foot in
the door, and she slammed it shut with forced bed rest and plenty of
liquids.

My father's family, upon hearing word of these strange goings
on, descended en masse to stand unbelieving at our bedsides, flab-
bergasted at the idea of confining otherwise healthy children to

their mattresses. Uncle Malvin, on the off chance we really were sick, brought along a replacement for the BB gun the sticky-fingered Mrs. Wower swiped from our yard and sold on her weekly rummage sale. Nothing puts the mother of a seven-year-old boy in a better mood than the unsolicited gift of a BB gun, particularly if it comes from the uncle who thoughtfully gave this same boy, when he was an exceptionally mature three-year-old, his very first BB gun. The relatives left, shaking their heads, and polio missed our house. No one will ever convince me my mother didn't do exactly the right thing.

A growing sense of alarm flowed from the newspapers we carried in the mornings and the radio news broadcasts we listened to at night. Polio hit Oakdale, the small Antelope County town just east of Neligh, particularly hard. In one two-week period in late July, Oakdale recorded five cases, more polio victims than twenty-one other Nebraska counties recorded for the entire 1952 season. By early August, Neligh had four children in polio wards in Lincoln and Omaha. The calls that poured into the parsonage that summer asking for my father's help only increased our sense of dread. Next to every cash register in town sat a miniature iron lung, a mute appeal from the March of Dimes. I never deposited my pennies without taking inventory through the cellophane sides. It was my belief that if enough money were raised, I might not have to live in a real iron lung. Usually the little banks were nearly full. It gave a person reason to hope. Sometimes in late evening, after most townspeople were sound asleep, my mother took us out in the cool night air for a constitutional walk around town. A light burning in an upstairs bedroom often marked the home of a new polio victim. Every time we walked, it seemed, there were additional lighted bedrooms.

Some counties had it worse. Polk County, to the south, suffered more deaths than Grand Island, Kearney, and North Platte combined. Polk closed its school on September 25 after a week in which two people died and eighteen others came down with the disease. Cedar County, to the northeast, was hit with fifty-two cases, trailing only four other more heavily populated counties. The Cedar

County Board of Health, in a desperate attempt to slow the epidemic, ordered all schools, churches, picture shows, bowling alleys, and other public places closed until September 29. Everyone was hoping the virus would follow its usual pattern and go into dormancy after the first frost.

People had every reason to be afraid. There was no general agreement on how the disease was transmitted. We worried about flies, mosquitoes, cockroaches, stagnant water, and running water. Some parents followed my mother's prescription of bed rest and crowd avoidance. Some painted their children's nostrils with an alum solution. It had little effect on the spread of the disease, but it destroyed the sense of smell. Polio usually finished the season in a stage of full-blown virulence, most often in a large population center. The next summer it popped up, ready to maim and kill, in some placid rural setting a hundred miles away. Sometimes it struck entire households. In other cases a child living fifty miles from the nearest polio victim might become dangerously ill in a matter of hours. A steady stream of planes and ambulances ferried patients into Lincoln and Omaha hospitals. Polio patients overflowed the wards, spreading into the halls and common areas. March of Dimes personnel worked around the clock finagling iron lungs from other states.

If Nebraskans experienced a rising sense of alarm, it was never as severe as the panic that hit Los Angeles during the polio epidemic of 1934, when some doctors and nurses refused to go to work. Some that did were so caught up in the hysteria that they wrapped their arms and legs in prophylactic casts, like self-basting Egyptian mummies, on the mistaken assumption they would be protected from the worst ravages of the disease.

My mother, and thousands of mothers like her, fought polio with the only weapons they had. My mother won her fight. Many others, equally diligent, did not. My third grade class in the Chappell elementary school showed plenty of obvious damage. Patsy wore a leg brace and had an oddly curved back. Loretta struggled with two leg braces and was often too tired to complete a full day of school. Toby, whose chest thrust out unnaturally, wore a built-up heel on one shoe. Even Margaret, one of the handful of kids who'd had a noncrippling form of polio, walked as if she were treading on light bulbs. Of course Margaret was such a complete weinie, she probably would have walked oddly without the polio.

The point was, I'd seen a whole slew of unlucky polio victims, whose braces and crutches accused me every day with my own good fortune. And I hadn't much liked that long terrible summer in Neligh. I'd done what I could to forget all about the dog days of 1952, when the lights in the neighbors' upstairs bedrooms burned all night. Now, two years later and clear on the other side of the state, my do-gooder father was arranging an early-evening encounter with yet another reproachful reminder of my completely undeserved healthiness.

*

After that much-dreaded car ride, we arrived at Big Springs. I was hardly inside the parsonage before the cozy warmth of the Roe household began to work on my hard little heart, gradually melting it down to an ugly, oily puddle. Enid, the family matriarch, wrapped me in the sort of soft southwestern-accented hospitality I might expect from an adoring grandparent.

"We're so happy to meet you, Bryan. It was good of you to come all this way on such a warm night. Ben will be so very pleased you chose to spend some time with him. He's been asking questions about you since last week, when we told him you might be coming. He gets tired of seeing the same old family faces for months at a time."

A certain two-inch-tall sniveling weasel couldn't quite catch his father's eye to apologize. Dad was busy talking shop with Ben's father, Joe. Every so often he'd ask one of Ben's three younger sisters a teasing question, and they'd flock around him like children always did. When Dad had his blue twinklies turned on, there wasn't a kid in Christendom could resist. He could light up a room just by being there.

The dreaded time arrived for some dutiful spreading of weaselly light and cheer. Enid deposited me in a small bedroom just off the kitchen. In the dusky light I could just make out a long skinny boy, propped up in a narrow bed. He had a mop of brown hair combed to one side, and was folding a piece of typing paper.

"You like paper airplanes?" he said.

"Sure."

"I met this smart kid at the hospital in Denver, and he taught me how to make really good airplanes. I'll bet you make airplanes like I used to." Ben set to work folding and crimping, producing in a few strokes the duddy blunt-nosed model I'd been making since second grade.

"That's it."

"Now look at this one." Ben made seven swift folds. What emerged was a needle-nosed, swept-wing beauty, not unlike what was manufactured many years later as a B-1 bomber. "Try it."

The thing shot across the room, true as a dart. I threw the duddy version for comparison. It wobbled in the air for a few feet before nose-diving into the floor. I was sold. Ben patiently taught me how to create the perfect paper airplane every time. After a bit I could have done it in my sleep. He moved on to other designs, experimental stuff that was still in the testing phase. Some crashed, some didn't. None flew as fast and straight as that first baby. I knew it was going to be a big hit with Zimmer, Fanoele, Boxbender, and all the other folks with an academic interest in aerodynamics. Unless I missed my guess, Old Man Hall was going to see quite a few of these new models before the year was out.

As he worked, Ben talked about his world, about radio waves, astronomy, about operations and hospitals. In the corners of his room odd bits of old radios tumbled over picture books on the solar system. He had a working radio next to his bed. Lousy radio reception was the norm in the Panhandle, but he dialed through several clear stations picked up with the aid of his jury-rigged antenna. I was thinking Zimmer would get a charge out of talking watts and crystals with Ben.

This last operation that laid him up for so long was tricky, he said.

Some strange business about slowing the growth in one leg so the other could catch up. The surgeon reversed one of Ben's knee bones and promised good results. Ben was hoping this deal worked out better than the cutting they'd done on his dropped foot. Not that Ben was complaining exactly; that wasn't his style. He had a normal personal interest in the whys of what he lived with every day, but he also had a scientific detachment that allowed him to take a visitor through the gory details without revealing a particle of self-pity. Certainly it never crossed his mind to blame anyone. "After all," he would say years later, "I always thought I gave myself polio by eating dirt."

SEPTEMBER 1948
Tillar, Arkansas

Joe and Enid, fresh out of Garrett Theological Seminary in Evanston, Illinois, returned to their old-home Arkansas roots. Joe had been in charge of the Methodist church in Tillar, Arkansas, for about a year when Ben took sick. Twenty-nine months old, savvy enough to find dirt and eat it. The family had just returned from a hundred-mile automobile trip to visit Joe's mother. Enid remembers Ben getting chilled on the trip home. The doctor diagnosed a sore throat and gave him some medicine. No one was particularly concerned since Tillar had experienced no polio cases that year. His condition worsened for two days. By the third day severe muscle spasms changed the diagnosis to infantile paralysis. A church member drove the family to University Hospital in Little Rock. The receiving staff made a single notation on Ben's admission form: "Refuses to stand." They dosed him with harmless medicine and waited for the polio to run its course.

"My earliest memory is seeing rows of beds. Hospitals didn't treat polio patients very well back then. We were isolated from our families, who were allowed only short one-hour visits. I think the damage from that was permanent."

Enid remembers the first month as being particularly hard:

"They put Ben in quarantine for thirty days. It was such a blow." Later, when the Roes were able to go to Little Rock for short visits, they had to leave their year-old daughter Phyllis in the care of friends who had a baby of their own. "Of course, back then, people didn't know for sure how the polio was transmitted. I've always marveled at the courage those friends showed by taking Phyllis."

Ben, now transferred to Children's Hospital, had no lingering paralysis, but had weakness in his stomach and in his right leg and bicep. "Treatments included heavy massage. And I'll never forget the smell of that hot wool. Sister Kenny came up with that brainstorm. I think she must have stumbled onto the wool business because she was from Australia. The packs were hot enough to hurt. I always knew when they were coming because of the smell. The nurses also put me in the whirlpool quite a bit. I didn't mind that so much. When I left I had a brace from my waist to my right ankle."

Ben came home in time for Christmas, came home to resume his wrestling match with chronic asthma. After two years of struggle, and on doctor's orders, the family set out for the drier climes of western Nebraska. Ben began his rotations in and out of the Denver hospital about the time I was meeting Richie Ashburn. While he learned to live with a dropped foot, I learned to swivel-hip my way through a crowd of tacklers. While I pulled an occasional shenanigan and fought the Churtedepriches and Bat C. Henrys of the world, Ben was doing his level-best to be good:

"My place was to be a good kid. My goal was to be good. Even if you didn't fit in with the rest of the world, you were better. The reality was extremely lonely. That's the emotional cost of that."

Ben's scientific curiosity led him to explore area dumps, where he scavenged the radio parts he used in his projects. Later he fell in love with ham radio. Chappell had no monopoly on jerks. Ben's training as Big Springs's school drum major ended when the boys in the band marched faster than he could walk. It became simpler to retreat to the warm bosom of his doting family, to study the stars from the safety of his telescope, to talk to his radio friends halfway around the world. "Our family very much had a sense that it was us against the world. We were close to each other, not so much to outside people."

*

Ben met wife Maggie when they were students at Nebraska Wesleyan. "After the doctors fused my ankle I walked with a small kick with a locked right knee, gave it a bit of a swing. At college they nicknamed me 'Bouncy.' Maggie says that was what attracted her to me." California's culture and climate drew Ben and Maggie to theology school in Claremont. The California School of Theology, heavy with German-trained biblical scholars and international ecumenicalism, eased Ben away from his comfortable brand of Nebraska Methodism into a different philosophical world. Ben worked in the communications lab, gaining a nodding acquaintance with computers. His doctoral thesis at Claremont explored religious sex education and the philosophy of Reinhold Niebuhr.

Ben and Maggie took a rural Nebraska pastorate for a few years, then moved to Lincoln. Ben launched a new ministry in human sexuality while Maggie worked at the Nebraska Energy office. Ben conducted workshops, worked with Planned Parenthood on sexuality education, developed sexuality education programs for the handicapped. The Roes moved west again when Maggie took a position with Bread for the World in Denver. Ben took a job as a Kelly temp worker, was sent to his present company, and never left. "The technical side of my life has resurfaced; the computer stuff is sort of like the early business with the radios. I think that's why I like psychology; it's sort of the same thing, seeing how people cook, a kind of technology." Ben joined the staff of Hope Care and Counseling in 1988, and continued to do counseling, in addition to his computer job, until very recently when he had to curtail some of his activities.

Ben's belief that he suffers from post-polio syndrome is mostly a "diagnosis of exclusion." The kid who, upon arriving in Nebraska from Arkansas, threw his leg brace away "with great ceremony," now gets around at work in a three-wheeled cart. He finds that if he overexerts, he loses the use of something permanently. His only option is to take it easy and not get overtired. Ben likens it to early aging: "Polio victims have fewer horn cells. Normal aging causes a loss of these cells. Since polio victims have fewer to start with, they age more rapidly. I've spent my whole life trying to keep going. I was not going to let polio stand in the way. I was going to overcome. Now if I overdo, the damage is done before I know it.

"With the technology we have now, when the time comes, I'll be able to work from home."

OCTOBER 1951
Neligh, Nebraska

The Wizard of Oz is back in Neligh for a Saturday matinee. Judith Ann and Miriam would like to view the entire movie in leisurely, uninterrupted fashion, eat some popcorn, maybe a box of Juigy Fruits. Under protest, they have agreed to take me along, "one last time." I have heard many good things about this Oz movie, mostly from Judith Ann and Miriam. I have also seen a little bit of the black-and-white part where the tornado carries off Dorothy and Toto. Every time the witch appears floating in the maelstrom, pedaling her bicycle and cackling, I become uncomfortable and have to be taken home. This is referred to in our household as "Bryan getting scared."

We are all back to try it again. If I do not watch this movie to the very end, I have promised to slit my wrists and swallow a large dose of strychnine or, if that doesn't do the job, lie out in the middle of the highway until a semi comes along and squishes my cowardly little brains all over the asphalt. I cannot claim credit for volunteering to do these things. Truth is, Judith Ann required me to make these solemn pledges before we left home.

I insist, for safety's sake, we take seats in the rear of the theater. Once we are settled in and watching a harmless cartoon, featuring a homicidal cat and a couple of cute mice, my confidence level rises to an all-time high. This time will be different. That silly witch is just a make-believe deal. Like Judith Ann says, "It's only a movie, you dope."

As usual I do not become alarmed when the tornado threatens. Miriam says it is a good thing Aunt Margaret isn't here or someone would surely be taking her home. Once Dorothy's house is airborne my old ter-

*rors return. Sure enough, the wicked witch pedals into view, cackling in a
particularly threatening manner. Only my foolish strychnine promise
keeps me in my seat. I discover that by covering my eyes during the distress-
ing sections, I can hold the panic to a manageable level. Dorothy's house
lands on a bad witch, smooshing her as flat as any semi would have done,
raising my spirits in the process. The recruitment of Tin Man and Scare-
crow go pleasantly enough. The Cowardly Lion is another matter. I have
not seen this part before, and his bloodthirsty roarings go on just a little
too long before he reveals his true status as an absolute wienie. I instantly
develop empathetic feelings for the lion.*

OCTOBER 1951
Ashland, Nebraska

Karen Rogers liked to sit way down front at the movies, lean back in
her seat, watch giant Indians mounted on giant horses gallop across
the screen above her head. When the nine-year-old came home with
a headache and a sore throat, everyone assumed she'd been looking
straight up for a little too long. The first killing frost was behind
them, and Karen's mother had relaxed her fierce vigilance. The doctor called to the house thought she had a touch of flu. The next
morning Karen collapsed on her way to the bathroom. "My legs
turned to mush," she says. A team of doctors at Children's Hospital
in Omaha determined she was suffering from three strains of infantile paralysis, including the deadly bulbar type that can shut down
the lungs in a few hours.

Lieutenant Don Bruno, an Omaha fireman, settled Karen into
the iron lung, her home for the next year, something she came to
call "my green convertible." He made a date to take her dancing after she recovered. For the next month Karen, now completely paralyzed, fought an uphill battle for survival. Although she did not realize how close she was to death, she remembers her mother's
frequent crying: "She had always been so afraid we would get polio,
kept us away from crowds in the summer, wouldn't let us go to the
beach." Karen remembers her mother being especially restrictive

when the Platte River was on one of its periodic rampages: "She thought flood water carried the polio virus, and we could never go look at the flood damage like other kids." When Karen was taken to the hospital, her parents had the house fumigated to protect the four remaining children.

Living in the iron lung meant Karen had to learn to talk all over again. She found herself starting a conversation, only to have the machine force her to inhale, swallowing up much of what she was going to say. "Once I was able to time the machine it wasn't much of a problem." When the total paralysis finally subsided, Karen, a confirmed stomach sleeper, figured out how to turn over inside the iron lung. Sometimes during the flipping process she knocked her pillow to the floor and had to call a nurse for assistance: "They gave me the dickens sometimes, but they gave up trying to make me stay on my back." If she awoke during the night, it was to the steady swooshing of the iron lungs punctuated by the plaintive cries of "Nurse" from the polio-afflicted children scattered around the hospital. Iron lungs were not equipped with call buttons.

Karen's rehabilitation began with Sister Kenny's hot-wool packs. "I detested those wool packs more than anything. The nurses pretty well covered me several times a day." Later she learned to breathe for brief periods with her iron lung turned off, and was able to read stories to the other children in her ward.

Somtimes she was placed in a rocking bed, whose motion was supposed to build polio patient's lung capacity. "I fell out, of course. They made a rule that everyone had to be tied in. Later, after I fell out of my wheelchair, they tied everyone in their wheelchairs. I was always active."

Her parents were allowed to visit two hours a week—Thursday evenings from seven to eight and Sunday afternoons from two to three. They missed one visit during the entire year. "My brothers took care of my little sisters while my folks were at the hospital. I think it helped make our family closer." The Cisco Kid and The Range Rider also visited her ward. The firemen who came to work the manual pumps during a power outage came back to take the ambulatory patients to front-row seats at a Barnum and Bailey circus.

*

When the flood of patients hit Children's Hospital in the summer of 1952, Karen and the other held-over patients were moved to a back room:

"There were so many critical cases coming in the door they almost forgot about us for a while. There were iron lungs everywhere, even up and down the halls. I was in a wheelchair part of the time by then. If a kid needed anything, I'd sometimes be able to help.

"When I think of polio I see all those kids in the hospital, some of the kids with me that didn't make it, those that died later of complications. I also think of how nice everyone was. The hospital administrator came to see me every day. She always asked me if I needed anything, if she should tell my folks to bring something on their next visit. She never missed a day. I'll always remember 'Lulu Bell' Roundtree, my favorite nurse. She was special."

Karen went home to her beloved Ashland. She learned to ride a bicycle again, this time with her feet tied to the pedals. She returned to horseback riding, feet tied to the stirrups. When she was unable to roller-skate, the roller rink owner designed a hoop on wheels. Karen skated inside the hoop, sailing around the floor with her friends.

"The other kids were always good to me. I don't remember a single instance when they were mean. I had one teacher that embarrassed me half to death. The school district had purchased new desks while I was gone. I was wearing a full leg brace and couldn't get in and out of my desk without leaving some scratches. She made the announcement in front of the whole class that I ought to bring a pillow from home so I wouldn't scratch the furniture."

Karen went back to the hospital twelve times between 1952 and 1961. Doctors fused her spine and an ankle, broke both legs and reset them. She suffered several severe cases of pneumonia. The March of Dimes paid for most of this care, something Karen never forgot. While building up her stamina to walk down the aisle at her brother's wedding, Karen tripped on a corn cob and broke her ankle. She made it down the aisle, but with a leg cast. She also began her work with the March of Dimes, first in Saunders County, then, by the time she was a high school junior, as state chair of the Teen March of Dimes. Karen spoke at schools across the state, urging students to fill their cardboard March of Dimes folders with dimes. Because future motherhood was Karen's primary goal, she was in tune with the changing mandate of the March of Dimes, the move from being a polio charity to one interested primarily in the problem of birth defects. Her standard speech always included "We, the teen-agers of today, will be the parents of tomorrow."

*

Blanche Sohl, who ran the El Blancho Cafe in Ashland, home of "real food," was a big fan of Karen and a regular viewer of Ralph Edwards's "This Is Your Life." Blanche alerted the show's producers to Karen's story, and a few months later Karen was on a train to Los Angeles, ostensibly to attend a national March of Dimes function.

"'I got so disgusted with the way the March of Dimes was spending money on that trip. Mom and I had two rooms, when one would have been fine. The prices on the menu were terrible. I tried to order the cheapest thing, but everything was expensive. I had no idea Ralph Edwards was paying for the whole deal."

Once in Los Angeles Karen stayed at the Ambassador Hotel, was shown the sights, taken to a Johnny Mathis concert. Karen says if she had tumbled to what was going on, her appearance would have been canceled. Her mother turned off the TV whenever a news program came on, made sure she looked through the newspaper before Karen read it. Waiting in line outside the theater with other tourists, Karen was incensed when the ushers came out to escort her straight to an aisle seat: "They said it was because I was on crutches. I figured I could wait as well as all those other people; I didn't need special treatment. I wasn't going to go in, but Mom said it would be less fuss to do what they wanted."

Complete surprise.

Karen was treated to guest appearances by her school chums, her father, her brothers and sisters, Lieutenant Bruno of the Omaha Fire Department, Nurse Lulu Bell, and Joan Gannon, who spent seven months in Children's Hospital as Karen's roommate. After trips to Disneyland and Knott's Berry Farm, the family flew back to Nebraska. They were met by Mr. Shimonek, the Ashland school superintendent, in a yellow school bus. He drove the family to a welcome-home party hosted by the school band and four hundred Ashland residents. The mayor presented Karen with a bouquet of red roses, and Mr. Shimonek announced the students and faculty of the Ashland schools had contributed $190 to the March of Dimes. "Ashland is a caring town," Karen says. "The people have always supported me."

Letters from all over the country flowed into Ashland. Some contained money, which Karen scrupulously accounted for and gave to the March of Dimes; some contained proposals of marriage. Many people wrote of their own troubles. Karen tried to answer all the letters personally, but she found it impossible: "I'd guess if you put all those letters together they would have filled a refrigerator box."

Requests for Karen to speak came in as well, first from local service clubs and then from all over the state. Regional March of Dimes meetings took her throughout the Midwest. She was offered the opportunity to chair the national Teen March of Dimes.

"Sometimes I think it was something I should have done, but I was interested in getting married and having children. That's what you did back then. I was young and in love. After graduating from high school, I made the decision to get married instead of taking the national office. I went back in the hospital and the surgeons broke my legs above my knees, turned the legs just enough to keep my knees from growing at a bad angle. I was in leg casts for several months after that. I got married, had two children. I had been worried I wouldn't be able to have children, even though the doctors told me I would have no trouble.

"Polio has made me a stronger person, made me more outgoing. I wouldn't have gone on planes, met all those interesting people. I wouldn't have learned how caring people are. I think what people did for me made me a more caring person than I would have been."

At fifty-two Karen finds she tires more easily than she used to, cannot always finish the tasks she set for herself. This is frustrating for the girl who usually did whatever she wanted. Sometimes she wonders if it's the post-polio syndrome she's heard about.

"Mostly I think it's just old age catching up to me."

OCTOBER 1951
Neligh, Nebraska

*My optimism returns. I uncover my eyes. Dorothy and crew are in good shape, skipping down the Yellow Brick Road singing a happy song. I stuff my mouth with Juicy Fruits. All is soul-satisfying, teeth-squelching, sticky-sweet gook. I add some popcorn to the mix. The music abruptly becomes ominous. The Yellow Brick Road enters a spooky woods. A familiar cackle erupts from the underbrush. There she is, up on a cottage roof, waving her nasty broom, threatening Dorothy and Toto with unimaginable evil. I cut loose with a wailing "*NAAAAAAAAAAAAAAH,*" blunder through a threatening forest of legs and feet in a mad dash for the exit. I burst through the theater doors into blinding sunshine. Judith Ann catches up to me on the sidewalk.*

"Do you want people to think you're a fraidy cat?"

"I d-don't care."

"I suppose you want me to walk you home."

Sniff. Nod.

"Okay, but don't expect me to take you to the movies again, little brother. This is it."

"M-maybe next year when I'm older it won't s-seem so scary."

"Wouldn't that be something?" Judith Ann grabs my hand and pulls me down the sun-warmed sidewalk toward home.

The Clan

We are heading down Highway 30 through the murky predawn. Foundered on sleep and Christmas delicacies, I sit in the peon's perch in the back seat, centered above the humming drive-shaft. My assigned space is rudely invaded by the sprawling limbs of my slumbering sisters. Unbearably chipper, as she is every morning, my mother explains to my father in excruciating detail every single stray thought she's produced since her head hit the pillow last night. Hers is not a brain that rests, and her nights and early mornings produce a blizzard of random theories about an astonishing array of matters domestic, international, and intergalactic. My father's job is to gently steer our ark eastward and murmur noncommittally in the appropriate places.

Like most families, ours has its peculiar Christmas rituals. After Dad holds Christmas Eve services, we invariably return home for oyster soup and the opening of presents. In the morning we stumble out to the cold car and the four-hundred-mile trip to Magnet in northeast Nebraska, the center of the Jones universe.

Up late with new games and too excited about the upcoming week with cousins to sleep much, I have been fighting drowsiness for the last twenty miles. There is mischief floating around in the front seat in the form of one of my mother's brainstorms. If I am not vigilant it may be adopted as official policy and not pass harmlessly into the discard pile. My father is being sold on the bizarre idea that I should spend the bulk of my upcoming visit under Aunt Margaret's roof. I am certainly not opposed to Aunt Margaret, who has a dry sense of humor and can cook. I am only opposed to spending more than a fraction of my precious vacation time in the company of anyone but cousins Carrol, Jim, and Larry. It is no secret my mother wishes to limit my contact with this trio of nonpareils. She is worried I will acquire too broad a vocabulary or, worse, a relaxed attitude toward the weaknesses of the flesh. I, on the other hand, am eager to expand my vocabulary and impatient to get next to the weakest flesh available. An objective observer would be hard-pressed to name three better qualified guides to impure knowledge than Carrol Jones and Jim and Larry Joachimsen.

"Last night, when I was kind of restless, I had the most marvelous idea, Lowell. Burt works so-o-o-o hard he's almost never home before dark. If Bryan went along with the girls to Burt and Margaret's he'd have a chance to talk with Burt. Don't you think Bryan would enjoy visiting with Burt?"

This is my mother's idea of subtlety. Uncle Burt is not only solvent, but well on his way to becoming rich. His John Deere dealership is minting money. He owns not one farm but several. In this he is markedly different from most other members of the Jones clan, who are one or two cream checks above the poverty line. Not only is my father being sold on my exile to Aunt Margaret's place, but, I suspect, is being tweaked a bit about his less-solvent relatives. If he is irritated by any of this, he gives no sign.

Visit with Uncle Burt? The very thought. Burt is too huge, a swarthy man-mountain, his thumb as big as my wrist. Too intimidating, communicating with the kind of rumbles and grunts popular among the larger species of carnivorous wildlife. At home he mostly eats—chickens, heaping platters of fish, mounds of potatoes and gravy, entire pies. A small child watching Uncle Burt inhale a meal can, without a serious stretch, imagine himself joining the platter of chicken in Burt's barreled gut. When Burt laughs, it is as if a freight train were loose in the room, blasting dorky little nephews clean out of their combat boots. The guy is scary. The theory that Burt and I would ever sit around like a pair of old-buddy plow-jockeys discussing hogs and machinery is simply preposterous.

"Mmmmm," Dad says. I am encouraged by this. So is my mother.

"I was thinking that Carrol just doesn't have the kind of meaningful activities he might have."

"Mmmmm?" Dad is as curious as I am about this brainstorm.

"I was thinking, and this is really wild, but maybe there's a Boy

Scout group he could join. They do so-o-o-o many things with projects. I'm sure he could find something he'd like."

Cousin Carrol, who is a fair hand with machinery and has been milking cows since the age of four, who has an encyclopedic joke repertoire, who can drive a car better than most grown people, who can spin a full bucket of milk overhead with either hand, who can hit a baseball farther than anyone in that rural neighborhood's recent memory, who has attracted the interest of a dozen pretty girls from towns as far away as Crofton—is a guy needing some putty-brained Boy Scout leader to show him "meaningful" activities? Apparently some activities, like joke-telling and making out and automobile driving, are less meaningful than others, like knot-tying and tent-trenching. Actually, lying somewhere in the bowels of my mother's motivation is the honest desire for my Jones cousins to get a few more of life's advantages. Their school, although large for a country district, has limited experience with good teachers. A crackerjack teacher like my mother could have real impact on my cousins' subsequent academic success. But mostly she wishes Cousin Carrol were not so robustly sinful. She might as well wish he would change overnight into a rutabaga.

"Mmmmm," Dad says. I take this cue to get my oar in.

"Didn't you say Jim and Larry have a pet burro?"

Dad chuckles. "He bucks. Those kids have a dickens of a time trying to ride. When they get bucked off they bounce a few clods off his head. They even got me on the darn thing last time I was up there. I wasn't on too long."

"I sure hope I get a chance to ride him."

"Oh, I'm sure you'll have plenty of chances."

Whew. Done deal. No Aunt Margaret's shipshape ship. No scary Uncle Burt. I'm on my regular vacation rotation. Once we spend the night with Grandpa and Grandma Jones in Magnet, I'll be let off at Uncle Doyle's place, where Aunt Alda rules Cousin Carrol with a loose hand and dishes out a chocolate chiffon pie I'm partial to. Then on to Aunt Mary and Uncle Wilbur's place, where easy laughter is the currency of choice, where Jim and Larry's daily spankings have never deterred misbehavior of any consequence. Plenty of cussing practice and sound sexual discussion all around. I can now slip off to sleep with perfect confidence. My father's decisions, once he makes them, are never subject to reversal.

*

I wake up to my sisters' poorly suppressed laughter. We are entering the western edge of North Platte. They have spotted a doofy-looking guy in a following car and are making jokes about him. Judith Ann says he has been formed by the dreaded Mr. Petrify, the legendary manufacturer of the highest mountain ranges of the West, who uses as his exclusive raw material the kind of bowel movements that instantly petrify once they reach the stage of finished sculpture. My father is laughing. Mom is busy with breakfast, handing out some kind of nutritious juice in pastel aluminum glasses and soft slices of freshly baked oatmeal bread. It never occurs to anyone to wonder how she had time to bake bread in all of yesterday's mad rush.

East of North Platte Judith Ann decides we should have a "Think!" sign counting contest. These are the little signs an insurance company plants along the highway to mark every traffic fatality. "Bloody Highway 30," as it is known, has plenty of these macabre reminders sprouting from its shoulders. She will take the north side of Highway 30 and let Miriam and me count everything in the south ditch. After ten miles Judith Ann has doubled our count. We accuse her of cheating, of knowing ahead of time the north side of Highway 30 is the deadlier. She protests innocence, but is laughing too much to be believed. She offers to swap sides. We take her up. Ten miles later she has doubled our count again. We accuse her of cheating, of knowing the precise location on Highway 30 when the south side becomes the deadlier. She is so tickled by this we have to pound on her with a few haymakers.

My mother is reading to Dad from a stack of late-arriving Christmas letters, another of our holiday rituals. She raises her voice to match the mayhem level in the back seat. Mom is a talented oral reader. We have listened to her musical voice for hours over the years, listened to her read thousands of pages after all of us could read competently on our own. Today we have little interest in long-winded Christmas letters from strangers, no matter how dramatically they are presented. Judith Ann says we should play the Burma-Shave game. This game is very simple: the first person to read the sign gets to read the sign. There is no score, no winners or losers. Burma-Shave advertising jingles are printed on six widely spaced signs. At times the signs are so rusty the lettering has mostly faded from view. Sometimes a sign has dropped off the post or been obliterated by shotgun vandalism. In these cases we supply our own lines. Judith spots the first distinctive red-and-white sign:

"The answer to"
Miriam blurts, "A maiden's"
They recite in unison, "Prayer"
Dad, erstwhile attentive Christmas-letter listenee, "Is not a chin"
Me, with gusto, "Of stubby hair"
All, "Burma-Shave."

We accuse Judith of cheating, of having memorized, by reason of her age and advantage in trips down Highway 30, the location of every "Think!" and Burma-Shave sign along the entire route. She giggles so guiltily we are forced to pound her again. She laughs harder. "Oh look," she points, "Mr. Petrify has been here." Sure enough, just south of the Union Pacific railroad tracks, which companionably parallel Highway 30 along much of its route through Nebraska, stands a huge mound of brownish frozen sugar beets. This sets off some very peculiar speculation about Mr. Petrify's food intake just prior to the sculpting of this most recent masterpiece.

"Sign." Dad is always alert.

Ben
Met Anna
Made a hit
Neglected beard
Ben-Anna split
Burma-Shave

*

We are between Gothenburg and Cozad. Dad goes very still. This unusual stillness is not necessarily easy to spot in a habitually quiet guy, but we recognize it when it happens. Everyone strains to see down the road to locate the terrible thing that has my father's attention. We expect a bad car wreck. We are right. Traffic slows to a crawl as we approach the accident site. One car, a mutilated ruin, its entire driver's side ripped open, sits astride the center line. My stomach turns over as I recognize the dark stains on the car's shattered windshield. Strands of wispy brown hair flutter weakly from the razored glass. Some distance down the road lies a blanket-covered body. I look away. Thirty feet off the highway in the wide south bar pit an ambulance is loading the injured from a crumpled station wagon. Brightly wrapped Christmas presents spill out of the open tailgate. Someone is screaming. We can hear the racket through our rolled-up windows. Like theater patrons watching a riveting movie we scrunch down in our respective seats, staring straight ahead. After a bit Miriam opens an adventure book. No one says much of anything for long time. Burma-Shave and "Think!" signs pass by uncounted.

A couple miles west of Kearney is what I call the Tipi Place, a set of gas pumps in front of a large red-and-white concrete tipi. Advertisements for all manner of authentic Indian artifacts appear on the billboards paving our approach. For several years I have turned whiny when we pass this place, wishing to pull off and buy a genuine Sioux tomahawk. On cue I ask my father if we can stop and "look around." On cue he says maybe we can stop on the way back "when we have more time." In summer when we make this trip, the Boys Training School vegetable gardens south of the highway will be populated by several hundred sweating apprentice criminals. My sisters will wave wildly, on the lame pretext of greeting a wayward Chappell youngster rumored to be a resident. Today the fields lie fallow, the neat yellowed rows of dead plants rulering the black Platte Valley soil.

It is lunchtime. Mom passes out turkey sandwiches. This too is a Christmas ritual. Members of Dad's congregation often make seasonal gifts of four or five turkeys. One guy always shows up with a fat goose. We save the goose for after New Year's. We are carrying one of our surplus frozen turkeys in the trunk, a gift for my grandparents. This morning we got as far as Ogallala without it. The fifty-mile return trip to Chappell was nearly soundless. I am glad it was not my job to remember the turkey.

I'm already thinking ahead to supper. My stomach slips into reverse gear. My grandparents live in a remarkably phlegmy household, with rheumy eyes and runny noses and much coughing and spitting. Grandma's lungs, weak from several death-defying bouts with pneumonia, have not improved from the years in close quarters with one of the world's more avid chain smokers. Grandpa spends a good part of his life hacking up the crap he sucks in when he isn't hacking. Walter and Pearl Jones have aged, not through some genteel process, but in the hard-working, hard-living way that produces bony chests, vast populations of liver spots, purple naked gums. I can muster little enthusiasm for witnessing Grandpa gum his way through yet another slice of ham. "Why don't Grandpa and Grandma Jones have any teeth?"

The back of Dad's neck reddens. Mom tries her brand of diplomacy. "I think his brother, Uncle Carl, might have had a bad experience with dentures. He always carried them around in his pocket, but he never put them in."

"Not even to eat?"

"Not even to eat. That would have been too new-fangled."

Dad cranks up his measured, patient voice, which means I had better lie very low for the next few minutes. "They haven't always had the most nutritious food. Mom did the best she could with what she had, but they didn't have the frozen vegetables and fresh fruits like we have. People of their generation just don't expect to keep their teeth. If they have one too many toothaches, and they're past forty, they'll pay some dentist to pull them out. I don't really know why. Maybe they think they're saving money."

I develop an intense interest in Miriam's book. The narrator-hero is exploring some Mayan ruins in the jungles of Yucatan. Looking into the remains of a temple pool, he hallucinates the visit of some poor sacrificed Mayan girl from the pre-Columbian past. She has plenty on her mind, what with being a beautiful virgin and managing handsome boyfriends and being ceremonially drowned by evil chief priests. Judith Ann wonders, since these Mayan pyramids are fairly brown and fairly large, if Mr. Petrify appears in any of this author's dreams. But Miriam is spellbound, and cannot be distracted by irreverent speculation on the chemical composition of Mayan pyramids.

On the east edge of Grand Island, we pass Bosselman's original truck stop. One summer day, several years ago, Dad surprised us by stopping here and treating the family to a sit-down restaurant meal. He must have had some unexpected wedding or funeral money burning a hole in his pocket because he hasn't done it since. We don't forget restaurants. It's not like we have many to remember. Sitting up straight in that spiffy red-and-white vinyl booth, surrounded by equal numbers of rough-talking truck drivers and nattily dressed company men, I agonized over Bosselman's extensive menu, debating between chicken-fried steak and something called a Denver omelette. The waitress grew snippy, fiddling with her order pad, snapping her gum. Then, just when matters were turning ugly, a genius bolt smacked me upside the head, and I haughtily ordered the Bosselman's Hamburger Deluxe, a coup of extraordinary originality. When it arrived, bun toasted to a warm gold, the plate heavy with lettuce leaves, onion and tomato slices, fat yellow French fries heaped on one side, I could only assume every diner in the room was green with envy.

Just past Bosselman's, rolling past scattered motels on the eastern outskirts of Grand Island, we strain to see the small buffalo herd north of the highway. In the 1950s buffalo are an exotic sight, and this sandy pasture can afford a tantalizing glimpse to the sharp-eyed. Today, because of the chilling north wind, the shaggy herd is bunched facing the breeze, naked tails clamped tight between their hams. Spring calves wander nervously on the lee side of the herd.

Another ritual. I ask Dad if there are more buffalo than last trip. He says he's sure the herd has at least doubled.

Once past the buffalo, conversation turns to Central City, the next sizable town on our route. This is where our family spent World War II; where I was born, the New Year's baby of 1945; where the Methodist sanctuary still sports a foot-sized hole in the ceiling incurred during one of my sisters' constant treasure-hunting expeditions. *The Secret of the Old Sampy Place*, first read to us by my mother, later read cover-to-cover by both Judith Ann and Miriam, featured, in addition to nail-biting danger, a loose fireplace brick behind which was concealed a sooty treasure sack. No brick in Central City was safe from my sisters' prying fingers. They became convinced that the Methodist church, by reason of being old and containing a fair number of bricks, was the likeliest treasure site. They worked over the basement first, paying special attention to the dingy coal bins, which they entered on a regular basis by way of the coal chute. What my mother thought about the condition of my sisters' clothing after these searches is not known. Almost as an afterthought, they tackled the church's unfinished attic, balancing precariously on the rafters above the sanctuary as they felt their way around the brick chimney. Judith slipped, poking a foot neatly through the ceiling plaster. Why this hole was never discovered and repaired, and why no one conducted a search for the guilty, is a continuing family mystery.

The main line of the Union Pacific passes through Central City, and during World War II, trains came through every six or eight minutes. I remember many-wheeled black engines pulling impossibly long trains, roaring past at full speed, emitting great clouds of steam and deep-throated whistles. Every time our family car passes the main railroad crossing, someone brings up Judith Ann's narrow escape. She was riding her bicycle, darting across the tracks just behind the passing caboose of an eastbound train. A westbound train, the thunder of its approach masked by its mate, missed her back tire by inches. The sight so unnerved the eyewitnesses that they trickled into the parsonage for a week afterward to report to my mother in shaken voices. Some of them scolded, wanted Judith Ann kept away from the tracks, kept home where little kids belonged, where she could never scare them again. My parents, as usual, chose freedom over fear, and my sister continued to roam. Restricting a free spirit like Judith Ann would have been problematical, even then.

*

Every Christmas the Jones family receives a large poinsettia from a Lincoln florist. Every Easter he sends us an Easter lily. On this Christmas trip, as we follow the curving highway through downtown Central City, my mother starts talking about the destitute Japanese family that arrived from California during the war, all their property in California, including house, bank accounts, and the family greenhouse, expropriated by West-Coast patriots. All that was salvaged was a handful of special flower bulbs carried in their suitcases. If they could find work here in the nation's heartland, far from vital defense facilities, they might be spared life in an internment camp.

"Somehow Dad found out about them, do you remember how, Lowell?"

"No."

"I don't think their English was ever very good, was it, Lowell?"

"No."

"Didn't you have to ask quite a few people before you found that gentleman a position?"

"Probably."

"Didn't he work at that greenhouse in the south part of town for a few years, Lowell? And then didn't they buy the greenhouse in Lincoln?"

"I think so."

"Twice a year they send the loveliest plants. As long as that man is alive I expect we'll keep getting them."

"Why did they lose all their stuff in California?" I ask.

"During the war there was a big panic," my mother says, "especially in California. People thought the Japanese people living here would help Japan in the war. Nobody was thinking too clearly and a lot of harm was done to innocent people just because they were different."

"Did people in Central City treat them mean?" Miriam asks.

"I don't remember if they did," Dad says.

"Wasn't it hard to find someone to hire them, Lowell?" My mother is persistent.

"I don't remember that it was." When my father is in his inscrutable mode, he can drive a seasoned KGB interrogator to hang up his electrodes and enroll in business school.

"Didn't Roarks move?" asks Judith Ann.

Jimmy Roark lived next door during our Central City years. He was a year younger than Miriam and addicted to cowboy boots and every form of cowboy play. Each morning he appeared on his front porch and yelled over in his peculiar foghorn voice, "Fiend or foe?"

If we answered fiend, Jimmy came over and played peaceful games. If we hollered foe, Jimmy became a blood enemy for the day, and we shot each other countless times, mostly with imaginary guns, although he possessed a pair of Gene Autry pearl-handled cap pistols I greatly coveted. In the years since we moved from Central City, we have had neither fiend nor foe as loyal as Jimmy Roark.

"Isn't this where Uncle Malvin made the antifreeze?" Miriam points to an old-fashioned stucco gas station with a large roof hanging out over the pumps. Another family ritual. Dad enjoys retelling the antifreeze story much more than my mother enjoys hearing it. She is still too embarrassed to see much humor. If Uncle Malvin, he of the Mephistophelian eyebrows, the uncle always suspected of some kind of chicanery, weren't the prime actor, hardly anyone would think the antifreeze debacle was anything worse than a small miscalculation. After the war, with Uncle Malvin, the guy with a nose for the million-dollar sure thing, in temporary residence from California, Uncle Willis home from a prisoner-of-war camp, Uncle Earl out of the Marines, the Jones clan reassembled most of its parts in Central City. Grandpa and Grandma held their farm sale and moved down from Bloomfield. Uncle Doyle, newly married to

Alda, was enticed from farming into the gas-station business with Uncle Malvin.

Antifreeze, never in abundant supply before the war, was still mostly unavailable. The county sheriff, who turned out to be a good old northeast Nebraska boy, came up with the magic formula. Calcium chloride, the highly corrosive chief ingredient in the fluid weighting down tractor tires around farm country, was mixed in a large vat with generous globs of good old American honey. The honey was supposed to keep the calcium chloride from eating its way through engine blocks in two minutes flat. Uncle Willis and Aunt Lucille mortgaged their house to secure the formula for the clan. Dad invested. If Malvin put in some small change, no one remembers. After all, he was supplying the brains. Doyle, with Alda firmly driving the buggy, passed on his chance at easy millions. Willis and my father, true believers both, filled their radiators with the gunk. And although it wormed its way through the engine blocks to coat everything with a thin scum of gelatinous ooze, the concoction did not kill their cars, nor did it allow freezing, although Willis always claimed both cars were so old and worn-out as to be past hurting. Malvin moved plenty of antifreeze. He could always sell.

According to Dad's version of the story, a few local cars came down with severe spazzums, resulting in some highly irritated customers and extreme embarrassment all around. Willis remembers the local customers as being generally well-satisfied. The exceptions were a couple of sorehead Iowans, who picked up some of the stuff on their way through town. The greedy buggers might have had visions of stealing the secret Jones Brothers' Anti-Freeze formula and making a killing, or, more likely, Malvin was secretly selling exclusive distributorships. At any rate, they sent the stuff to a lab for testing, something Dad wishes the Jones boys had done before Willis mortgaged his house. The test results weren't all that bad, according to Malvin. True, the stuff did almost freeze, turning downright mushy, making it too marginal to sell as true antifreeze. But the honey worked, neutralizing the calcium chloride into a noncorrosive substance. If someone had figured out a use for an almost-anti-freeze that flowed through the sides of engine blocks without damage, the Jones brothers might still have made their pile.

Since no one did, Malvin folded the tent and took Aunt Laura back to sunny California. Doyle and Alda, heartily sick of the gas-station business à la Malvin, returned to farming. The sheriff gave back most of his formula windfall, allowing Lucille to pay off the mortgage. Willis and Lucille, always on the lookout for a small-town grocery store, took Grandpa and Grandma with them to Edison for a brief fling with commerce. Uncle Earl eventually followed, leaving us as the lone Jones representatives in Central City. No more Grandma Jones–hosted Sunday dinners, with the entire local clan available for fried chicken and vinegar pie and spirited Rook games. No relaxed afternoons of cigarette smoking, joke-telling, and just plain sitting around doing not much of anything.

If this gauzy little family interlude in Central City accomplished nothing else, it assuaged the gut-hammering fear that paralyzed everyone some years earlier when Uncle Willy's B-17 was shot down over Germany. The day the news arrived my father stood lonely watch in his garden, staring sightlessly off to the east, as if he could will his brother safe harbor. Even the delayed notice that Willis was alive in a prisoner-of-war camp did not entirely dispel the family's apprehension. But with everyone home, circled safe and sound around that laughter-filled Sunday table, where they could touch and be touched, the Jones family was made whole, free once again to allow its more adventurous members to roam.

*

Our car continues east under a lowering sky, rolling down the wide Platte Valley, through Clarks, Silver Creek, Duncan. On this barren Christmas, the flat sandy corn ground, rank with twisted corn stalks, displays hues of faded yellow. Frost-backed Hereford cows, butter-fat from easy living on dropped ears, move nonchalantly through the harvested fields. We cross the Platte and Loup Rivers at Columbus, following Highway 81 up and out of the Platte Valley and into the steep hills of the Elkhorn River watershed. The conversation turns to Aunt Margaret, specifically the impressive range of matters she chooses to worry about. My father attributes her permanent state of high anxiety to the tornado that turned their farmhouse on its foundation and drove straw deep into the fence posts. Margaret is the one, after all, who views each cloud, no matter how pale and scrawny, as an imminent threat to life and limb. Nor does she take comfort from cloudless skies, knowing in her bones they conceal nothing but treachery. She worries about floods when it might rain and drought when it might not.

Talk of long automobile trips worries Margaret.

"Why would they want to do that? They might get in a bad wreck."

Talk of airplane flights worries Margaret.

"Why would they want to do that? Their plane might crash."

Talk of fishing trips worries Margaret.

"Why would they want to do that? I hope they don't get so far out in that little dinky boat that they can't get back and everybody drowns."

This is the woman who continued to worry herself silly over the Orson Welles radio broadcast of *The War of the Worlds* long after most of the audience had pretty well sobered up. I have heard her, more than once, caution adults about the dangers of crossing the street. On the last leg of this familiar Christmas trip I am also remembering a time, not so long ago, when Margaret had a right to be worried.

*

It was early spring after one of the big blizzard winters, maybe spring of 1950. A carload of women—and me. A sunny afternoon drive between two unremembered points in the Plainview–Norfolk area. Aunts Mary and Margaret were in the car, maybe Alda. My mother was there, holding me close as the air swirled with womantalk. I was five and more interested in the passing scenery than in conversation. Between the receding snowdrifts, patches of green were poking through. Every pasture was a maze of drifts and rivulets. Sometimes we crossed a creek and looked down into churning gray water hurrying toward the swollen Elkhorn. I was dressed in my heavy winter parka, the only member of my family to own such a garment. The heater was going full-blast. It was an open question whether I would be fully cooked before I fell asleep.

We crossed a larger creek. I perked up and was rewarded by the sight of angry whirlpools spinning madly downstream. The car crept along, slowed by the nearness of high water, now filling the road ditches. I spotted a boy, near my size and age, playing along the creek. He was wearing red overshoes and was poking a long stick in the water. Perhaps he was as interested in the workings of whirlpools as I was. Aunt Margaret spotted him too. A mere child off by himself having what very much resembled a reasonably good time threw her into a complete tizzy. Nothing would do but that we turn up the driveway of the nearest farm and send out the authorities. I was mortified to my toes. Why did I keep getting mixed up with interfering old bats? The memory is a bit frayed here, but I may have given voice to my outrage at this gross violation of an innocent boy's constitutional right to mess around in a creek. Perhaps I sat mute, thinking affronted thoughts. There were many more full-grown women in that car than there were of me.

Margaret, in an absolute toot, marched up to the farmhouse stoop and harangued an invisible person behind the screen door. A few minutes later Margaret was back in the car, telling us with a hint of smugness that the boy in question was NOT where he was supposed to be. An older sister, wearing a short jumper and a pair of those ubiquitous red overshoes, ran by our car on her way to fetch her brother. She was running hard, her boots splattering into the soft ground with every step. Margaret worried that she was already too late. Without wanting to, I caught some of Margaret's hysteria. Sure, the entire business was a lesson in silly-assed meddling, but it became important to see the little guy was safe, if only to show my aunts the folly of their intrusive ways. Our car paralleled the hurrying sister, now wending her way through the slushy drifts. She never faltered, her bony legs stretching for the next firm bit of green turf, her long brown hair streaming out behind. Her mouth opened as she called her brother. We were almost to the bridge. Everyone in the car studied the creek bank. No kid. No stick. Probably he walked downstream, someone said. "No," said Margaret, "I think something terrible has happened." We made a U-turn at the next intersection and headed toward our original destination. The indelible picture I have is of a frail shivering girl in muddy red boots, bathed in brilliant sunshine, squinting disconsolately across the sullen water.

Margaret demanded we listen to the car radio, certain we would hear the worst. I, on the other hand, recovered my senses. The kid had merely wandered off. If his sister searched behind the right snowbank she'd find him building a fort. Then his family would be thanking Aunt Margaret for all the hysteria, wouldn't they? There was no reason for him to go in the water, not with all that pasture to play in. Didn't someone say he was supposed to be fetching the milk cows? Why didn't we assume he went about tending to his own business, an object lesson for a couple of busybodies very near me. I was secretly hoping the kid had found his Holsteins, had them headed for home through the shrinking drifts, milk-heavy bags swinging in the sharp breeze. I was hoping his sister was helping him, maybe doing some mild chewing for his tardiness but too relieved to make much of a job of it. I desperately wanted Margaret to be wrong. Because if she was right, against all laws of probability, then not only had a little boy perished in that frigid stream back there, not only would his family be completely devastated, just as my own would be if I were to drown under such tragic circumstances, but his big sister would be forever haunted that she didn't run just a little bit faster. Worse, from my point of view, Margaret's brand of nosy anxiety would gain credibility, perhaps to the point where small boys would be locked in their rooms every time there was a hint of rain somewhere in the Western Hemisphere.

The sun was almost down. We were nearing our destination. The radio news broadcast informed us a little boy had drowned in a snowmelt-swollen creek on his own farm. His body had been discovered by a sister a short distance from where it was presumed the boy had slipped under the water. Authorities speculated that the five-year-old attempted to wade the creek and slid on the icy bottom, possibly hitting his head. The family was alerted to the situation by concerned passersby, but was unable to get help to the boy in time. I felt lightheaded. Someone in our car was crying. My mother hugged me closer. There was nothing left for anyone to say.

*

This Christmas there are no drifts and no floods. Once we pass through Norfolk we have a clear shot to Magnet. My father's mood lightens. He starts kidding Mom about pie. This is standard procedure. "I wonder," he says, "if Grandma will have any of those mysterious things?"

"What mysterious things?" I have played this game before.

"Oh, you know, they're kind of round."

"Like this?"

"No, they're more like this."

"Humph." Mom takes the bait. She has been feigning indifference.

"What do you suppose those things are?" Dad asks with eye-batting innocence.

"Gee, I dunno. What do you think?"

"I don't know either. Maybe we could call in some university experts, and they could tell us. I just haven't seen those things often enough to have an opinion."

"You're just being silly." My mother is boiling. "You know very well I baked you three pies last week, a cherry, a butterscotch, and a lemon meringue AT YOUR SPECIFIC REQUEST, LOWELL JONES! I even had to make a special trip down to Red & White just before closing time to buy eggs when I was supposed to be sending out Christmas cards."

But Dad is laughing, too gleeful to be chastened. Indeed, everyone but my mother is red-faced with laughter, mostly because she can never resist the bait, as predictable as a ten-pound carp. She is still steaming, knowing she's been suckered by the same routine for the umpteenth time, when Dad slips in the next needle.

"That Grandma is really a good cook."

Everyone dutifully agrees that Grandma is a good cook.

"And Margaret, she's also a good cook."

Everyone agrees that Margaret can also cook.

"And that Mary, she can *really* cook."

Everyone agrees that Mary's cooking is something special.

"And Alda. That Alda can make everything so it tastes scrumptious. Mmmmm. Makes my mouth water just thinking about it."

"Humph." My mother has taken the hook again.

"What do you suppose Alda will serve us this time?" He is asking me.

"Chicken and homemade noodles? Brownies?"

"How about her yellow cake? Baked ham? Tapioca pudding? I guess the possibilities are just about endless."

Mother is squirming. Despite being a pretty fair cook in her own right, she is always sensitive to comparisons, particularly to the storied kitchen doyennes of the Jones family.

"You don't suppose," Dad says, forming a circle with his hands, "that Alda would have made one of those mysterious round things?"

"Lowell Jones! The way you talk, everyone will think you haven't had a decent meal since you left home."

"We were just talking."

"Humph. Talk, talk, talk. You ought to hear yourself." But Dad is chuckling again. He can't help himself.

We turn off Highway 81 onto a narrow gravel road. The western horizon, glowing with shaded swirls of apricot and crimson, signals the end of a late-December day. At our urging Dad takes the steep hills fast enough to ensure our stomachs do roller coasters. Neat farmsteads with red barns and bulging corncribs border our path. Patient queues of muddy Holsteins wait outside milking parlors. It is suppertime.

Once across the weed-strewn railroad tracks and past the first solitary house, we are inside the loose confines of Magnet, Nebraska, another town too tough to die, hardy survivor of periodic visitations by conflagration and tornado. Home, in the mid-1950s, to perhaps one hundred tenacious souls, most of them sharing blood with either the Black or the Jones families, Magnet is my father's geographic center. He has moved around Nebraska a good deal, as is common with Methodist ministers, but when he says, "my home," he is talking about Magnet. His fraternal grandparents were descendants of a long line of hard-mouthed, sin-butchering Missouri Baptists, steadfastly opposed to almost anything a normal person would do for fun. His mother's parents, the Blacks, wasted little time gnawing holes in their own humanity. In fact, Grandma Black smoked a corncob pipe when it wasn't stashed in her apron pocket. Growing up, my father was bright-eyed, curious about his fellow man, always a good listener. It was not surprising he became the object of much doting by the community. The editor of the *Magnet Mail* worried in print when the Jones boy lost an altercation with grumpy bees and took note when he got his hand caught in a wringer washer. Grandma Jones welcomed him to her table for plain fare and moral dictation. Just down the street was Grandma Black's fragrant kitchen, a piece of lemon meringue or vinegar pie always set aside for a favorite grandchild.

In his mature years, my father came to see Magnet as a Nirvanic paradise, a standing metaphor for the better side of the human spirit. Writing of Magnet in his book, *When My World Was Young*, he asked,

> And what is to be said of the village itself, our town? Is this just a nondescript little town in a far-off forgotten corner of the world? Did we, in fact, in our time rub shoulders with greatness in a pathetic desire to escape oblivion? Is the town itself, now faded, indeed to be consigned to oblivion, as though it never was, never could be?
>
> One answer is that we, like the citizens of Thornton Wilder's *Our Town*, by our citizenship here, are thereby a part of the universe, both we and our forebears. For like Grover's Corners, Magnet's proper address is not the one the United States Postal Service gives us, but the more accurate one, "Magnet,

Morton Township, Cedar County, State of Nebraska, United States of America, Northern Hemisphere, the Earth, the Solar System, the Universe, the Mind of God." While we lived in this place we were made aware that we too are creatures of that universe. And its impact, mediated through the environment of days and nights, nurtured in us qualities of dignity and meaning as citizens of the great cosmos.

It should not be surprising that my father shrugs off the snobbery his wife and children show to his beloved birthplace. He knows implicitly that someday the veil of ignorance will be lifted from our eyes and we will see Magnet as the same spiritual place he does. He does not care that B. J. Tupper, on his first visit, declared it a nest of card-playing, joke-telling ne'er-do-wells, most of whom were some kind of Jones. Nor does he care that B. J. disapproved of the way the Jones family depended on the generous ministrations of my great-uncle George, nor that B. J. was made uncomfortable by the towns-people's lack of hard-bitten business acumen. For my father, commercial success is relevant only to the extent people share what they have. He is as much a confirmed believer in tribal redistribution of wealth as any traditional Sioux or Cheyenne.

*

Grandma Jones greets us in the doorway of her simple house. She is wearing a light-blue gingham dress under a fancy lace-trimmed apron that has all the markings of a recent Christmas gift. I am always appalled at how thin and unhealthy she looks, never much more than eighty pounds dripping wet, her arms little more than withered sticks, her tiny concave chest continually wracked by labored coughing. But her eyes are so joyful at our arrival, her tendings to our needs so prompt and so solicitous, that she quickly becomes less the vaguely threatening symbol of decay than the warm heart and soul of the Jones clan. I am even persuaded to eat some of Grandpa's home-cured ham. In spite of my misgivings, I find it delicious. Grandpa is ensconced in his preferred spot next to the oil space heater, rolling and smoking one fragrant Prince Edward cigarette after another. His hands are no longer steady, and he can usually only get enough tobacco rolled up in the paper for three or four prodigious puffs. The process pretty well occupies his waking life. He is pleased that his notoriously finicky grandson has eaten some of his ham.

My father plops a quivering slab of ugly gray gelatin on my plate. "Vinegar," he says. "Pie doesn't get any better." Everyone is watching, Grandma especially. Firmly convinced I am fatally poisoning myself, I take a tiny forkful. Vaguely butterscotch, but much lighter, livelier, the barest whiff of apple, a pinch of allspice, all dancing around my tongue with exquisite electricity. An instant convert, I eat three pieces. Grandpa hacks his way through a short-lived fit of amusement.

After supper we play with Grandpa's wind-up toys on the dining room table. He has a large assortment of fuzzy dancing bears, all manner of clowns, and goofy-looking creatures, who dutifully perform for as long as their well-worn internal springs allow. Tonight he brings out his most treasured Christmas gift, a bright-red and -yellow cymbal-playing tin monkey. The monkey's antics so pleasure Grandpa that he almost expires from coughing.

*

Why am I half-awake on the living room couch? A clock has just struck three. Something alive is in the room. A black shape looms over the foot of the couch, then retreats out of sight. Maybe I am having a nightmare. A single Cyclopian eye glows evilly in the dark. The ruddy eye moves in a regular circular pattern, always keeping me under surveillance. I am afraid to move, afraid to call for help. Is this one of those visits from the devil incarnate Mr. Steele is always talking about? I'm not sure what a devil incarnate looks like, but this one will serve until something worse shows up. What is devil incarnate protocol anyway? Do I talk to the guy, maybe confess to a few small-scale acts of recent sin in the hope he goes away? What would a devil incarnate make of the recent incineration of Mr. Hockersmith's lilac bush? Too piddly. What about cold-cocking Miriam's most recent beau with a fist-sized rock? Nah, that wasn't sinful, I was just protecting my sister's virtue. Besides, watching the kid's eyes roll up in his head just before he pitched down on his face was almost a religious experience. Remarkable as it might seem, despite all my frantic soul-searching, I can't come up with a single instance of personal wrongdoing worth confessing.

The Cyclops dissolves in a waterfall of showering sparks. The devil incarnate erupts with familiar grumblings and hackings. The lid on Grandpa's Prince Albert can snaps shut. There is a faint crinkling of paper, the wet sound of slobber. A kitchen match flares in the dark. A fog of sweet, heavy smoke rolls over the couch. I cover my head with the quilt. Every dream is punctuated with Grandpa's harsh barking.

*

Uncle Doyle decides I should learn to milk. I am balanced precariously on a one-legged stool, gingerly kneading the yielding freckled teat of an imperturbable Guernsey. Doyle and Cousin Carrol have their heads sunk in the flanks of their respective cows, but I am afraid to get that close. I sit as straight as possible on my treacherous stool, groping uneasily for a handle that will give some milk. Mostly I am hoping I don't get my head kicked off. Doyle's cow has erupted once today, upsetting a bucket and Uncle Doyle, who imprints all manner of novel invective on my budding lexicon. Carrol assures me that my cow is much gentler than the fit-thrower, but he is not above having some fun with a city cousin, and I do not completely trust him. Uncle Doyle—no one but a complete dope would ever trust *him*. This is the guy who once risked death and dismemberment at the hands of his wife for the simple pleasure of shoving an entire raisin cream pie in Judith Ann's face.

Ten minutes of hard kneading results in barely enough milk to cover the bottom of my bucket. My right hand is exhausted. I switch teats and hands and am rewarded with a white trickle. Carrol has already finished two cows and is working on a third. Great streams of milk froth into his half-full bucket. Doyle shouts a warning. The cow behind me is spreading her legs. A torrent of hot piss pours into the manure trough, spattering my legs and combat boots. Doyle's cow starts the same process, but he belts her with a milk stool, and she changes her mind. The frigid barn air is full of eye-watering ammonia.

My left hand is cramping, about to give out. There is less than an inch of milk in my bucket. "I think she's done," I announce.

"Let me strip her out."

Carrol brings his stool and bucket over. He pumps milk for five minutes, not piddly little squirts, but bucket-rattling jets. He uses all of his bucket and half of mine before he finishes. "You about had her," he says without a hint of sarcasm. The humiliation is not as bad as it could be. Carrol, an eighth grader, is stronger than most full-grown men. His huge square hands hang from long arms corded with work-hardened muscle. He has beaten the crap out of tough guys from Omaha, who thought they could swagger into the Skylon Ballroom and mess with the local women. His buddies run to him for protection, and he is happy to oblige. Having Carrol Jones on your side stops most fights before the start. The opposition just sort of melts away. So I am not ashamed to struggle out of the barn under the weight of a half-bucket of milk while he steps lightly, dangling a brimming bucket easily in each hand.

It is a good thing a kid as strong and agile as Carrol is hard to rile. For despite his occasional scraps and his tough talk, Carrol is easygoing, would always rather laugh at a new joke than fight. On this Christmas, with Carrol seven months away from his first high school football scrimmage, it is easy to project what is about to happen. He will break all the records. He will lead his team in both rushing and tackling. On the basketball court he will be an animal force, tearing down rebounds, shooting his smooth outside jump shot, muscling defenders out of the way for another offensive tip-in. Watching this young Adonis run the court, with his unique swinging, broad-shouldered, narrow-hipped lop, will be like watching a great cat on the hunt. This is the happy genetic blend of his mother's big-boned MacFarland strength and the long-waisted Jones traits of quickness and agility. Track season will see him among the state's leaders in the shot-put, the high jump, and the discus throw.

Wayne State College wants to give him a track scholarship the first time they clap eyes on him. In baseball he will keep doing what he has always done—throw the ball harder, hit the ball farther than any baseball fan in that part of the state has ever witnessed. Less easy to predict is the generous disposition Carrol will display despite the kind of mass adulation that sometimes turns high school heroes into big-headed jerks. As a senior he will continue to drive twenty miles out of his way to give pimply freshman kids a ride home from late basketball practice. His manner with the countless squirming girls who eye him with open invitation is polite and respectful. The only human beings that earn his scorn are the hard-cases that occasionally follow popular rock-and-roll bands to Hartington's legendary Skylon Ballroom. Carrol and his buddies will relieve the invaders of their knives and chains, beat them up, and send them home with a warning not to come back.

What will happen after high school is not so easy to predict. Carrol does not have the academic credentials to star on the Wayne State track team. Vietnam is heating up. He certainly would be subject to the draft. Given his instinctive bravery and automatic loyalty to his friends, he would be a ready-made hero. Maybe he would have even survived his heroism. But he does not go to Vietnam.

*

It is a Fourth of July wedding dance at the Skylon. Carrol and his best buddy, Wally, have brought back a surprise from a fireworks factory in South Dakota, a brutish eight-inch firecracker. The fuse is also a monster, over three feet long. It is nearing time for the band to take a break. Sweating dancers will be abandoning the tropical innards of the Skylon for fresh air, perhaps another cherry vodka Coke, some furtive back-seat fumbling with straps and rayon. They will be dumbfounded when this colossal firecracker explodes high over their heads, which is where Carrol is going to fling it after Wally lights the fuse. This thing has more power, the Yankton fireworks salesman assured them, than a quarter-stick of dynamite. The first sweat-soaked dancers appear in the doorway. Carrol braces himself for the heave, feet wide apart, great shoulders poised to roll skyward. Wally sticks his Zippo under the end of the ridiculously long fuse. He spins the wheel. The world blows up.

Wally lands on his back behind a car thirty feet away. Carrol is still upright, dazed at the sight of his empty wrist. The entire side of the car he is standing beside is blown inward, glass scattered over the interior. Two miles away Aunt Margaret lies in bed, awakened from a sound sleep by the explosion. So worried that something bad has happened to Carrol, she does not sleep for the rest of the night.

The doctors give him a steel hook, and in time he can light his own cigarettes. He moves out to Oregon, finds work as a parts man. Sings in a rock-and-roll band for a while. Buys his own auto parts business. Becomes a pretty fair pool hustler, using his hook to discourage sore losers. "I sometimes wish," he jokes, "that I'd had this hook all along. Wouldn't I have been something?"

*

It is well after midnight, and Jim and Larry are hungry. We have slipped downstairs once tonight and conducted a successful raid on Aunt Mary's pantry. Those toothsome cookies are long gone, and we have stirred up another hungry with our nonstop joke-telling and incessant giggling. Jim and Larry giggle about as often as most people breathe. By now we have belabored every joke in our collective memories countless times. It is no longer necessary to actually tell the joke to get a laugh. "Tell the one about Titswiggle again" is enough to spasm everyone senseless. I am not as sanguine about sneaking around in my underwear as Jim and Larry. They are back from the kitchen by the time I locate my jeans. My share of the booty is half an angel-food cake. I am pretty sure, come morning, that Aunt Mary is going to miss something this large, but the element of imminent discovery only adds savor to the cake. Jim and Larry make short work of a cold fried chicken, thoughtfully throwing the discarded bones out of sight under the bed.

Uncle Wilbur is much on our minds. Our mostly unbridled hilarity has brought him to the foot of the stairs once tonight with dire warnings to be quiet. If he comes up, Jim and Larry will certainly be paddled, and perhaps their dorky little cousin as well. I have never been paddled by Wilbur, but I have seen Jim and Larry swinging upside-down while their little butts were being warmed often enough that I don't want to push things too far.

"Eek! A bald-headed mouse!" We collapse instantly, muffling our guffaws under the pillows. This is followed by some ignorant speculation on the physical configuration of Oriental women.

Then we turn to the serious business of telling tales of major mischief.

"Tell the pig story."

*

It was a midsummer's day in the not-too-distant past. All the Jones cousins, including Earl's boy, Curtis, for the lone time in family history and for reasons no one remembers, were gathered in one location on Mary and Wilbur's farm. This meant that Willy's boy, Warren Lee, was also present. Having Warren Lee on the premises never failed to drop Uncle Wilbur into a state of deep depression. He knew from bitter experience that during any Cousin Warren visit at least one piece of expensive, hard-to-replace machinery would, for no apparent reason, become a twisted pile of junk. Kindly uncles undergoing pleasant afternoon ablutions would look up to the shattering of glass. Errant footballs would land in the bath water. Formerly dependable lawn mowers would explode. Hitches would bend. Tractors would refuse to start. On reflection, it is something of an enigma why advance word of Warren Lee's coming did not cause Wilbur to hurriedly pack his bags and head for the border.

The adults were sitting around smoking and talking. The cousins had finished the noon meal and were on the lookout for amusement. Pelting Wilbur's fat hogs with clods and corncobs held only brief interest. We talked about riding them, perhaps rigging up some kind of rope bucking harness, but were discouraged by the smell and all the shoe-sucking mud. Our attention wandered to a small pen beside the barn, where a brood sow and a late litter of pigs were rooting contentedly. Someone proposed that we kidnap one of the smaller pigs. This was certain to enrage the sow, my country cousins assured me, and everyone was eager to see what a pissed-off six-hundred-pound sow might accomplish. This was surely a job for Carrol, the strongest and swiftest among us. He deferred to me, not wanting, he said, to deprive me of a rare opportunity. The rest of the crew wholeheartedly concurred. The idea of covering myself with glory in front of all the cousins had a certain irresistible charm.

We stole into the adjacent milking parlor. The sow, sensing danger, moved her litter to the far end of the pen. The runt was left behind, a bare twenty feet from our hiding place. He stuck his soft pink nose in the mud, unaware of our intentions or of the alarmed snorts of his mother. I decided to abandon stealth for speed, vaulting over the barn door and covering the ground to the pig in short order. I grabbed the little devil and lifted. This piglet seemed to be made of lead. I failed to budge him. He cut loose with ear-splitting squeals. Carrol yelled a warning. I fled for my life. The sow was gaining. She was threatening all manner of bodily harm. As I approached the barn door I expected a kind cousinly hand to throw it open for me. Perhaps they were too transfixed by the arriving spectacle to tend to my safety. I would like to think that was the case. The sow was at my heels, snapping like a mad, slavering she-bear. I dove over the barn door head-first, landing wetly in the manure trough. The sow almost made it. She got both front feet over but couldn't quite pull the rest of her bulk across the top. Disappointed, she bit a four-inch chunk out of the door before sliding reluctantly to the ground and returning to her squealing litter. I was too exhilarated by my narrow escape to be much bothered by my cousins' noticeable state of amusement. Because of my remarkable fleetness of foot, I was appointed chief pig thief by acclamation. Pointing to the disreputable state of my clothing, I begged off from further kidnappings until a later date.

"Tell about Good Time Charlie."

*

We were exploring the dusty granary when we stumbled upon a box of Jim and Larry's outgrown clothing. Good Time Charlie was a name borrowed from a Damon Runyon book of short stories lent by the Chappell Memorial Library. Runyon's Good Time Charlie

Bernstein operated a New York speakeasy with singular open-hearted generosity. Our Good Time Charlie was a dummy, fashioned from a pair of cast-off pants and a near-new sport coat, a few sticks, and a stuffing of oat straw. Tied to the bottom of Charlie's stick legs were Larry's best Sunday shoes. We decided Charlie would like to spend a sunny afternoon with his legs sticking out of a cardboard box in the middle of the highway that marked the northern border of Wilbur and Mary's farm.

Once Charlie was up and operating we were hard pressed to keep him together. One passing motorist after another came to a sudden stop shortly after passing Charlie's box. Apparently they confused Charlie's lithesome limbs with those of an actual child. When they marched back up the road, fully intent on reprimanding this foolish tot for its poor choice of play location, and discovered instead a harmless pile of clothes and sticks, they reacted not with the relieved shrug of the shoulders one might expect but with ugly hostility. From our hidden vantage point deep in Wilbur's shelterbelt, we saw Charlie torn to pieces, his mutilated carcass thrown in the ditch, his box mashed and kicked off the road. We wasted a great deal of time reassembling Charlie after each abuse encounter, allowing many potential customers to pass by unmolested on the highway. Jim volunteered to take up residence in the culvert directly under Charlie's position. After this move the vengeful motorists were scarcely back behind the wheel before Jim was out in the ditch gathering up Charlie's essentials.

Cousin Curtis became a problem. He was possessed of a loud, honking laugh, not unlike that of a braying donkey. With each new concerned motorist, he began honking at an earlier stage of the proceedings. Before long he was braying before the motorist was safely back in his automobile. Some of these soreheads charged into the shelterbelt with what appeared to be murderous intent. Carrol volunteered to keep Curtis quiet. This was a big job, even for a guy of Carrol's talents. Curtis was not used to our peculiar variety of play activities, having spent most of his life in California. He was acting more like a spectator than a participant in a game that was mostly harmless good fun but nonetheless entailed a slight element of risk.

A gasoline transport under a full head of steam sailed by honking frantically. Air brakes hissed. It came to a full stop a half-mile up the road. Rather than walk back to Charlie's box, the sensible course followed by most of this afternoon's drivers, this idiot backed his semi the entire laborious half-mile. The suspicion circulated that a truck driver this stubbornly stupid might prove to be a tough customer. We decided, long before the truck finished its painful journey back down the road, to retreat to more distant lookout points. Jim scurried out of his culvert hidy-hole to join us. Carrol, in a rare loss of concentration, failed to get Curtis moved in time, and he was left in a relatively exposed forward position. We hoped for the best. The truck driver, once he arrived, was particularly vicious, sailing Charlie's parts in several different directions, jumping up and down on Charlie's cardboard home. "Hah-yongk, hah-yongk, hah-yongk." Curtis, you silly-assed dinkphod.

We were in full flight even before we heard the trucker crash through the first row of Russian olives. Incredibly, Curtis caught up with us almost immediately, running easily. The kid had more speed than we realized. We would have been more pleased about this if he weren't still hah-yongking to beat the band. Even truck drivers of unsurpassed stupidity have no trouble tracking that extraordinary sound. Carrol led us through the nettles and barbed-wire fence along a ditch bank, and under the bridge to the country school across the road from Wilbur and Mary's farm. We were now exposed in open country, but no one doubted we could outrun any truck driver in creation. Carrol showed the way, with Curtis hard on his heels, hah-yongking gleefully. We heard a shout and turned to see the distant trucker bent at the waist, catching his breath in the schoolyard. Although he was some distance away, it appeared that he had lost a wrestling match with the barbed-wire fence. His shirt and jeans were flayed open in numerous places. He gestured weakly with one hand, giving us some sort of singular salute. Taking his motions for a white flag of surrender, we happily returned his salutation.

"Tell about Larry's shoes."

*

Before we put Good Time Charlie back in business, something had to be done about Curtis. We discovered he was too good-natured and too trusting to take our grave promises of physical brutality seriously. Warren Lee finally took him to the far end of the shelterbelt, told him to hah-yongk to his heart's content. If the motorists were tearing after Curtis, they wouldn't be bothering us much. Fast as he was, there wasn't much chance of their catching up.

Charlie hardly had time to settle into his accustomed spot on the highway before a station wagon filled with the scowling members of a porcine Iowa family lumbered off onto the shoulder. A black-haired fat man waddled over to Charlie's box. He looked around, studying with particular care the trees we were hidden behind. His attention was diverted momentarily by the loud hah-yongking coming from the east end of the shelterbelt. Charlie took his usual tragic ride into the ditch. His box followed. The fat man waddled back to his car. The driver's side sagged. A door slammed. The car got up a slow head of steam, rolled over the big hill to the east. Jim was in the ditch sorting madly through Charlie's parts.

"He stoled Larry's shoes!" he yelled. "That dirty bastard went and took Larry's Sunday shoes! What's Wilbur gonna say?" From the far end of the shelterbelt came the now-familiar racket of Curtis hah-yongking up a storm.

"Tell about Leola."

*

A more perspicacious observer, one less occupied with recent outbursts of obnoxious laughter, might have guessed, after witnessing Curtis's effortless running that green afternoon, that he had a future in track. It would have been impossible, on the other hand, for even the most extrasensory mind to predict that Curtis would vanish from our lives completely. We lost contact with him soon after this special family gathering. He and his two sisters disappeared back to California, taken away by their sly, strange mother.

Leola, tall and absurdly thin, with high-arching eyebrows drawn in dark pencil high on her forehead, latched onto Earl when he visited Willy and Grandpa's ill-fated grocery store in Edison. Leola, daughter of the town mortician, was running the cash register. "The minute she laid eyes on Earl I knew he was a goner," Willis said later. After ten years of fairly easy life in California, Leola did not share Earl's desire to return to his old home country. But return they did. She was plainly unhappy living in the humble Nebraska housing Earl earned as part of his farmhand wages. No visiting cousin looked forward to mealtimes at Leola's table. She warmed up some week-old oatmeal, threw sticky gobs of the stuff in the middle of our plates, told us she could not afford anything better on the wages Margaret's son-in-law Rod was paying Earl. Her children giggled at this act, knowing once we left they would eat hamburgers and hot dogs and potato chips.

Earl came home one day to find the car gone and the house empty. Why Leola flew the coop is another family conundrum. No adult ever offered a remotely plausible explanation. We missed Curtis for a while, wondered how he was doing, if he still laughed the same old way. Years later Uncle Willis looked him up in California. He was married, had a nice family. He told Willis about his career as a collegiate steeplechaser. Curtis was pretty good in high school. UCLA gave him a full ride. He got to the NCAA finals a couple of times. His senior season was a dream come true.

Going into the final race at the NCAA national meet, Curtis was in great shape, with none of the usual nagging injuries common to steeplechasers. After miles of jumping hurdles and water hazards, Curtis had a comfortable lead over his nearest competitor, a guy who had beaten him the last two years. Curtis approached the last hurdle, one with a four-foot water hazard on the other side. At this point in the race, he said, he was not even particularly tired. A lapse, a tiny break in concentration. Curtis speared his foot straight through the hurdle, started a long, agonizing barrel roll through the dirty water, a contorted mass of hurdle, red hair, lanky legs, flailing freckled arms.

"You know that ski jumper they show at the beginning of ABC's 'Wide World of Sports,' the guy that represents the agony of defeat, the one that loses it and nearly kills himself?" Curtis asked Willis. "Well, that guy was not the first agony of defeat. For a couple of years after that NCAA track meet they led off the 'Wide World of Sports' with a film of me going through that last water hazard. They played it over and over. I guess you could say I was the original agony of defeat." Willis said Curtis laughed at this, and he sounded just like a donkey.

*

Margaret and Burt are hosting a post-Christmas hoorah at their spacious home in Hartington. This will be our family's last stop before we head for Red Cloud and a New Year's visit at the Tuppers. Burt's John Deere dealership is doing well enough they are talking of building a new home. Burt also has plans to replace Mary and Wilbur's sagging farmhouse, which he owns, with a new ranch-style model. Mary is giddy at the idea of having a new house with indoor plumbing. Burt has traded for a new Oldsmobile. Times are good.

The male cousins are in Burt's basement shooting snooker on a regulation table. Carrol is beating our brains out. In a corner my sisters consort with Margaret's three daughters, talking the whispery, nonsensical girl-talk that gives them such inexplicable satisfaction. Doyle's girls, Karna and JaVae, are several years younger, and they amuse themselves bouncing between the two rigidly segregated basement groups. Aspiring and current beaux of Margaret's girls show up all afternoon. Carrol cordially suckers them into playing him "just one game" of snooker. While Carrol nonchalantly cleans the table, Jim and Larry make sure each and every victim gets a fresh rendition of the immortal Titswiggle joke. In late afternoon Margaret calls us upstairs for an early supper of holiday leftovers. She says Wilbur and Doyle are making the stirring noises that invariably signal the approach of milking time.

The aunts and uncles are around Margaret's dining room table. They have not moved for hours, sharing stories, kidding unmercifully. Periodically the room is rocked by gales of laughter, Grandpa and Grandma's nap in a back bedroom unaffected by the uproar. Uncle Doyle asks Judith Ann if she's tried Aunt Alda's most recent raisin cream pie. He warns her not to make a pig of herself like she did last time. This earns him a belt on the arm from Alda, and causes the room to erupt again. My father's family nickname is Toad, a corruption of the Toby his mother called him as a child. There is a general call for Toad to tell about Old Nort and the pancake batter. I have heard this story before, but I take my plate and sit on the floor behind Dad.

"Old Nort was our bachelor neighbor when we lived up by Niobrara. We used to visit him once in a while. He didn't have much, maybe fifteen acres of farm ground. He had a stud horse and probably got a little money from that. He had plenty of cats."

"Did you ever eat a meal there, Toad?" A burst of knowing laughter.

"No, and I don't know anyone but Nort who ever did. He had this wonderful system for doing dishes."

"He did, too."

"You should have seen it."

Dad waits for quiet. "You see, he nailed all the plates to the table so all those mangy yellow cats could lick them off." Groans around the table.

"I thought he just sat the dishes on the floor."

"Didn't he let the dogs lick too?"

"What about his great big, real ugly dog that bit people?"

"No, that was that other old fella that never picked his corn."

"Tell about the pancake batter."

"Well, you see Old Nort was a creature of habit, and he always used the same bowl to mix up his morning pancakes. But because he never washed the bowl, a crust built up. Over the years it got thicker and thicker, until there was only a small little place in the very middle of the bowl to mix up new batter. It got so he could barely get a spoon in there." My father holds his thumb and finger two inches apart to indicate the size of the batter hole. People groan and wrinkle their noses.

"Tell about Harvey and Louie, Toad."

My father tells about the half-idiot brothers, neighbors who barely knew enough to come in out of the rain. One day they were standing under the windmill in a powerful state of thirst. Louie, the older, dumber brother, picked up the bolt that locked the windmill shaft into the pitcher pump. He fumbled around and dropped it into the well pit. If the boys weren't thirsty before, they were now totally parched. Louie worked the loose pump handle to no effect. "Hey, Harvey," he said, "stick your finger in that bolt hole until I can pump us enough water for a drink." Harvey, always willing to oblige, stuck his finger in the bolt hole. The moving shaft severed his finger as neatly as any guillotine. He stared in amazement at his spurting stump. "How did you do that?" Louie asked.

"Just like this," Harvey said, sticking a second finger in the bolt hole and losing yet another digit.

In unison, a chorus of Jones voices say, "Just like this," as they imitate Harvey poking his finger in the bolt hole. Everyone laughs uproariously.

"I thought he only lost one finger."

"Malvin always said two."

"I'm sure it was only one."

"Could have been one."

"Do you remember, Margaret? You were around when that happened."

"I don't know about that. They sure wasn't very bright. Time they growed up they was probably lucky to have any fingers at all."

"Remember the time Toad walked home for Christmas?" My father smiles at the memory. He starts the story. The room grows still.

He was something of a late-bloomer, having quit high school after his freshman year to help his father on the farm. He farmed with his dad until he was twenty-one, when LeRoy Blough, the local Methodist minister, saw some talent and encouraged my father to go back to school. After zipping through three years of high school in a year and a half, Dad was attending Yankton College during the week and serving the Wynot Methodist Church on the weekends. The Wynot deal was supposed to pay sixteen dollars a month, but mostly Dad had to settle for whatever was in the collection plate. One week all he netted was fifteen cents, in pennies. Dad walked or hitchhiked the eighteen miles between Yankton and Wynot because he was too broke to buy, let alone operate, a car. He made friends with the toll-taker on the Yankton bridge, who sometimes forgot to charge him the dime toll to walk over. This was fortunate because he often did not have a dime. "Of course, that was during the worst part of the Depression," Dad reminds us, "and nobody had any money."

The Wynot church put on a Christmas Eve program, with little kids reciting memorized verses and some desultory hymn singing. After the last bundled child scooted homeward, after the old coal furnace was dampened and the church closed up, Dad buttoned up his thin jacket and started the twenty-mile walk toward the Jones family farm east of Bloomfield. "People back then," he stresses, "didn't have the warm clothing they do now. We weren't used to much."

"You had on your long johns, didn't you?"

Dad agrees that he most likely was wearing long johns. It was bitter cold, even with the long johns, and though he stuck to the roads no friendly car gave him a lift. He passed the shuttered Bow Valley store, the darkened hulks of a hundred farmhouses. The last few miles he began to question whether he would make it before his feet froze.

"I knew Mom would put that old yellow oil lamp in the window. She always did when she expected me. Every time I topped a hill I'd hope that light would show. When I finally came over that last cold ridge and saw that old yellow light, it was the most wonderful sight I ever saw."

"Mom sure was glad to see you come through that door."

"We all was."

"Remember that tornado that hit . . ."